Theatre for Children
Guide to Writing, Adapting, Directing and Acting

Plays and Musicals by David Wood
(published by Samuel French Ltd)

ALADDIN, THE BFG (based on the book by Roald Dahl), BABES IN THE MAGIC WOOD, CINDERELLA, DICK WHITTINGTON AND WONDERCAT, DINOSAURS AND ALL THAT RUBBISH (based on the book by Michael Foreman), FLIBBERTY AND THE PENGUIN, THE GINGERBREAD MAN, HIJACK OVER HYGENIA, THE IDEAL GNOME EXPEDITION, JACK AND THE GIANT, JACK THE LAD (co-written with Dave and Toni Arthur), LARRY THE LAMB IN TOYTOWN (co-written with Sheila Ruskin, adapted from the stories of S. G. Hulme-Beaman), MEG AND MOG SHOW (from the books by Helen Nicoll and Jan Pieńkowski), MORE ADVENTURES OF NODDY (based on the stories by Enid Blyton), MOTHER GOOSE'S GOLDEN CHRISTMAS, NODDY (based on the stories by Enid Blyton), NUTCRACKER SWEET, OLD FATHER TIME, OLD MOTHER HUBBARD, THE OWL AND THE PUSSYCAT WENT TO SEE ... (co-written with Sheila Ruskin), THE PAPERTOWN PAPERCHASE, THE PIED PIPER (from Browning's poem, co-written with Dave and Toni Arthur), THE PLOTTERS OF CABBAGE PATCH CORNER, ROBIN HOOD (co-written with Dave and Toni Arthur), RUPERT AND THE GREEN DRAGON (based on the Rupert stories and characters by Mary Tourtel and Alfred Bestall), SAVE THE HUMAN (based on the story by Tony Husband and David Wood), THE SEE-SAW TREE, THE SELFISH SHELLFISH, THERE WAS AN OLD WOMAN ..., TICKLE (one act), THE WITCHES (based on the book by Roald Dahl)

also:
THE OLD MAN OF LOCHNAGAR (based on the book by HRH the Prince of Wales; published by Amber Lane Press), ROCK NATIVITY (with music by Tony Hatch and Jackie Trent; published by Josef Weinberger Ltd)

also by Janet Grant
THE YOUNG PERSON'S GUIDE TO BECOMING A WRITER (Free Spirit Publishing, Minneapolis, Minn., USA), THE WRITING COACH (Pembroke Publishers, Markham, Ontario, Canada), THE KIDS' GREEN PLAN (Pembroke Publishers), KIDS' WRITERS: BOB MUNSCH, JEAN LITTLE, DENNIS LEE AND LUCY MAUD MONTGOMERY (Fitzhenry & Whiteside, Markham, Ont., Canada)

Theatre for Children

Guide to Writing, Adapting,
Directing and Acting

David Wood
with Janet Grant

Ivan R. Dee
CHICAGO

THEATRE FOR CHILDREN. Copyright © 1979, 1999 by David Wood and Janet
Grant. All rights reserved, including the right to reproduce this book or portions
thereof in any form. For information, address: Ivan R. Dee, Publisher, 1332 North
Halsted Street, Chicago 60622. First published in Great Britain by Faber and Faber
Ltd. Manufactured in the United States of America and printed on acid-free paper.

Library of Congress Cataloging-in-Publication Data:
Wood, David, 1944–
    Theatre for children : a guide to writing, adapting, directing
and acting / David Wood with Janet Grant.
        p. cm.
    ISBN 1-56663-232-3 (cloth : alk. paper). — ISBN 1-56663-233-1
(pbk. : alk. paper)
        1. Children's plays—Presentation, etc. 2. Theater—Production
and direction. I. Grant, Janet, 1957–   . II. Title.
PN3157.W57 1999
792'.0226—dc21   98-46033

This book is dedicated to everyone
for whom working in children's theatre is,
was, or will be special.

Contents

Acknowledgements

For permission to use the photographs on the back cover, the authors and publishers are grateful to the following:

The BFG: Anthony Pedley as The BFG, Ruby Evans as Sophie, Andy Couchman, Oliver Gray, Marcia King, Tristan Middleton, Katie Purslow, Mary Waters as Giants. Designer: Susie Caulcutt. A Clarion Production. (David Wood's *The BFG* is based on the novel *The BFG* by Roald Dahl.)

Meg and Mog Show: Maureen Lipman as Meg. Designers: Jan Pieńkowski and Vikie Le Saché. A Unicorn Theatre Production. (David Wood's *Meg and Mog Show* is based on *Meg and Mog* books by Helen Nicoll and Jan Pieńkowski.)

The Gingerbread Man: Tony Jackson as The Gingerbread Man, Susannah Bray as The Old Bag, Beejaye as Pepper, Michael Kirk as Herr von Cuckoo and Adam Stafford as Salt. Designer: Susie Caulcutt. A Unicorn Theatre Production.

The authors are also grateful to Birmingham Hippodrome for permitting photographs for the front cover to be taken during performances of Whirligig Theatre's production of *The Gingerbread Man*.

The authors would also like to thank all those people whose comments contributed towards the research for this book.

For permission to reprint material from other sources, acknowledgements are due to the following: Thames and Hudson for permission to use an extract from Bruno Bettelheim's *The Uses of Enchantment (The Meaning and Importance of Fairy Tales)*; HarperCollins Publishers Limited for permission to quote from *How Not to Raise a Perfect Child* by Libby Purves; Casarotto

Ramsay Ltd for permission to quote from *The See-Saw Tree, The Selfish Shellfish* and *Rupert and the Green Dragon* by David Wood (published by Samuel French Ltd); RUPERT characters TM and © Express Newspapers plc, © 'Rupert and the Green Dragon' Nelvana Limited and David Wood 1997.

Every effort has been made to trace or contact copyright holders, but in some cases this has proved impossible. The editor and publishers would be grateful to be notified of any additions that should be incorporated in the next edition of this volume.

Foreword

For three decades I have written and directed plays for children, for me the most important audience of all. Over the years my work has become widespread in Great Britain, and I have achieved the unofficial title of the "National Children's Dramatist." My plays have traveled as far as Germany, Japan, Australia, South Africa, and many other countries, but until now they have enjoyed only occasional success in the United States—the best known being *The Owl and the Pussycat Went to See . . .* and *The Gingerbread Man.*

Back in the 1970s I was privileged to be interviewed on British radio alongside Aurand Harris, the eminent American children's playwright. We shared many beliefs and theories about what "works" for children. In New York I met Joanna Kraus, another distinguished practitioner, and in Minneapolis I observed the directing skills of Jon Cranney. Our work had a great deal in common, and I was sure that my plays, given the chance, would please American children.

This year it seems to be happening. Soon after finishing the manuscript of *Theatre for Children*, I began an adaptation of *The Sheep-Pig*, Dick King-Smith's delightful children's novel which inspired the film *Babe*. During the play's successful tour of the UK, news came that the Dallas Children's Theater wanted it for an American premiere. I was thrilled to visit Dallas, enjoy Nancy Schaeffer's warm and colorful production, offer storytelling sessions in local schools, and feel part of Robyn Flatt's excellent theatre team.

A second excitement was thanks to my friend Marta Suarez, who came to Britain to further her children's theatre studies. She became my assistant director on a production of my adaptation of Roald Dahl's *The Witches*, which toured extensively and played a season in London's West End. When Marta returned to the States to work for the Chicago Children's Theatre, she persuaded Nan Zabriskie and Scott Ferguson to mount a production of my adaptation of Roald

Dahl's *The BFG*. Again I was fortunate to see this delightful production and to meet Professor Rives Collins, who kindly asked me to work with his theatre students at Northwestern University.

I dedicate this book to all my American colleagues who have believed in my work, and to the many more whom I hope will find this book useful. To give children the excitement of live theatre especially created for them is vital in this age of sophisticated technology. It is up to us to trigger their imaginations and widen their horizons. Children are the future.

D. W.

November 1998
Wimbledon, England

Introduction

In the mid-sixties, while I was at Oxford, I went to see a big commercial pantomime at the New Theatre. It was a matinée and the audience was mostly children. As a child my favourite theatre treat had for several years been *Peter Pan*, but I had also enjoyed pantomimes. Now, having grown up a little, I watched the show rather differently. I noticed that the story-line was very thin. The entertainment was really a succession of variety acts. The children in the audience were often restless.

After the story had rather perfunctorily been disposed of, the star comedian embarked upon his half hour obligatory spot. It was quite enjoyable, if, in my view, out of context. At one point he cracked a slightly blue joke. The children didn't understand it. A few of the adults did and cackled in the stalls. Whereupon the star walked eagerly down to the footlights, leant over and said: 'Oh, come on, let's get the kids out of here and then we can get started!'

It was as though an electric shock had jolted me. I even blushed. How on earth, I thought, can this man, who is being paid a lot of money to entertain these children, blatantly tell us that he would rather be entertaining his late night cabaret audience. Surely those children deserved better. It struck me that there was very little theatre aimed at children. That moment was a turning point in my life.

The seeds for my career in children's theatre were sown early. At first it was *Peter Pan* and pantomime and then, by the age of eight, I had developed an interest in conjuring and puppetry. I loved my Pollock's toy theatre and performed puppet shows in the back garden. By the age of eleven I was part of a cabaret act, singing and performing magic tricks.

In my teens I started performing magic at children's parties. In retrospect I realize this taught me a great deal about how children respond *en masse* and how to encourage and control audience participation. (My interest in magic has continued. I am a member of the Magic Circle and perform my own *Magic and Music Show* in theatres. I often try to incorporate magic and illusion into my children's plays. Incidentally, magic helped me get into Oxford; Christopher Ricks, my long-suffering tutor, once confessed that although my academic abilities were no more than average, he thought I might be useful to have around – he had three young children at whose birthday parties I entertained.)

As a teenager I took part in school plays, local amateur theatricals and youth drama festivals. For several years I attended residential youth drama courses run by a wonderful teacher/writer/director called Frank Whitbourn, who at eighty-five is still my mentor and is the first person to see the first draft of anything I write.

Before going to Oxford to read English I was lucky enough to get two jobs. The first was as a bingo caller in Bognor Regis, where I developed a rapport with my audience by trying to entertain them as well as call the numbers. The second was as an extra in the newly opened Chichester Festival Theatre. Being a small part of Sir Laurence Olivier's star-studded season added to my resolve to turn professional. I loved the excitement of dashing off stage at Chichester, stripping off my *Saint Joan* soldier's costume, jumping into a taxi in my underpants, changing *en route* into my dinner jacket, then leaping on stage at the Theatre Royal crying, 'Welcome to Bognor's Biggest Bingo.'

At Oxford I managed to do more acting and writing than I might ever have done at a drama school. Plays in the Oxford Playhouse, a European tour in Shakespeare, several Edinburgh Festivals and, perhaps the greatest thrill, writing songs for and appearing in *Hang Down Your Head and Die*, the anti-capital punishment revue that transferred to London's West End.

After scraping through my degree, I co-wrote and appeared in a University revue called *Four Degrees Over,* which was also lucky enough to transfer to the West End. The other performers were John Gould and Bob (now Sir Robert) Scott, with whom I later presented *The Owl and the Pussycat Went to See ...* in London, and Adele Weston, who, by a strange coincidence, also became a children's writer, and a highly respected one, under her married name, Adele Geras.

After a period of enforced 'resting', during which I tutored a prep-school boy in Latin and a Swiss ski-instructor in English, I co-wrote a documentary musical for the Traverse Theatre in Edinburgh and spent a very happy few months doing Theatre in Education at Watford, sharing in the early days of this new form of theatre which had been pioneered by the Belgrade Theatre, Coventry. It taught me a hell of a lot about playing to cynical teenagers at 9.30 in the morning. I also learnt the importance of keeping moving and having eyes in the back of your head when playing in the round; one day I didn't and got spat at. Maybe that influenced me later to concentrate on younger children. For Watford TIE I also wrote a participatory play about Boadicea. From this I learnt a lot about taking children seriously.

1967 found me in repertory at the Swan Theatre, Worcester. I directed The Knack and a new musical called A Present From The Corporation, and as an actor I gave my Feste in Twelfth Night, played the juvenile lead in Caste and dragged up for Charley's Aunt. Then I had my first break as a film actor, playing Johnny, one of the rebel schoolboys in Lindsay Anderson's If..., which became something of a cult film. This taste of the high life might well have detracted me from any idea of pursuing a career in children's theatre, but I was inadvertently hijacked from any thoughts of stardom on the big screen by my return to Worcester, and by the request of John Hole, the director of the Swan, to do some children's theatre.

First of all it was limited to Saturday mornings. I regularly compèred and performed in a show with the other actors in the company. We presented a hotchpotch of stories, magic, songs and audience participation. Audiences grew and soon we were having to do two performances instead of one. I found that I loved doing these shows. Indeed I began to wonder whether I was enjoying it too much. I sensed a feeling of power over the audience. They were so willing to join in and to follow my lead. I felt that if I asked them to, they would do absolutely anything. I could understand how Hitler's youth rallies had been able to brainwash young Nazis into blind obedience. Children are impressionable. I now realized how responsibility is a quality vital to the children's entertainer.

Next John Hole suggested I wrote an adaptation of Hans

Andersen's *The Tinder Box*. He didn't want a pantomime. The theatre was too small to present a traditional pantomime and in any case, he didn't really like them. He told me he wanted me to write a 'proper' play for children. I was not to worry about the adults in the audience – if the children enjoyed it, the adults would. He wanted the story clearly and imaginatively told. Audience participation was fine, but it had to be made part of the story. There were to be no speciality acts or irrelevancies. It may seem strange now, but at that time his brief was quite unusual. Most Christmas entertainments then were jolly romps or extravaganzas. Even adaptations of *Alice in Wonderland* or *The Wizard of Oz* were aimed at a wide audience and had to have a broad appeal. John's insistence that we concentrate on the children was refreshingly novel.

I never saw a performance of *The Tinder Box* – I was giving my Wishee Washee at Watford at the time – but I don't think it was very good, even though the cast and director were very talented and worked hard on making the story come alive. The writer still had much to learn. Luckily, John Hole didn't give up on me, and the following year asked for another musical play. Sonia Davis, his secretary, suggested *The Owl and the Pussycat*. This was the play that got me hooked.

My acting career continued. I did a play, *After Haggerty*, for the Royal Shakespeare Company. I was in films like *Aces High* and *North Sea Hijack*. I did lots of television including classic serials and even starred opposite Shelley Winters in a two-hander called *The Vamp*. In 1970 I created the role of the Son in John Mortimer's *A Voyage Round My Father* and was nominated Best New Actor; later I played the part again in Toronto opposite Sir Michael Redgrave.

But all the time my commitment to children's theatre was developing. By the time I wrote my fourth play for Worcester we reckoned that the audiences trusted us and that familiar titles were no longer necessary. I wrote my first original play, *The Plotters of Cabbage Patch Corner*. This subsequently came to London and was directed spendidly by Jonathan Lynn, who was later to achieve a wider audience by co-writing *Yes, Minister* and going to Hollywood to direct feature films. Jonathan's work reinforced my belief that children's plays should be directed seriously. He made the conflict between the insects in the garden totally real. The success of this production in 1971 and 1972 was also due to Sheila Falconer, the choreographer and Peter Pontzen, the musical director, both of whom have worked with me ever since. Their contribution to the style of my productions has been invaluable. Susie Caulcutt provided the brilliant set and costume designs. She had first worked with me on the London *Owl* and has since designed most of my own productions. Her sympathetic interpretations of my work have never been equalled.

For some years thereafter I rather turned up my nose at the idea of adaptation, thinking grandly that the original art of children's playwriting was the be all and end all. For Worcester, I wrote *Flibberty and the Penguin*, *The Papertown Paperchase* and *Hijack Over Hygenia*. But when John Hole departed to open the new Queen's Theatre at Hornchurch he persuaded me that the larger stage and better facilities now at our disposal might offer openings for adaptations of pantomime subjects. Also, there were many books and stories which had such splendid ideas in them that it was foolish to ignore them as subject matter. I called them my 'pantomime substitutes'. They were conceived as musical plays for children rather than traditional pantomimes. They retained certain elements of pantomime, but sometimes, as in *Babes in the Magic Wood* and *Mother Goose's Golden Christmas*, had original story-lines.

Looking back, John's continued confidence in me had a huge influence on my development. I ended up writing thirteen Christmas productions for him. A regular annual commission, a writer's dream.

Cameron Mackintosh came into my life in the early seventies, when he offered to co-produce a Christmas season and national tour of *The Owl and the Pussycat Went to See* ... Since then he has often financially supported my productions. For this I will always be most grateful. But perhaps his major contribution to my development began in 1976. I had been asked to write a new children's play for the Towngate Theatre, Basildon. Presented by the Theatre Royal, Norwich, *The Gingerbread Man* was directed by Jonathan Lynn.

Cameron came to see the play and immediately offered to co-produce it with me in London the following year. He secured the Old

Vic, which proved to be a splendid venue, and the play ran there with considerable success for two Christmas seasons. We subsequently produced the play in several other West End theatres, as well as on tour. We never sought subsidy and the play was never commercially successful, mainly because the seat price was kept low to encourage school parties to come. But the response was always positive and *The Gingerbread Man* became my most popular play. It has been performed all over the world, and one of my happiest memories is seeing Japanese children reacting to it in exactly the same way as their English counterparts. I subsequently adapted the play into a book and a television model animation series.

The response of audiences throughout Great Britain to the touring productions of *Owl* and *The Gingerbread Man* convinced me that touring was the best way to introduce the work to the widest possible audience. Ideas for a national touring children's theatre began to be discussed seriously, and in 1978, WSG Productions, the company I ran with John Gould and Bob Scott, presented a pilot tour of *Flibberty and the Penguin*. The tour was well received, but it proved conclusively that in order to maintain our standards and in order to keep our seat prices low, we needed subsidy or sponsorship or both. Commercial sponsorship was beginning to make its mark on theatrical projects, and we were lucky enough to secure funding from Clarks Shoes. They proved ideal sponsors, providing splendid give-aways for every child and never asking me to write a play all about shoes.

We decided to give the touring company a new name, Whirligig Theatre. It would be run as a public service rather than a commercial venture. The first tour for the new company was a revival of *The Plotters of Cabbage Patch Corner*. Arts Council Touring took an interest in our work, and supported it through the eighties. An average tour would play in middle-scale and large theatres to over 100,000 children. Most of the performances were day time matinées to which school parties could come. Teachers became our allies and we regularly presented seminars for them, as well as offering Teachers' Packs and competitions.

When Whirligig's second production, *Nutcracker Sweet*, was safely on the road, I went to Unicorn Theatre and wrote and directed *Meg and Mog Show*, based on the books by Jan Pieṅkowski and Helen Nicoll. Maureen Lipman made a wonderful Meg, and the production was revived many times. This play introduced me to even younger audiences than I had written for before. Although parties of five to seven year olds came from primary schools, the show was especially popular with groups of pre-school children from kindergarten and playgroups.

Talking to teachers in the eighties about children's growing interest in and concern for the environment led me to write *The Selfish Shellfish*, *The See-Saw Tree* and *Save the Human* (originally commissioned by the Cambridge Theatre Company). In these plays many of my own ideas from children's theatre became fused with some of the aims of Theatre In Education and led to what I believe is some of my best work.

In the nineties, it has become increasingly difficult for Whirligig to maintain its touring programme to the major theatres. In 1989, the Education Reform Act began to make its impact on theatres across the country. It stated that school theatre trips that had been traditionally subsidized by parents, now had to be paid for by the schools. As schools had no budget for such trips, the Act allowed them to approach parents for a *voluntary* contribution. However, when something is labelled 'voluntary', approximately one third of people are reluctant to pay. Therefore, many theatre bookings had to be cancelled. For example, for Whirligig's 1989 Sadler's Wells season we had seven thousand advance pencilled bookings, but by the time we opened three thousand had been cancelled. This was echoed across the country. School party bookings dropped and theatre managers began wondering whether to include children's theatre in their programming. Children's theatre companies in turn found it very hard to survive. The Education Act is still in place, but many teachers seem to be ignoring this aspect of it, and schools do seem more willing to bring parties to the theatre. I sense that the tide has turned. The recent Whirligig production of *The Gingerbread Man* at the Birmingham Hippodrome appears to prove this point. The Hippodrome offered the production to schools at only £5 per ticket, including transport. This was an initiative inspired by the visionary attitude of Professor Tim Brighouse, Birmingham's Education Chief, who has stated that every child in Birmingham is *entitled* to a theatre visit. In Birmingham, approximately 10,000 children attended the performance in one week, and the experiment was declared a great success. The Education Reform Act, therefore, seems to be less of a deterrent, but nevertheless had a devastating effect, which children's theatre is only just getting over.

This coincided with a shift in attitude by theatres where it was no longer feasible to present a children's play even as an important community service because its low seat prices might prevent it making money or even breaking even. Sponsorship and Arts Council funding have simultaneously become harder to achieve. The costs of mounting our relatively large-scale productions have increased, yet the seat price must be kept low (a third, say, of an average adult seat price). Thus the gap between expenditure and potential revenue has increased; filling that gap has proved difficult, sometimes impossible.

As a result, some of my most recent plays have been more commercial, adaptations of very familiar and popular children's books. In 1990 James Woods and Justin Savage of Clarion Productions invited me to adapt and direct *The BFG* by Roald Dahl. This toured successfully and played to well-attended Christmas seasons in the West End. It was followed up by another Roald Dahl adaptation, *The Witches*, which also toured and played in the West End, and two adaptations based on Enid Blyton's *Noddy* books. All these productions were mounted with care and integrity. Many of them employed members of the Whirligig 'team'. I was very pleased with the results.

But I live in hope that it will soon be possible once again to present plays with lesser known or new titles for school parties. This does not mean to say that school parties do not come to the more commercial titles – many do. And it does not mean that the plays are not suitable for family audiences at the weekends. But the shift away from public service to pure commercial viability is a trend that threatens the future of children's theatre.

My tally of plays for children stands at approximately forty. I have been very fortunate in that most of them have been commissioned and that all of them have been published by Samuel French Ltd.

Many of the plays are regularly performed by professionals and amateurs all over Great Britain. Some of them have played successfully abroad. But so far the costs of transporting one of my own productions to other countries have proved prohibitive. Even *The Gingerbread Man* (one basic set, six actors) was unable to play the Vancouver Children's Festival because it was 'too big'. It required a theatre rather than a marquee and a day rather than a couple of hours to 'set up'.

In spite of the problems, I know I was right to concentrate on children's theatre, even though it has always been something of a crusade to keep up the momentum and persuade the theatre establishment to accept the work as important. Writing and directing the plays takes up far less of my time than trying to arrange productions or secure funding. But every time I witness an audience reacting positively to my work I know it has all been worthwhile. And I am greatly encouraged by the number of young actors, writers and directors who are now not simply interested but genuinely determined to make a career in children's theatre, sharing the ideals of those of us who started in the sixties, and who still believe that children are the most important audience.

I find children's theatre more challenging, and the rewards – though not necessarily financial – greater. For me, as writer, director and often producer, the creation of a new piece of work, the writing and the build-up, via casting, pre-production meetings, and rehearsals to the opening performance is always a daunting yet exciting journey. Nothing gives me greater satisfaction than to sit in an auditorium witnessing a full house of children unequivocally approving my work.

The challenge is to give a unique theatrical experience to an audience, many of whom will be first-time theatre-goers, to involve them emotionally, to sustain their interest in a story, to inspire and excite them using theatricality, to make them laugh, to make them think, to move them, to entertain and educate them by triggering their imaginations. Over the years the challenge has never faded. If it had, perhaps my single-minded dedication to children's theatre would have long since waned. But every new play, every new production stimulates the adrenalin, brings on the nerves and invites me to the fray.

Janet Grant is responsible for encouraging me to write this book; she mapped out its structure and scope and helped me analyse the way I work. I am truly grateful for her patience and persistence and for her skilful ability to ask me the right questions. Janet expressed a professional interest in children's theatre which made me realize how little there is in the way of formal training available for people seriously interested in children's theatre: books, courses, and/or work-shops. Yet since I began my career there has undoubtedly been a sharp increase in the number of young theatre practitioners considering a career in children's theatre as a serious option. I am also concerned that the assumption that children's theatre is somehow second-rate compared to adult theatre is still prevalent. Maybe this is our own fault. Maybe we haven't banged our drum hard enough. Maybe we haven't yet convinced our adult theatre colleagues, the critics or indeed the general public of the importance and vitality of our work and the enormous improvements it has seen in quality and variety over recent years. Maybe now is the time for those of us involved in all aspects of children's theatre to speak up and wave the flag.

In this book I want to share my enthusiasm for children's theatre and encourage others to enter this exciting field. I want to erase the myth that writing, acting in or directing children's theatre is an easy option. It is not easy and is often done badly because there is little about the dramatic theory of theatre for children in print and there-fore theatre practitioners haven't understood the depth or breadth of the art form. I want to pass on the knowledge I have gained through many years of practical experience of writing, directing and performing for children, in order to inspire all drama practitioners who enter the world of theatre for children to provide the highest quality theatrical productions possible.

The scope of the book has been defined by my own experience. By children's theatre I mean plays performed in theatres for children by adults, professional or amateur. I'm not writing about pantomime, although certain pantomime techniques often come in useful. Nor am I writing about youth theatre in which young people perform. And, athough I have learnt a great deal from Theatre in Education, toured to schools by actor/teachers, I have not included a study of it in these pages. But I hope that everybody interested in theatre of all kinds for children will find I have something relevant to say, and I am certainly not implying that my particular area of interest means that I don't value the aims and achievements of other disciplines.

I have never received formal training in writing, adapting, acting or directing. It seems somewhat impertinent to be writing a book about all four. But by getting up and doing it for so long I feel I have learnt a lot that might be useful both for teaching purposes and as a platform for future discussion. There is no one way to write, adapt, act or direct. This book is not intended to be the 'be all and end all' on the subject of children's theatre. It is based on one practitioner's experiences, opinions and insights into what makes theatre for children so very special.

David Wood

When I returned to England in 1993, the Unicorn Theatre in London was kind enough to invite me to every one of their new productions. On one occasion, I watched a children's musical that was so cohesive, I was left mesmerized. As I walked in the lobby, I read the credits and saw that a David Wood had not only written the play but had written the lyrics and music too, and directed it. No wonder the play fitted together like an enchanted piece of Swiss clockwork! So awed was I by the talent I had seen displayed, that for half an hour I tried to get up the nerve to approach David at the after-show reception and say, 'Congratulations. What a wonderful play.' Not normally a shy person, that day words failed me. In the end I took the easy way out and wrote him a letter. This book is the result.

Janet Grant

Theatre for Children
Guide to Writing, Adapting, Directing and Acting

Part 1 Theatre for Children:
A Unique Art Form

What an audience!

I shall never forget standing at the back of the auditorium of the Swan Theatre, Worcester watching the first production of *The Owl and the Pussycat Went to See...*, my second play for children, co-written with Sheila Ruskin. It was January 1969. I had been acting in an adult play in Manchester and returned in time to witness twelve sell-out performances in a week. The children responded with huge enthusiasm, rooting for the Owl and the Pussycat as they pursued their quest to get married, beset by marauding Jumblies and the ever-hungry Plum Pudding Flea. One minute they listened attentively, the next they participated with ear-splitting excitement. The way they willingly suspended disbelief and entered into the spirit of the performance was incredibly exciting and strangely moving. They laughed, they shouted warnings, they became emotionally involved, they cared. And the victorious, abandoned cheer when justice prevailed and the Plum Pudding Flea was vanquished was sheer joy to behold. A couple of years later Braham Murray, director of the prestigious 69 Theatre Company in Manchester witnessed the same triumphant moment with tears rolling down his cheeks. 'This,' he said, 'is what theatre is all about!'

Such uninhibited displays of happy enthusiasm are all too rare in adult audiences. After that Worcester production I knew I had to give more children the chance to see *Owl* and eventually managed to bring it to London. Finding a suitable director proved difficult and potentially too expensive, so I directed the play myself and began to understand how working for children was different from working for adults. Then an actor fell ill, so for a week I acted the roles of the Pig and the Turkey, thus experiencing first hand how much energy is necessary and how the actor has constantly to monitor the audience reaction and adjust to it.

The London response to the play echoed Worcester's. Good reviews led to *Owl* getting large audiences. And Samuel French Ltd, who had twice previously read the play and turned it down, sent a representative actually to see it and immediately offered to publish it. This, looking back, reinforces my belief that in children's theatre the audience becomes an integral part of the success or failure of the play. If, when preparing a play or production, we don't consider the audience as a major factor, we may well get the chemistry wrong.

The enormous pleasure *Owl* gave me was the clincher; from now on I needed the adrenalin, the 'buzz' of a children's audience, and the challenge to give children exciting theatrical experiences began to dominate my professional life.

It is interesting how, when theatre folk are reminiscing, stories concerning adult theatre almost always involve funny things happening on stage – props not working or lines forgotten, actors 'corpsing' – whereas stories concerning children's theatre almost always involve the audience – the isolated funny remark, the gasp of wonder greeting a magical lighting effect, their vitriolic disapproval of unfairness, the toddlers playing 'can't catch me' up and down the aisle.

> It was the first performance of the tour at the Theatre Royal, Newcastle, and Herr Von Cuckoo (David Bale) was about to eat the contaminated honey. A lone six- or seven-year-old boy in the audience, anticipating the coming disaster, shouted in a loud, clear, and thick Geordie accent: 'Nooooo! Don't eat the huneeeeeey!' Of course, this is the desired and usual reaction of the audience for the end of the first act, but it was the 110% commitment and sincerity of that lone voice which I shall never forget.
>
> Neil Smye, ASM/understudy, *The Gingerbread Man*

> MR PLOD: Hey! My poster! It's gone! (*to the audience*) Who took it?
> TIMID VOICE FROM THE AUDIENCE: It wasn't me.
>
> David Burrows, Mr Plod, *More Adventures of Noddy*

Over the years children have given me many heart-stopping moments of theatrical pleasure. In 1977 I arrived late, thanks to a delayed train, for the opening performance of the first London (Old Vic) production of *The Gingerbread Man*. As I entered the auditorium mid-song, the entire audience was swaying and clapping in time with the music. School parties of inner-city children, many of them from ethnic minorities, possibly attending a theatre for the very first time. The goodwill and warmth radiating from these children was overwhelming. It was one big, happy party. Yet they listened too, eagerly following the plot. As Irving Wardle said in his review in *The Times*: '... the loudest audience participation I have ever heard, and, much more remarkable, the most absolute breathholding silences.'

The first performance of *The See-Saw Tree* in 1986 was truly nail-biting stuff. Would the audience, who, at the start, had voted in favour of chopping down the tree to make way for an adventure playground, be persuaded by the play's depiction of the plight in store for the creatures who live on the tree? How would they vote at the end? As their hands vehemently shot up in the air in favour of saving the tree, I felt a lump in my throat and couldn't hold back the tears. You wouldn't get that from adults. Give me children every time.

Why do children need their own theatre?

Theatre for children is a separate art form with qualities that make it quite distinct from adult theatre. It is *not* simplified adult theatre; it has its own dynamics and its own rewards. Quality theatre for children is valuable in that it opens the door for children to a new world of excitement and imagination.

I once read that a healthy theatre scene is a sign of a civilized society. It naturally follows that children, as an important part of that society, should have their own theatre. Indeed, Adrian Mitchell, the well-known poet and playwright for both adults and children, once commented that in every city where they have a theatre, they should also have a children's theatre. He was referring to the provision of a theatre building specifically for children. In Antwerp they have one right next door to the adult theatre, but in Great Britain most children's productions take place in adult theatres and tend to be low on the list of priorities. Indeed there is a view that children don't need special plays. A trip to the pantomime or to a spectacular ice show or a production of Shakespeare or a big musical is perfectly good enough as an introduction to theatre.

I cannot accept this. The world of literature has a flourishing tradition of specialist books for children; it is accepted that before being able to appreciate Dickens or Keats children need to cut their teeth on the Ahlbergs or Michael Rosen. To gain their interest and encourage an enthusiasm for reading, children need books that appeal directly to their world, their pleasures, their fears and their experiences. In a similar way, children's theatre can open doors to a new world of imagination, excitement and thoughtfulness.

Some people believe that drama for children is best employed as an educational tool. Certainly drama classes can develop communication skills, instil confidence and encourage teamwork. And Theatre in Education can bring to life all kinds of curriculum topics and, through participation, make learning more palatable and fresh than constant reference to a textbook. But, however educationally valuable such work is, it should not be seen as a substitute for a visit to the theatre to see professional actors performing a quality piece of theatre. I'm sure that art teachers would agree that teaching children to paint and draw doesn't mean they shouldn't go to an art gallery to see what is regarded as fine art; teaching children to play football does not negate the value of taking them to a premier league football match; a child learning to play the piano surely benefits from hearing a professional pianist in a concert hall.

It also strikes me that there is nothing wrong with the notion of children going to the theatre to be entertained. Why should theatre for children always be educational? Just as adults unwind by going to see farces, thrillers or musical comedies, so children deserve relaxation. And most teachers would agree that *any* theatre experience that has a modicum of worth can be educational with a small 'e', inviting discussion and follow-up writing and art projects. And most teachers agree that entertaining lessons succeed more than purely factual ones.

The quest for quality

And the first step, as you know, is always what matters most, particularly when we are dealing with those who are young and tender. That is the time when they are easily moulded and when any impression we choose to make leaves a permanent mark.

Plato, *The Republic*

Quality is the keynote. We must give children the best we can. We must fight the offhand attitude 'It's only for kids.' Production values and the quality of writing and direction must be high. If we fail? The words of Alan Hulme, the *Manchester Evening News* theatre critic, say it all. Reviewing a big commercial pantomime which clearly failed to cater successfully for the large number of children in the audience, he wrote: 'Ah well, bang goes another generation of theatre-goers.'

Kathleen Hale, the creator of Orlando, the Marmalade Cat, once told me, 'Of course you have to remember that children have terrible taste. They can be fobbed off with all kinds of rubbish.' This lack of critical faculties in children makes our responsibility to entertain them with integrity all the more crucial. For children are often inexperienced theatre-goers. They must not be short-changed. If we are to trigger their imaginations, emotionally involve them and give them an exciting, memorable new experience; if we are going to encourage them to enjoy theatre-going in their adult years; if we believe that theatre can be educative as well as entertaining, then we must endeavour to give them the best.

A music critic recently appeared on television attacking a populist production of the opera *La Bohème* at the Albert Hall. He pointed out that many of the thousands of people attending the performances would be 'virginal' opera-goers. Though he welcomed the fact that with low seat prices many people would now experience opera for the first time, he nevertheless felt that the production, with its use of microphones and 'pop' lighting, would not really introduce opera properly to the masses. They deserved more, he felt. They should be witnessing the real thing.

Children, too, need the real thing. They don't need tinsel or candy-floss. The idea that children's theatre offers little more than whimsical tales of elves dancing on the village green belies the developments that have taken place in recent years. It need not be primitive, jokey, superficial or patronizing.

Michael Billington, The *Guardian* critic, once wrote: 'I begin to doubt the whole notion of a special ghetto area called "Children's Theatre". That belongs to a fast-fading, stratified culture in which serious things were for grown-ups, and children, supposedly innocent of the world, had to be fed an anodyne substitute devoid of sex, violence, death and harsh reality. If you relied on the British Theatre solely for your information about children, you would assume that they loved only furry animals, fairy tales, glove puppets, gingerbread men, dwarfs, giants and audience participation.'

Mr Billington had perhaps not seen much quality children's theatre. His mention of gingerbread men may have been a dig at my play *The Gingerbread Man*, written in 1976. *The Gingerbread Man* is a fantasy, but, as Robert Hewison said in his *Sunday Times* review, 'Behind the antics of the inhabitants of a kitchen dresser lie themes that have inspired the greatest grown-up drama: Death (cuckoo clock has lost his voice and is facing the Dustbin); the Stranger (the newly baked Gingerbread Man who disrupts Pepper and Salt's domestic routines); the Outsider (the horrid old tea bag lady who lives alone); the Invader (Sleek the Mouse, a threat to the whole community) ... the kitchen dresser is a home: the family must care for its members.'

In fairness to Mr Billington, he later reviewed with enthusiasm my adaptation of Roald Dahl's *The Witches*, and gave favourable coverage to other children's plays at the Young Vic and Polka Theatre.

Pioneers and Practitioners

This book is not a history of children's theatre, but it is worth remembering some of the pioneers who paved the way and led to the children's theatre movement. A full history of children's theatre in Great Britain has yet to be written, but Alan England, in his book *Theatre for the Young*, devotes an interesting chapter to it.

It is generally accepted that the first widely successful children's play was J. M. Barrie's *Peter Pan*, which first appeared in 1904. But for many decades the play could only be seen in London.

In 1927 Bertha Waddell founded the Scottish Children's Theatre, the first professional company of its kind. They performed mainly in schools.

Since the First World War, children had been encouraged to go to the Old Vic, with special matinées at low prices. But the plays were not specially written for them.

In 1929 *Toad of Toad Hall*, A. A. Milne's adaptation of Kenneth Grahame's *The Wind in the Willows* appeared, and played for many years in London and elsewhere. Peter Slade in the thirties and Brian Way in the forties were highly influential in developing performances in which the audience of children participated. Both worked mainly in schools.

The years following the Second World War saw the formation of several children's theatre companies including John Allen's Glyndebourne Children's Theatre, John English's Midland Arts Centre in Birmingham, and George Devine's Young Vic Players. Caryl Jenner's Mobile Theatre subsequently became the Unicorn Theatre, the first full-time professional theatre for children in London, taking over the Arts Theatre in 1967. Finance was a major problem for all these companies, whether playing in theatres or schools. And it was not until the sixties that Arts Council funding, albeit limited, became available for children's work.

A most significant step forward, in 1965, was the arrival of Theatre in Education at the Belgrade, Coventry. In the same year, the Royal Shakespeare Company, which has sadly since shown little interest in children's theatre, presented Robert Bolt's *The Thwarting of Baron Bolligrew*.

It was in the late sixties and early seventies that I first became involved in children's theatre. There was still not that much activity, but I remember seeing Brian Way's *Pinocchio*, performed by his company Theatre Centre, which had begun in 1953. I enjoyed an excellent children's play at the Royal Court, presented by the mime artistes who later formed Theatre Machine. And at Unicorn, I much enjoyed Ken Campbell's *Paraphernalia* (later retitled *Old King Cole*). Ted Hughes, Adrian Mitchell, Peter Terson (notably in his work for the National Youth Theatre) and Joan Aiken wrote successful plays for children. But the work was still being produced by dedicated pioneers. There was no real pattern or integrated policy.

Over the last twenty-five years we have seen the blossoming of Theatre in Education and small-scale touring children's theatre, although many companies have not been able to survive ruthless financial cuts. Polka Theatre, founded by Richard Gill, is a unique purpose-built children's theatre in Wimbledon. The Young Vic has presented several splendid productions for children. The National Theatre has occasionally included a children's play in its programme, notably the work of Michael Bogdanov and Alan Ayckbourn. Guy Holland's Quicksilver Theatre Company has toured successfully and David Holman's splendid plays have been presented in both schools and theatres. Some regional theatres regularly present children's plays, including the Sherman Theatre, Cardiff, Contact Theatre in Manchester, and the Birmingham Stage Company. Many writers have chosen to concentrate on children's theatre, including Mike Kenny, Bryony Lavery, Diane Samuels, Vicky Ireland (who is also the Director of Polka Theatre), Charles Way, Shaun Prendergast, Nona Shepphard, Neil Duffield, Andy Rashleigh and Richard Williams (former Director of Unicorn Theatre).

In Great Britain, however, there are few theatre buildings exclusively for children. And it is hard to persuade the managements of the 'adult' theatres to make productions for children an integral part of their programming. Despite this, the twentieth century has seen a growing interest in children's theatre as an art form, and since the sixties more and more practitioners have dedicated themselves to it.

Children's theatre is obviously aimed fair and square at children. But it is important to remember that different plays may be aimed at different age-groups. There is, for instance, a growing interest in catering for pre-school children. Some plays are most appropriate for primary school-age children. The most exciting audiences for this age-group are often uninhibited school parties. Older children, on the brink of joining the adult audience, are perhaps more difficult to write for. Many performances of all kinds of children's plays will be attended by families.

My own work has mainly targeted the primary school-age child, although I am aware that many of my plays have a wider appeal. They are performed by amateurs and professionals (and sometimes schools) in theatre buildings or halls. My aim has been to channel them into the theatre mainstream, rather than separating them into some sort of children's ghetto that is ignored by the theatre establishment.

Raising our standards

Children's theatre has come a long way since *Peter Pan* paved the way. But the quality of productions, both professional and amateur, remains variable. The same could be said of adult theatre. But the difference, in my opinion, is that the lack of specialist training in children's theatre has led to some very basic problems and misunderstandings:

- many practitioners don't understand their audience and how to create productions to involve and enthuse them.
- the writing often lacks clarity and focus, expecting too much, or worse, too little of the audience.
- the acting often lacks sincerity and truth; some actors assume children need constant jollity and surface enthusiasm rather than honesty and depth.
- many directors take their own adult understanding of dramatic theory and superimpose it unchanged on to children's theatre; consequently their productions miss much of the potential humour, excitement and energy.
- the general overall attitude towards children's theatre and its practitioners still tends to relegate it and them to the second or even third division; it fails to recognize theatre for children as a separate art form.

This book tries to dispel such myths and offer practical advice on how to avoid fundamental failings.

Part 2 The Nature of the Beasts: What Children *En Masse* Respond To

The Dynamics of a Children's Audience

> The whole audience – hundreds and hundreds of children – were creating a storm to blow the Great Slick back out to sea and save the creatures living in a rock pool. What made it so fantastic was that you could feel that they were all totally into what they were doing. They were all fully involved and willing to play their part in the survival of those small rock pool characters. It really was the most powerful and moving experience. The big lesson was that if you play it for real, if there is no hint of tongue-in-cheek, then you will gain the respect and interest of the young audience because they are willing to be involved.
>
> Adam Stafford, Sludge/ASM, *The Selfish Shellfish*

When I'm entertaining children with a magic show or entering a class of young children to talk about books, I always introduce myself with one word. 'Hello!' I say, not too loudly, but with a broad smile on my face. I get an immediate response: 'Hello!' It is said in chorus, and not too loud in case the teacher disapproves, but the children are willing and curious to see where things are leading. I say 'Hello!' again, much louder this time. The children smile. I have given them licence to make a bit of noise. 'Hello!' they shout. The ice has been broken ...

If I were to adopt the same approach with a class of teenagers, the reaction would be very different. Total silence, probably. No eye contact. Maybe the odd raised eyebrow or curled lip. A general atmosphere of 'Who is this idiot?' For teenagers, indeed most young people above the age of about eleven, have developed a sense of self-awareness. They would feel embarrassed and patronized by this smiling middle-aged twit bouncing in and trying to be affable – until I had established a safety zone and it was clear I wasn't there to make fun of them. Any enthusiasm or willingness to join in 'the game' is carefully guarded.

If I said 'Hello' in exactly the same way to a group of adults the response would be different again. Some adults would be rather embarrassed and self-conscious and decide not to react. Others would show a certain generosity and a willingness to enter into the spirit of the entertainment, tongue-in-cheek. In Britain, this is most noticeable in old-time music hall, where the audience is invited to join in certain phrases – the Chairman knows that his audience enjoys being part of the entertainment and introduces situations in which they can participate. In music hall and pantomime, audience participation has become part of the fun, part of the game, linking the stage with the audience in a warm complicity.

Yet the acting in pantomimes is often insincere. The actor performs in a tongue-in-cheek style, winking at the audience, the implication being that the story need not be taken too seriously. 'I may be playing Aladdin,' the actor seems to say, 'and I may have been shut up in this cave by Abanazar, but really I'm your favourite star from that soap opera on the television and I'm not really in any danger.' This style may appeal to adults, who like seeing their favourite television names or pop singers or comedians cast in fantasy roles, and welcome the fact that part of the tradition is sending up the story, but children do not understand this sophistication and will often simply turn off. They lose interest in the story because they see and hear nothing to make it particularly important.

Children love stories and do not welcome deviation or interruption in the narrative line or insincerity. It is all too easy for an adult who enjoys pantomime to think that a child enjoys the same thing. This sums up one of the major considerations when embarking upon a theatre project for children. The audience is different from an adult audience. How children differ, what they respond to, what makes them turn off and how they react when confronted with a story acted out for them – knowledge of these areas is vital.

How Children Differ

1. Children enjoy being active participants rather than passive spectators

One of the most successful routines I perform in my children's magic show involves a flower which wilts whenever I'm not looking at it.

The energy with which the audience informs me of the fact is amazing. The children build on each other's vocal energy, thoroughly enjoying the 'crowd chant'. Time and time and time again they shout and point. Of course, I can never turn round in time to see what they can. The flower has always righted itself. When with amazement and concern I finally catch sight of the flower in the wilted state, I invite the audience to revive it. The whole audience treats the exercise with great seriousness, making rain noises, blowing pretend clouds away, smiling broadly to represent the sun coming out. When the flower slowly but surely straightens the audience cheer triumphantly as if to say, 'We did it! We made the flower get better.'

If a children's play is really working well, it is exciting to witness the way in which the audience will galvanize itself into one organic being, swept along by the twists and turns of the plot, following the story and reacting with laughter and, if encouraged, participation. For instance, when the lighting in the theatre dims before the start of the play, children will often erupt into wild cheering. As the play progresses, children often react like a crowd of football spectators, allowing their emotions to run free, enthusiastically encouraging or hindering the characters, and sharing with the actors moments of triumph or disaster.

While it is true that adults watching an adult play can become totally absorbed and react as one, they will seldom demonstrate the uninhibited exuberance or lack of self-consciousness displayed by children.

2. Children, far more than adults, generate a sense of electricity in the theatre

Most children enjoy sharing a communal sense of occasion. The theatre trip is special – a treat, sometimes even a day off school. Their expectations are high. The stage becomes an arena on which their eyes and minds are focused. It is bigger and more immediate and therefore more important and exciting than a television screen; and far harder to ignore or walk away from.

The excited chatter in the auditorium before curtain-up paves the way for something special, an event in their lives, not – as for adults – a run-of-the-mill theatre visit. The actors register this and must respond to it. They realize they are working on a knife-edge and that every performance will be different.

> The thing that stands out most strongly in my mind about playing to an audience only of children is the belief they have in the story and the situation. Children can project their imaginings into reality. In the theatre, when you have convinced a young audience of your character's plight, the silence and stillness is deafening. I have felt this many times: in *The Gingerbread Man* when he may be eaten, or in *Dick Whittington* when Dick is accused of stealing, or in *Cinderella* when the Ugly Sisters tear up Cinders' ticket to the ball. Only once playing to an entirely adult audience did I feel this energy and then I was strung up on the cross in the Mystery Plays, and there I was assisted by a huge emotional history.
>
> Peter Duncan, The Gingerbread Man, *The Gingerbread Man*

3. Children can become over-excited

Their enjoyment is infectious. They spark off each other. The actors' skills may be stretched to the limit to retain control. They need to keep their wits about them, taking in and adjusting to the audience reaction far more than they might have to for adults.

4. Children willingly enter into the spirit of the entertainment

They will happily participate, helping or hindering the characters as the story unfolds. They enjoy taking sides, identifying with a likeable character, getting angry with the behaviour of an anti-social character. Their ability and willingness to become emotionally involved is more overt and instinctive than adults. They will openly release their feelings, reacting instantly to a change in direction, not just sitting there listening and weighing up the debate in their heads, as adults do.

5. Children can be uncompromisingly direct

An audience as generous and willing can, it follows, be a wonderfully rewarding audience to play to. Their lack of inhibition and their open enthusiasm make them a potentially more exciting prospect than an adult audience. But their ability to assess instantly what is going on on the stage and respond instinctively to it can be unsettling for the unseasoned children's practitioner. Add to this the fact that children have not had years of training in theatre 'manners' and you get a sometimes surprisingly direct, honest reaction. If a visitor with a large wart on his nose comes to tea, the parents will politely avert their gaze and pretend the wart isn't there. The child will probably point at it straight away and enquire, 'What's that at the end of your nose?' In the same way, a children's performance may be peppered with unwanted individual cries from the audience: 'I don't like you!', 'You're fat!' or (kind but distracting), 'You're funny!' Children also have an uncanny gift for sniffing out untruthful acting. They don't sit there and say, with adult vision, 'This actor is being insincere,' or, 'This actor is playing tongue-in-cheek.' They simply turn off. They decide that what is happening isn't interesting and that until something more enjoyable comes along they may as well kick the seat in front.

6. Children let you know when they are bored

Even if they are hating every moment of the play, adult audiences tend to sit quietly and even clap politely at the end. But children rarely grant you the right to fail. They react rather more like the adult audiences of Shakespeare's day. If they are bored, they won't keep the fact to themselves. They will probably start talking. They will take their eyes off the stage and look around for something more interesting. They will get fed up with sitting and stand, walk around or see what it's like to hide under the seat.

Many will decide that this strange dark place is the very last place on earth they want to be. They will think of ways of leaving. Younger ones may resort to talking loudly or crying in order to get the attention of an accompanying adult. They'll ask their parents, 'Can I go home now?' in loud tones for the rest of the audience to hear. Children seem to know this will embarrass the adult, who may well feel, not wanting to spoil the play for others, that the best course is to

take the child out. Another common ploy is to decide that they want
to go to the lavatory. This has nothing to do with the limited capacity
of a child's bladder. It has to do with the fact that the child, from a
remarkably young age, knows that wanting to go for a wee is the
most likely lever with which to force a parent to act. It never fails.
The majority of children who want to go to the lavatory do not really
want to go at all; they want to alleviate the tedium of the performance
they are being forced to watch.

7. Children respond to direct audience participation

If asked a question, they will answer. Most children actively enjoy
vocal and physical participation, giving advice or warnings or helping
achieve a goal. It is up to us carefully to channel and co-ordinate this
participation to use it profitably and 'clearly'.

8. Not all children respond in the same way

We should never forget that the audience *en masse* is composed of
individual children, some of whom may resist the experience. Some
children may be first-timers. Depending on their age, they may find
initially that the experience of being in a theatre is a strange one.
They may find it intimidating being part of a large crowd. They may
be frightened by the noise levels. They may become disturbed when
the lights go down. While some children may find it thrilling to be
frightened by a scary character, others may quickly turn to their
parents and ask to be taken out. There will be times when the individual child will not be swept along with the rest.

9. Children don't always choose to come

The children file into the theatre and take their seats. Some of them
have been brought by teachers, some by parents. In most cases, the
decision to come in the first place was not theirs. Whereas adults
know what they are letting themselves in for when entering a theatre,
for some children the expectation may be daunting rather than
exciting. Not all children will find it natural to sit in rows of seats

watching actors on a stage. Do not expect them all to understand immediately the theatrical convention of watching a play performed.

10. The composition of an audience for a children's play is so variable

There are four types of audience for a children's play: weekday performance for school parties, weekday public daytime performance, weekday public after school performance, and the weekend or holiday public performance. Audiences that include many more adults (most of whom are parents) often have an inhibiting effect on their own children. Plus, babes in arms or toddlers who are too young to understand what is happening can be irritating distractions.

A Children's Audience – Common Characteristics

So let's imagine we are confronted with an audience of children – several hundred of them maybe. What is the nature of this beast? How can we best manoeuvre to get it on our side and give it a good time? What are the common characteristics we can capitalize on? What are the common characteristics that might cause us problems?

1. Children eagerly respond to justice

I believe that children are born with an innate sense of justice. This has nothing to do with morality, or knowing the difference between right and wrong. It is to do with fairness. From a very early age children seem to understand that everyone should be treated equally. So, in a play, a situation where one character is unfair to another is an automatic trigger to set the child's blood boiling. Emotional involvement is guaranteed. The common instinct to support the underdog provides us with a very basic, powerful lever with which to manipulate the audience's response. It is very rare to find a child who backs the baddie. The vast majority of children instinctively want justice to prevail.

2. Children like being frightened – within limits

The next time we tried this phobic child in a theatre – at her own request – I took an emergency Granny in the party to stay with the older one and his friends. There were smiles and confident announcements that she wouldn't be afraid. Curtain up, pretty dancing-girls, smiles. Then BANG! The Demon King appeared in red tights and orange smoke, going HAAHAHAAHAHAHAHAHA! I fled up the aisle (we had booked end seats, suspecting trouble) like an out-of-control bagpiper, with a wailing bundle under my arm. In the foyer, we reconsidered our position. Ten minutes later, we progressed to peering round the door at the back of the theatre. Later still, we resumed our seats. Well, my seat: she clung to me until her confidence returned. Unfortunately, it returned so thoroughly that by the second half she was standing on her seat shoeless, shrieking 'PISS OFF DEMON!' Oh, the shame.

Libby Purves, *How NOT to Raise a Perfect Child*

In a controlled situation, most children do get a thrill out of a scary situation. Most of us can remember being frightened by an episode of a series like *Doctor Who* or by the Wicked Witch in *The Wizard of Oz*. We would hide behind the sofa and peep out at the screen, seeing how long we dared keep our eyes open, but we always had the reassuring presence of a parent in the room, and the room itself was a familiar environment. So the power of the frisson never became too close for comfort. The experience in the theatre is similar. Children are surrounded by their friends, parents and others, and a certain amount of horror is really rather appealing.

I think this is the reason why so many fairy-tales, for so long the most popular examples of literature for children, have genuinely scary moments. Neil Postman, in his book *The Disappearance of Childhood*, points out that: 'As Bettelheim has demonstrated in *The Uses of Enchantment*, the importance of fairy-tales lies in their capacity to reveal the existence of evil in a form that permits children to integrate it without trauma.' It is true that we cannot hide from children the nasty things of life. What we must endeavour to do is introduce them in such a way that children will not be scarred, rather prepared for some of the unpleasantness they are bound to face. Theatre, along with literature, can take a major role in this process.

This also explains the considerable appeal to children of the world of the supernatural, magic and monsters, all of which have great theatrical possibilities. I know that some people would like to ban the use of magic and characters like witches from the entire canon of children's literature. They feel it introduces children to a darker world which is unhealthy. I once toured a production of *Meg and Mog Show*, based on the well-known books about a witch, her cat and her owl. A born-again Christian vicar captured the front pages of the local newspapers of one Midlands town, advising parents not to take their children to see the play because 'It could encourage child abuse.' I found this sad. Meg, the witch, is renowned for her lack of success with spells, and for her kindness to her familiars. I cannot believe that the vicar had ever seen the play because by no stretch of the imagination could the play be said to be a danger to its audience. The banning or expurgating of stories with supernatural themes is a sad mistake. Much of the richness of our culture would be denied to our children, and the world of the imagination would be shackled, leaving only a bland diet of pleasantry.

3. Children are healthily subversive

They find 'rude' things fascinating and funny. Smelly socks, under-pants and bodily functions, subjects that aren't quite 'nice' in the realms of polite adult society, spark off children's giggly appreciation of 'naughtiness'.

Alison Lurie, in her splendid book about subversion in children's literature, *Not In Front of the Grown-Ups*, points out how many classics of children's literature, from *Alice in Wonderland* to *Peter Pan*, involve the subversive view of a child in a world peopled by adults:

> These were the sacred texts of childhood, whose authors had not forgotten what it was like to be a child. To read them was to feel a shock of recognition, a rush of liberating energy. These books, and others like them, recommended – even celebrated – day dreaming,

disobedience, answering back, running away from home, and concealing one's private thoughts and feelings from unsympathetic grown-ups. They overturned adult pretensions and made fun of adult institutions, including school and family. In a word, they were subversive, just like many of the rhymes and jokes and games I learned on the school playground.

In more recent years, Roald Dahl has achieved enormous popularity amongst children by incorporating taboo and often rather revolting things in his books. He knew, when he wrote *The BFG*, that his audience would be fascinated with the ghastly child-eating preoccupation of the giants. He knew they would fall about with laughter at the 'whizzpopping' of the Big Friendly Giant – for breaking wind is something we are all familiar with but rarely talk about. He knew, when he wrote *The Witches*, that children would be intrigued by the idea that ordinary women in everyday life might in fact be child-hating witches. He knew they would revel in a story in which a child protagonist could, even after having been transformed into the shape of a mouse, defeat the wicked witches of the world. Certainly both these stories adapted like a dream to the stage and I can still hear the gales of laughter that erupted when the BFG 'whizzpopped' in front of Her Majesty the Queen. The ultimate embarrassing moment.

4. Children are logical

In *More Adventures of Noddy*, a wasp dive-bombs our hero, who leaps around trying to flap it away. A young voice from the stalls in one performance shouted encouragingly, 'It can't sting you, Noddy, you're made of wood!'

Such a sense of logic means that even the most fantasy-based ideas must be clearly and rigorously carried through. In *The Owl and the Pussycat Went to See...* I made the Runcible Spoon a character. She was timid and wouldn't say boo to a goose. But I thought it would be amusing if she was the only character of whom the villainous, ever-hungry Plum Pudding Flea was frightened. This would make her useful in warding him off when he tried to eat the Owl and the

Pussycat. My logical reason for her own strength was that, in real life, plum pudding (of which the Flea is made) is eaten with a spoon. I was a little unsure that children would make the necessary connection. But I needn't have worried. When asked by a rather patronizing radio interviewer why on earth the Plum Pudding Flea should be frightened of the Runcible Spoon, a little girl in the audience replied long-sufferingly, 'Well, what do *you* eat plum pudding with?'

Their logical approach means that children like a story with a beginning, a middle and an end. It is not always necessary to perform these in the traditional order. The use of flashback is understood by children, as long as it is done with clarity. Unlike adults, children do like all the loose ends tied up by the end and a satisfying resolution. They don't like too many sub-plots meandering away from the central through-line.

5. Children will respond differently and unpredictably

No two performances will feel the same. Some audiences will laugh more than others. Some audiences will be quicker than others to respond to plot developments.

A children's audience is unpredictable. You have to be ready for anything. Expect the unexpected. Do not expect to rehearse, then perform it as you rehearsed it. The audience can leave you spellbound by their imagination and confused by their logic, so that you are holding back tears of laughter or completely dumbfounded as to what to do next. It can happen with any part of the production, including audience participation.

For example, some audiences will pick up a comment made by one child and latch on to it like a limpet. This can be very frustrating when the solo initiator has actually got the wrong idea. Take one audience's reaction to Salt's predicament in *The Gingerbread Man*. Salt consulted with Pepper on ways to catch the marauding Sleek, the Mouse. He said the line, 'Something to make him freeze, still as a statue', to which Pepper is meant to respond that Sleek himself had done that once when the Big Ones had shouted and screamed at him. Unfortunately, Salt paused for a fraction of a second after the word 'freeze'. One quick child, fiercely involved in Salt's problem, shouted the word 'ice'. Ice would indeed make Sleek freeze. It was a perfectly reasonable suggestion. But there was no ice on the Welsh dresser where the play took place. The whole audience took up the word and chanted it mercilessly for a couple of minutes, while the confused cast tried to maintain their cool. 'Ice, ice, ice!' In this case, the actors rightly ignored the audience and carried on until they reached the next exciting piece of action which regained the audience's attention. To have answered or entered into an argument would have been impossible. The actors simply couldn't be heard.

6. Children make noise during the performance

Remember that however involving and entertaining the performance, the auditorium will rarely be an oasis of total silence. A certain amount of noise is inevitable.

Constructive noise can be the sound of children talking to their parents or whispering to help explain something to a younger sibling or friend. It is not a sign of boredom, but a quite natural reaction for them to talk about what they see and hear on stage. Some noise is caused by the physical movement of the children themselves. In moments of excitement children will often jump up and down unable to contain themselves. For example, the appearance of a hopping kangaroo guarantees that many children will echo the movement. Children cannot really be expected to sit motionless in seats not designed for their small bodies. Tip-up seats in some theatres can be a real pest and cause quite a racket. Children find them uncomfortable. They even slip through the seats or decide they are fun to play with.

Not all noise, however, is inevitable. Some of it is unnecessary and not the 'fault' of the children. Most destructive noise – catcalls, 'I want to go home' cries or uninterested talking – can be traced to a problem in the writing, acting and/or directing: someone integral to the production has not fully understood the importance of the story and the need to involve children emotionally. It is up to children's theatre practitioners to acknowledge the realities and challenges that an audience of children brings, and to reduce the possibilities of boredom to such an extent that the children have no time or desire to think of alternative activities.

Some people blame noise on short attention span. It may be true that the attention span of a child is shorter than an adult's, but I feel it is far more useful to focus on the question of content. Although a children's play will probably be somewhat shorter than an adult play, for both adults and children just five minutes can seem interminable if the content is not interesting. Conversely, many children will happily continue an activity for a long, uninterrupted period of an hour or more if what they are doing thoroughly involves them.

7. Children respond to action

Language will be the main means of communication in most children's plays. But conversation must be linked to action, which gives movement and visual interest. Always be suspicious of a play for children in which two characters sit around doing nothing but talking. Characters doing things are just as interesting, sometimes more interesting, than characters talking. Theatre for children should not be an arena for debate, but rather an arena for getting things done. I can't imagine that ancient Greek children got pleasure out of the plays in the amphitheatres. So often they would have witnessed a messenger coming on to tell the assembly all the exciting things that have happened offstage on the battlefield. The children would have been far more interested in seeing those events rather than hearing about them. Perhaps, however, the concerted movement of the traditional Chorus would have held their interest.

8. Children don't like being patronized

Children resent being talked down to. We underestimate their intelligence if we simplify things to an extreme degree or address them rather like we sometimes talk to our pets, in a singsong, smiley sort of way. Such tweeness in writing or performance is guaranteed to turn them off.

9. Children don't like lovey-dovey stuff

Beware of princes and princesses gazing doe-eyed at each other singing gooey love songs. On the whole, children can't stand love scenes, especially sung ones. In a pantomime, there is nothing better guaranteed to start the chat and the queue for the loo than the onset of such romance. Or worse. Once, as Prince Charming and Cinderella kissed, I heard a precocious nine-year-old shout, 'Go on, give her one!'

Children are not interested in the process of falling in love. They are quite happy for two people to love each other, but they are more interested in the problems that beset them. Love thwarted gives the audience an opportunity to root for the lovers and foil the killjoys. In other words, we return to the theme of justice.

10. Children love animals and toys

Aesop knew what he was doing when he chose animals to be the characters in his moral fables. Just look at how many of the favourite characters in children's literature are animals. Most of them are anthropomorphic in that they appear to have human emotions and often live in communities reminiscent of our own. But children's writers know that their audiences will respond to animals more positively than to their own kind. Why is this? Is it because children feel they have a certain power over them? Is it because they have a vulnerability that children sense and which encourages them to feel protective? Is it simply that animals are attractive? It is certainly true that if I am looking for a character to immediately emotionally involve the children in the audience, I will probably choose a mute animal to whom life is giving a raw deal.

In the same way, children enjoy toy characters. Toys are familiar to them, friends with whom they share their own games and make-believe stories.

11. Children love stories

A good story-line is essential for any children's play. Ideally, avoid the use of too many sub-plots. Even a play with an overtly educational aim, such as a play about the conservation of the environment, must have a strong, coherent, logical, interesting basic plot. The focus must be well-defined. There is no time for superfluous detail. The script needs to be so tight it is virtually impossible to cut anything without losing the meaning.

A useful exercise is to compare an adult novel with a successful children's novel. The children's novelist will waste little time. He or she won't spend the opening pages describing the scenery and telling you the sun has come out. Unlike the adult novelist, the children's novelist will not feel the need to embark upon long detailed psychological profiles of the characters. There is clear punchy dialogue and narrative, and the concentration will be on action rather than reflection.

The story must be within a child's understanding, but it does not need to be simplistic. A simple basic plot is not the same as a simplistic plot. However, the starting point may be the same. For instance, the simple basic plot of *The Gingerbread Man* is that the cuckoo in the clock loses his voice and gets it back again. This would remain simplistic if the play focused only on that one 'journey'. In fact, the one basic idea becomes the through-line for a story involving other characters. It becomes a saga of life on a Welsh dresser, but Cuckoo's voice remains the spur. In *The Owl and the Pussycat Went to See...* the basic plot is very simple. The Owl and the Pussycat want to get married and, having sailed away, find an island on which there is a pig who gives them a ring and a turkey who marries them. If only that basic plot were used to create the play, I would suggest it could be called simplistic. As it is, the Owl and the Pussycat encounter many hazards along the road. Their quest is peopled with other exotic characters from Edward Lear's imagination, but, again, the main through-line keeps the whole thing together. Any sub-plots need to relate directly to the main theme and contribute to it.

Stories and Themes that Children Love:
Ideas that Work on The Stage

Children respond to certain themes, ideas and stories:

Fantasy within Reality

On a school visit I once asked a group of children why Roald Dahl's books were so popular. A bright ten-year-old put up his hand. 'Take *The Witches*,' he cried. 'All those extraordinary happenings like the boy turning into a mouse ... but it's all so plausible!'

He was right. The extraordinary springing from the everyday provides a rich vein for children's stories, and indeed theatre. Children are intrigued by impossible happenings. They are fascinated by the inexplicable.

In *Peter Pan*, the first children's theatre classic, the story starts with the children of a typical middle-class Edwardian family going to bed. Admittedly fantasy creeps in early on when we discover that the children's nanny is a Northumberland dog. This apparently mundane, familiar routine is interrupted by the arrival of Peter, who flies in through the window. We have all thought how exciting it would be to fly. Here is someone who can actually do it – and, of course, Peter subsequently teaches the children to fly and carries them off to an exciting sequence of adventures in the Neverland.

Fantasy does not mean airy-fairy. The reality in a fantasy story can be as gritty as the reality in a biographical study or the story of a child living on the streets in Victorian London. The story can be rooted in reality or fantasy or a combination of both.

More recently Allan Ahlberg's stories have worked well on stage. He often starts with a normal situation and then changes the rules. In *Ten in a Bed*, a girl complains to her non-believing parents that her bed is regularly invaded by fairy-tale characters. We witness the events and therefore have to believe them, even though we know they couldn't really happen. In *The Giant's Baby*, a fairly normal family is suddenly lumbered by the arrival on their doorstep of a huge baby, temporarily abandoned by a giant. The idea is immediately appealing, but great skill is applied in continuing and developing the idea.

Although I have seen a number of excellent plays for children firmly rooted in reality, I cannot resist for long the use of fantasy, particularly for younger children. Occasionally, the whole play can be a fantasy, yet still rooted in a real world. My play *The Ideal Gnome Expedition*, starts off with two rather bored garden gnomes, Mr Wheeler (who pushes a wheelbarrow) and Mr Fisher (who wields a fishing rod), who are forced to spend their days in the Big Ones' (human beings) backyard. Answering a cry for help from the dustbin, they rescue an abandoned clockwork toy duck. They mend him and, longing for adventure, take him on an expedition over the wall into the concrete jungle of the city beyond. The problems they encounter feature situations and places familiar to children of today, yet the story is basically fantasy-derived.

Myths and Legends

Myths and legends spring from the superstitions and fears of human beings throughout the centuries. Stories from the myths and legends of different countries are a natural source of material for children's plays. They abound in adventure, quests, monsters, battles against the elements, incredible journeys and struggles for survival. Man's position in the Universe, the Underworld, fate and destiny, 'why are we here?' – these are stories on a grand scale and they can be made accessible to a children's audience.

I much enjoyed Diane Redmond's version of Homer's *Odyssey* at the Polka Theatre in which the imaginatively staged perils and excitements of the journey were tempered by the humour of Homer being portrayed as a harassed war-reporter, struggling reluctantly to keep up with events in order to file his latest column. At Unicorn Theatre I saw a highly impressive production of *Beowulf*, which made the whole legend come to life much more appealingly than when I studied the epic poem at University.

My own versions of *Robin Hood* and *The Pied Piper* (co-written with Dave and Toni Arthur) were exciting projects to work on. We set *Robin Hood* within the celebratory atmosphere of a medieval village's May Games. Every May Day, villages throughout England would celebrate by acting out stories of the legendary Robin Hood and his outlaw band. We incorporated other May Day traditions, such as the arrival of the Jack-in-the-Green, the Maypole ceremony, and the choosing of the King and Queen of the May. The 'plays-within-a-play' structure worked well and the audience became part of a major celebration. The legend of *The Pied Piper* – in which the Piper, having rid Hamelin of rats, is denied payment by the villainous Mayor and gets his revenge by using his pipe to entice the children away from the town – proved to be a thought-provoking piece of theatre for children. Again, we used a 'play-within-a-play' device, whereby Hamelin's children of today were told the story by the townsfolk. A modern-day busker is cajoled into playing the Piper. In a twist at the end, he reveals himself to be the real Piper, who has returned to claim his fee, or he will do the same thing again. This updating made the storytelling easier, although we still incorporated much of the famous Robert Browning poem within the text.

In today's multi-racial society, children's theatre can be a useful way of re-telling the legends and stories from foreign lands. India, Africa, Asia and the Americas all have their own tales and their own versions of universal traditional stories. David Tse has written a splendid adaptation of a Chinese story, *The Magic Paintbrush*, which was beautifully directed for Polka Theatre by Vicky Ireland. This production employed many Chinese theatre techniques, which added a unique flavour.

Old Wine in New Bottles

It is worth exploring the idea of taking an age-old theme or story and using it within a new, more modern, framework. When we think of giants and witches, our most potent memories are probably of the giant in *Jack and the Beanstalk* or of the witch in *Hansel and Gretel*. Giants and witches belong in the world of fairy-tale or legend.

Now think of Roald Dahl's modern classics, *The BFG* and *The Witches*. In one sense both stories are timeless; they won't date. Yet both seem contemporary in atmosphere. Sophie in *The BFG* is a modern child. She is an orphan, yet she is self-confident and resourceful. The Big Friendly Giant lives in Giant Country, a timeless world straight from the dark realms of fairy-tale. Dahl's treatment of the giants feels in no way old-fashioned. When Sophie enlists the help of the Queen of England to save the children threatened by the giants, Dahl may not refer to her as Queen Elizabeth II, yet we are undoubtedly in the world of today. The Queen uses a modern army and air force, complete with helicopters, to effect the capture of the giants. It is also interesting to note that fairy-tales are full of Queens, the parents of Princes and Princesses. Dahl knows that children are used to reading about such characters in stories, but he chooses to update the idea by using the Queen they can actually see on postage stamps.

Similarly, Dahl takes the well-worn theme of witches and brings it slap up to date. His witches do not wear cloaks and pointed hats. Their familiars are not owls and cats. Dahl's witches look remarkably like ordinary women. He even suggests that his readers' teacher could be a witch. This gives the story more immediacy and an extra sense of danger.

Charles Way imaginatively took the biblical story of Noah and created a modern play called *The Flood*, in which the wife of a materialistic businessman has a vision of world ecological disaster. She buys a boat and leads her family through the rising flood towards a new, secular form of spirituality, a world in which children's values are recognized as the true way forward.

Tales of the Anthropomorphic

It may be unscientific to suppose that animals can think, act and speak like human beings, but children's writers know that their audience loves animals and loves reading stories about them. Beatrix Potter's *Peter Rabbit*, Kenneth Grahame's *The Wind in the Willows*, A. A. Milne's *Winnie the Pooh*, Dodie Smith's *The Hundred and One*

Dalmations, and Richard Adams' *Watership Down* are all classics involving a community of animals. They may behave as animals to a large extent but their great appeal to the reader is that they feel and speak like human beings. The appeal of animals for younger children is overwhelming. Rupert Bear, Paddington Bear, Spot, Pingu, Orlando and Disney characters like Mickey Mouse, Donald Duck, Dumbo and The Lion King all exploit the lovability of animals – but the characters are really human adults and children given animal form.

Amongst the earliest examples of this device must be the fables of Aesop. These tales, like *The Tortoise and the Hare*, offer moral advice and common sense, made more palatable by the fact that animals rather than human beings are the protagonists. Plays about animals can work very well for children. Fables tend to be rather short and to the point and may need considerable developing, but it is well worth considering them when creating a new play, as I did with *Save the Human*.

The Quest

The quest provides an ideal theme for a children's play and gives it an immediate shape and structure. A character wants something, sets out to find it, faces hurdles and hazards on the way, but eventually triumphs. *The Wizard of Oz* is a perfect example. Dorothy sets off to find the Wizard, picking up an assortment of friends on the way; by the end of the journey everyone has benefited.

I first used the quest form in *The Owl and the Pussycat Went to See...* (co-written with Sheila Ruskin). The Owl and the Pussycat set off to find a ring and somebody to marry them. By introducing characters from Edward Lear's other poems and stories, it was possible to flesh out the original poem and introduce more obstacles for the central characters to overcome.

In *Meg and Mog Show*, I used several of the books by Helen Nicoll and Jan Pieńkowski, weaving them together into a quest. Meg, the friendly witch, sets off to find the ingredients for a spell to get rid of a rampaging Stegosaurus whom she has inadvertently conjured up and who is devouring all the vegetables in her garden. The quest format provides great opportunities for audience involvement. The audience wants the quest to succeed, so they do everything in their power to help the travellers and to hinder those who attempt to prevent them from reaching their goal. The happy resolution should be as exhilarating for the audience as it is for the characters.

Toys and Inanimate Objects

Toys and inanimate objects coming to life has always been a favourite device of children's playwrights. When children play with their toys they often breathe imaginative life into them, sharing games and adventures with them. Their toys become their friends. Maybe this explains the success of characters like Enid Blyton's Noddy, a wooden doll living in a world of toys who are all 'alive'.

A story about toys is therefore good subject matter for a children's play. Just like anthropomorphic animals, inanimate objects and toys can think, talk and behave like human beings. The Disney cartoon, *Beauty and the Beast* features an animated Teapot and Candelabra, plus a dancing dinner service. There have been books written and illustrated about live vegetables and fruit. In my adaptation of HRH The Prince of Wales' *The Old Man of Lochnagar*, I used three crazy Haggis. Such characters are fun and can throw up all sorts of interesting ideas for plays.

Real Life

History can be a rich source for stories, especially for plays for older children, aged 8 and up. Familiar historical figures, particularly men and women of achievement, those who have triumphed over adversity, or those who have displayed extraordinary resilience in the face of danger, will be of interest to children. For example, Marco Polo, Florence Nightingale, Louis Pasteur, William Wilberforce, Boadicea. Several successful plays have been written about the childhood of famous people from history. Helen Keller, Anne Frank and the young Charles Dickens have all been the subjects of successful plays at Polka Theatre. Their heroism and struggle against extreme odds, all set in the harsh reality of the age they lived in, proved harrowing and eye-opening.

A straightforward documentary play will not easily engage the audience. It is probably more useful to find an interesting historical figure whose life affected children, for example, Dr Barnado, who opened children's homes for orphans living on the street in Victorian England. Or you could turn a piece of history into a play in which children take a central part. The plight of a child in wartime is likely to be more involving than a political debate about the causes of the war. An adult playwright might explore political diplomacy or war strategy, or even the effect of the war on ordinary families. A children's playwright would be more likely to concentrate on the plight of a young evacuee, forced to leave his or her family and cope with a new environment, new people and new problems.

Contemporary Themes

There are many contemporary issues which are potentially good subjects for children's plays. For example, just as the Canadian children's bestseller Jean Little's books about blindness encourage children to have a new appreciation of what it is like to be blind, a play about a disabled child could encourage understanding and tolerance. It need not be overtly political, rather an investigation of the human problems faced by the disabled, and how the able can help. Roy Kift's play, *Stronger than Superman*, is an excellent example.

In recent years the increased interest in Green issues has offered playwrights an interesting area of work. My play *The Selfish Shellfish* is about oil pollution. I wrote it not to investigate the political reasons why oil has to be transported across the sea or why it is once in a while dumped, but to increase awareness of the problem. That seemed to me the most important thing. The way I could best do this was by focusing on a small community of creatures in a rock pool and looking at the problems they would face if an oil slick threatened to engulf them. The subject was a good one, because I thought that nobody, but nobody, could look at the tragic image of a dying seagull coated with oil and actually say they approved. My theatrical instincts also led me to imagine the dramatic impact of an oil slick played by an actor with an enormous, rippling, oily cloak, covering the whole stage. A very powerful image.

Social issues, such as drugs, bullying, alcohol and solvent abuse, sex and Aids are all worthy subjects for plays for older children. Personally, I would hope these issues could be dealt with in a theatrical way, rather than being offered as straightforward documentary reportage. Children's theatre is a suitable arena for debate but not political propaganda.

Fairy-tales

Perhaps the most universal theme for children's entertainment is the fairy-tale. Pantomimes, cartoon films, storybooks and plays all make use of the classic stories most children hear and read from a very early age. The classic tales of Perrault (*Cinderella* and *Sleeping Beauty*), Grimm (*Snow White* and *Hansel and Gretel*), Hans Andersen (*The Ugly Duckling* and *The Tinder Box*) and others manage to survive any amount of re-working, updating or adaptation. Stories of rags to riches, virtue rewarded, magical transformations, good versus evil – the basic appeal of these stories has been handed down through the ages by storytellers, 'performed' in the oral tradition, honed and personalized, spread worldwide in varying versions.

No wonder they appeal so directly to our emotions. They appeal to our most basic instincts. We don't like Cinderella being bullied by her Ugly Sisters. We are appalled that Hansel and Gretel's parents can abandon them in the wood. We identify with the loneliness of the Ugly Duckling. We cheer when the baddies get their come-uppance and when fairness and right win through. However old the stories may be they can still come up fresh, sparkling and emotionally involving, as the Young Vic production of *Grimm Tales* triumphantly proved.

Suddenlies and Other Ingredients of Good Theatre for Children

A Canadian children's book publisher, with whom I was once interviewed on television, when trying to explain what works for children, told how her own daughter, aged 8, put down a book, saying how much she had enjoyed it. 'Why?' asked her mother, mainly out of professional interest. 'Lots of suddenlies,' came her daughter's reply.

Most children of that age would have embarked upon a detailed exposition of the story. The perception of this remark has been engraved on my mind ever since. The suddenlies, the changes of gear and surprise events of the story, made the book impossible to put down. The child was ever eager to turn the page and find out what happened next. In dramatic terms, suddenlies work in a similar way. When writing a play I consciously count the number of suddenlies on each page. I'm never happy unless there are three or more.

Suddenlies

What is a suddenly? It is anything that, by shifting gear with a logical jolt, helps to hold the attention of the audience. A suddenly can be:
- a new character entering or the sudden return of a character
- a sudden thought or realization or idea which can be vocalized in a way which changes the rhythm of a scene
- a sudden interruption, for example, a telephone call which changes the direction of the scene
- the advent of dramatic news
- a sound effect or a sudden lighting change
- a magical transformation or a pyrotechnic flash
- a scene change
- a musical 'sting' to emphasize a particularly dramatic moment
- a character speaking or entering from an unexpected place

- a sudden question posed to the audience by a character
- a character's movement suddenly stopping or changing because they have seen or heard something, for example when their movement changes to a stylized slow-motion to suggest a nightmarish chase

At their best, suddenlies force the audience to be attentive, simply because they can't bear to miss anything. They should always be natural and logical and not superimposed for the sake of it. When suddenlies are used well, they can help considerably in maintaining interest and giving an immediacy to the experience. The experience should be rather like listening to and watching a very good storyteller varying the pace, acting out the dramatic moments, pausing for effect, then suddenly making the audience jump at an exciting moment.

> Meg has to be the best part ever written for an actress in a children's play – or in any play! The part gives an endless supply of 'suddenlies'. The 'thought moment' of a 'suddenly' was what used to get my audience back if they had wandered off a bit. Children are intrigued by moments of silence, and I found that was the magic magnet rather than shouting. When you held that 'thought moment', they began to realize something was going to follow, hopefully a very interesting 'suddenly'.
>
> Leni Harper, Meg, *Meg and Mog Show*

What are the other aspects of a theatrical experience children respond to positively?

Humour

Humour is a vital ingredient in children's plays. Children love a good laugh.

A child's sense of humour is not exactly the same as that of an adult. For example, time and again I have worked on scenes in rehearsal which have yielded laughter from the other actors or the stage management in the rehearsal room. Almost invariably these moments prove to be 'in' laughs, which are not shared by children. This so-called 'wit' often passes over their heads.

Whereas repetition of something funny may dilute the joke for adults, it often enhances the joke for children. The familiar 'rule-of-three' where an identical bit of business is repeated three times can develop a child's initial giggle into a huge, unleashed roar of sheer delight. A very bald and basic example is that of a character tripping over a banana skin. The first time, the audience will find it quite funny. When he trips over it a second time they find it very funny. A third time and the joke is hilarious. For example, in the opening sequence of *Meg and Mog Show*, Meg, Mog and Owl are discovered asleep in bed. The alarm clock goes off. Meg stirs and reaches out to turn off the alarm. But she misses the clock and hits Owl on the nose. Owl reacts, waking up bemused, rubbing her nose. Laughter. The alarm is still ringing. Meg reaches out and hits Owl's nose again. More reaction from Owl. More laughter. A third hit. Owl reacts. Even more laughter.

I remember how funny the audience found the scene in Open Hand Theatre's adaptation of Ahlberg's *Ten in a Bed* where Baby Bear asks 'Why?', time and again as his father tries to explain something. There is an element of recognition here. The children seemed to understand that this was a heightened version of their own conversations with parents.

Even the most serious subject matter can be enhanced by humour. In *Dreams of Anne Frank*, Bernard Kops manages to heighten the tragic story by incorporating humour into Anne's daydreams. The occasional lightening of the mood succeeds in making Anne's predicament and eventual demise even more harrowing.

Characters

If drama is heightened reality, it follows that the characters in a play will be larger than life. This is particularly true in a children's play, even in a naturalistic play for older children. Children respond to characters who are drawn clearly and in broad strokes. They also respond to characters who are strongly defined, interesting, identifiable, and fun. Whether the characters are human beings, animals or inanimate objects who come to life, they ought to be full-bloodedly funny, sad, flamboyant, frightening, eccentric, magical or exotic.

Characters need not be simplistic. Subtlety is desirable. While the characters may appear on the surface to be one-dimensional, their traits will have probably been exaggerated to make them more accessible. They should certainly develop. For example, a villain need not be irredeemable and a foolish character can receive wisdom.

It helps a child understand the story if each character has a very definite purpose within the plot. It also keeps children's interest and helps them distinguish one character from another if the characters are richly varied.

Children relate to a child as the hero or protagonist of the play. Dorothy in *The Wizard of Oz* and Boy in *The Witches* are immediately identified with by the audience, simply because of their childhood status.

Children also relate to one or two characters who are 'normal'. These are characters with whom the audience can most readily identify, and through whose eyes they follow the action. In *The Owl and the Pussycat Went to See...* the Owl and the Pussycat may be animals, but they are played as a young man and a young woman who want to be married. The eccentrics they meet along the way take them by surprise, frighten them or help them – and all the time the audience see them through Owl and Pussycat's eyes. Owl and Pussycat become the 'norm' against which the other characters are judged.

Another useful device is to introduce characters who are innocent of the world and its ways. The willingness of the audience to help such characters quickly bonds them and the children enjoy using their superior knowledge to further the story. In my adaptation of *Noddy*, the audience sympathize with Noddy when he has trouble getting dressed. They know the feeling. Giving the audience superior knowledge in this way gives them a feeling of security and flatters them. They are not used to being considered wise. They are always having to listen to other people telling them things and giving them advice. Now the situation is reversed.

Life or Death Situations

> I believe that an element of threat is crucial ...
>
> Bruno Bettelheim, *The Uses of Enchantment*

From time to time, having found a world in which to set a play, I have deliberately asked myself what would be the worst thing that could happen to destroy the peaceful existence of that world.

Conflict has always been the stuff of drama. Conflict of personality, view, or desire can lead to a thought-provoking clash of ideas. Children's theatre is no exception. Indeed, I would suggest that conflict is an invariable ingredient of a good children's play. The arguments posed need to be clear and accessible to the audience. It is often useful to create a very serious life or death situation. When Beauty goes to live with the Beast, she genuinely fears for her life. When the BFG snatches Sophie and carries her off to his cave, her life is in danger. The child-eating activities of the other giants, although they do not directly threaten any of the characters we actually see, pervade the atmosphere of the story with a genuine threat.

Language

In most plays for children, language will be the main medium of communication with the audience. A child's vocabulary and use of language is more limited than that of most adults, but this does not mean that the playwright has to use the simplest words.

For example, in *More Adventures of Noddy*, Mr Plod the policeman dashes into the Square to stop everybody dancing to the music of the Great Tootle's magic tootle (whistle). He cries out 'Stop!' a couple of times, then in effect he says, 'What's going on?' I thought for some time about how to phrase this question. The simple route would have been to say 'What's all this noise?' But in order to emphasize Mr Plod's rather pompous nature, I gave him the line, 'What's all this abandoned activity?' Children may well not understand this phrase, but in context, spoken by the scandalized Mr Plod, it is quite obvious what it means.

Here is a simple example of the use of rhyme and enjoyable word-play to make a mundane thought more interesting and entertaining. In *Rupert and the Green Dragon*, Rupert meets a Squirrel. The Squirrel is complaining about the cold weather. The simplistic way of writing this scene could have been:

RUPERT: Hello, Squirrel. How are you?
SQUIRREL: I'm fed up. It's so cold.

Here are the lines I eventually came up with to lift the gloom with a bit of humour. The basic idea remains intact, but the language is less prosaic.

RUPERT: Hello, Squirrel. How are you?
SQUIRREL: Fed up.
RUPERT: Fed up?
SQUIRREL: Me nose is froze, me teeth are chatter-chattering, me paws are freezing and I keep sneezing. Atishoo!
RUPERT: (*handing her a hanky*) Use my hanky.
SQUIRREL: A hanky! Thankee! (*she blows loudly into the hanky held by Rupert*)

I'm not saying this dialogue is hugely witty or funny, but it is more entertaining than the simplistic version. Plus, the audience found the sneeze extremely funny.

It is quite acceptable to use difficult or challenging words as long as the sense within the context is clear. However, it is advisable to keep sentences, speeches and conversations relatively short. Clarity is still the aim.

Where possible, characters should have their own way of speaking, their own individual tone and style. This adds variety and helps characterization. A character who hops everywhere might have a staccato style of speech, a lazy, languorous character might employ a more melodious tone. Characters might have catch-phrases or specially created oaths which echo their personalities. For some characters it may be appropriate to use rhyme or onomatopoeic sounds instead of words. Children relish sounds.

When I worked on *The Owl and the Pussycat Went to See . . .* I went through every single Edward Lear poem and story, making lists of all the nonsense words he used. Many of them were incorporated into the play, giving it Lear's distinct flavour. The sheer fun of such language worked well.

Silence

While emphasizing the importance of language, it should never be forgotten that silence on stage can be very powerful. An action scene with no dialogue can speak louder than words. A silent scene can also encourage the audience to follow carefully and interpret the action. I'm always rather sad when producers or directors of *The Owl and the Pussycat Went to See...* decide to leave out the optional silhouette mimes. It is true these are not absolutely necessary to the understanding of the plot, but they restate the situation of the characters in their quest. They echo who is chasing whom, and because they are done to music, offer the audience the chance to talk to each other about the characters without missing any plot developments.

A character who cannot speak gains the immediate sympathy of the audience. Children enjoy helping such a character. They are eager to interpret whatever ideas are being communicated through mime or movement. For example, in *Flibberty and the Penguin*, the Penguin cannot speak. He is lost. Flibberty meets him and tries to find out about him. The Penguin mimes and Flibberty interprets with the help of the audience.

FLIBBERTY: Where have you come from?
(*The Penguin mimes being very cold, shuddering, slapping himself to keep warm. From now on the audience is encouraged to interpret the Penguin's mimes. Flibberty appears to be somewhat slower than the audience, so that half their fun is guessing what the Penguin is 'saying' before Flibberty can guess. Flibberty will have to improvise somewhat, but as long as the sequence of mimes is always the same there should be no problem*)
(*To the Audience*) What's he saying? He looks cold, doesn't he? Where? Iceland? (*To the Penguin*) Is that right?
The Penguin nods

(To the audience) Oh, well done! *(To the Penguin)* How did you get from Iceland all the way here?

The Penguin mimes 'walking'. The audience shout this out

You walked?

The Penguin nods, then mimes 'swimming'

And swam across the sea?

The Penguin nods, then mimes 'climbing mountains'

And climbed mountains? My, no wonder you look tired. But why have you come here, to this forest?

The Penguin mimes 'searching for someone'

Looking for someone?

The Penguin mimes 'not one person, two people'

Two people. *(To the audience)* Who could they be?

The Penguin opens his case and takes out a framed photo of his father and mother

Who are they? *(Helped by the audience)* Your mother and father?

The Penguin nods

Well, where are they?

The Penguin shrugs his shoulders

Where? Oh, you don't know. Of course, that's why you're looking for them. What happened to them?

The Penguin mimes 'I don't know, they just disappeared'

What? They disappeared?

The Penguin nods and begins to sob

And you've come all this way to find them?

The Penguin nods, sobbing

Oh! *(To the audience)* Well, I think we ought to help him , don't you? Shall we help him?

Hearing the audience reaction, the Penguin brightens considerably and jumps around, delighted

The effect on the audience is twofold. First, they enjoy working out the mime and helping Flibberty. Second, they become emotionally involved with the Penguin and become protective towards him and eager to assist him in his quest to find his parents. (Incidentally, it was many years after I wrote and directed this play that someone kindly pointed out my ignorant *faux pas* – penguins don't come from Iceland. Funnily enough, children never shouted out 'The Antarctic!')

Audience Participation

This is an important ingredient of children's theatre, but an entirely optional one. For some children's stories and plays, it would be irrelevant and out of place. Anyone writing or directing a play should however consider using audience participation as young children suffer few inhibitions when given the chance to join in.

I often write in the audience as a character predicting the responses they will give. I see it as my job to predict what they will say. I believe that no play for adults or children really exists until the audience is watching, therefore it is natural that in a play with audience participation, the audience should become a character in the script.

In pantomime, audience participation is often used to galvanize a family audience: 'Oh no I didn't!', 'Oh yes you did!' Such passing of the ball between the stage and the audience is fun, but often the aim seems to be to get the audience to shout as loudly as possible and create a diversion from the story. As the story is key in a children's play, audience participation needs to retain its element of fun while contributing to the telling of the tale. This is a vital distinction.

Simple warnings – 'He's behind you' – work well, but they work better if they are not directly asked for. If the audience has been grabbed by the plot, and genuinely wants to warn a character of the arrival of another unwelcome character, that generosity should be encouraged; but its effect is diluted if the scene has been prefaced by the character directly requesting assistance of this kind. Far better for the warning to come spontaneously as a result of the audience being unable to contain their desire to be helpful.

Advice can be sought from the audience. For example, a message has been left and the finder cannot read it – the audience will readily show off their reading skills. It can be dangerous for a character to ask the audience what to do next, unless the playwright has worked out very carefully what is the required response. This is manipulative but necessary. It is often useful for a character to ask the audience for confirmation of something that they have witnessed and he or she has not. If such a request is not made, it may well be that the audience may feel impelled to tell the character anyway. Better to incorporate the request into the script.

Children like joining in magic spells. I have often increased their importance by making the spell not work when chanted by the magician alone. In desperation he appeals for help, and gets it. The consequent success is thus made even more gratifying to the audience.

Once in a while it is interesting to involve the audience to such a degree that they are willing to lie in order to help a character with whom they identify. On its simplest level, this can involve the 'baddie' asking which way the 'goodie' has gone. The children will almost invariably send him off in the wrong direction. However, this device should not be tried on very young children. Connaught Films made an interesting television documentary in the *Horizon* series which revealed how a three-year-old found it very difficult to lie, even when it was for good reason. A psychologist showed the child two dolls. One represented Snow White, the other the Wicked Witch. Using a kindly voice for Snow White and a nasty cackle for the Wicked Witch, the psychologist played out a scene in which the Wicked Witch expressed her determination to catch Snow White. The child must have realized that Snow White was in danger. Then Snow White told the child she would hide. There were two possible places – a castle and a hollow tree. She chose the tree and, before the psychologist placed her inside, earnestly entreated the child not to give away her whereabouts. The Wicked Witch returned and asked where Snow White was. We expected the child to help Snow White by lying and pointing to the castle, but the child pointed immediately to the hollow tree. She didn't seem to know how to lie! She was asked a question and had to answer it honestly. Then the psychologist repeated the experiment with a four-year-old, who had no hesitation in helping Snow White by sending the Wicked Witch to the wrong place.

Capitalizing on the audience's willingness to help can lead to major audience participation, in which they are in effect rehearsed in a sequence of lines or actions. In *The Selfish Shellfish* the audience is asked to create a storm to frighten off the Great Slick, the invading, life-threatening oil slick. The audience make a succession of noises to represent lightning, raging wind and fierce thunderclaps. After a practice, they create the storm 'on cue', and find it very satisfying when their efforts triumph.

In *The Plotters of Cabbage Patch Corner*, the audience, unaided, captures three characters to stop them destroying the garden. They are given lines to say and rehearsed by the actors. Then, the characters instigating the trap exit, leaving the audience to do their bit. During rehearsals for the original production, the director was concerned that the audience would not participate, would not be able to remember what they had to say, and that the whole scene would end up as an embarrassment. He took out an insurance policy by writing all the lines on large boards ready to be brought on in case of emergency. Much to his surprise, they never had to be employed. Needless to say, the sincerity of playing such scenes must be stressed upon the actors. They must somehow retain the urgency of the situation, while rehearsing the audience. It must never seem like a lesson.

In *The See-Saw Tree*, I tried an even more important level of audience participation. This time the audience have to vote on whether or not the tree should be destroyed. At the start of the play, they are at a public meeting at which the proposal for redevelopment of the land where the tree stands is put forward. They are told that a splendid new children's playground will be built in the area once the tree has been cut down. They are asked to vote not for the destruction of the tree but for the idea of the children's playground. Most of the audience vote in favour. At the end of the play, we return to the public meeting, but by now the audience have had the chance to witness the effect the destruction of the tree will have on the animal community. This time they are asked whether the tree should be destroyed. Invariably they answer 'no'. I would hate to think that such manipulation went too far. The play still gives the children ample opportunity to make up their own minds, but to leave open too many possibilities and choices would make it very difficult for the audience to think clearly.

If you are intending to write a play with audience participation make sure that when you write the dialogue you don't confuse the children by asking over-complicated or convoluted questions. For instance, 'Don't you think I ought to do this?' quickly followed by, 'Or do you think it's better if I don't?' Both these questions invite the choice of 'yes' or 'no'. Double negatives lead to confusion.

Scale

There is something immediately appealing to the imagination about giant-scale or small-scale objects or people. Most of us have enjoyed playing with a doll's house, a toy shop, a toy garage, a model car or a train set. Books like *The Borrowers* or *Gulliver's Travels* or fairy-tales such as *Jack and the Beanstalk* or *Snow White* feature tiny folk or intimidating giants. Adults as well as children enjoy miniatures or huge inflatables.

In children's theatre the use of different scales can be very effective. Giant sets against which the actors look small are fun and can provide scope for imaginative ideas and danger. In *The Plotters of Cabbage Patch Corner*, the use of a giant garden, a huge cabbage for Slug to live in, a giant apple to catch Maggot in and big flowers all add a special dimension to the story.

Sometimes the scale can change as part of the plot. In *There Was an Old Woman...*, a spell goes wrong, reducing the giant shoe to a normal-sized one.

In *The Old Man of Lochnagar*, the Old Man is given a potion to shrink him so that he can go to meet the tiny Gorms. Unfortunately, the three Loch-Haggis accompanying him naughtily drink some of the potion, thus shrinking themselves. In fact, they turn into puppets. In the same play, the villainous Giant Gormless, searching for the Gorms, tries to catch them by inserting a butterfly net into their burrow-like cave. In the enlarged scale the Gorms are thus terrorized by an enormous butterfly net sweeping the stage, trying to snatch them up. Such devices keep the audience on their toes and stretch the imagination.

Puppetry

Children like puppets: glove puppets, rod puppets, shadow puppets, large puppets or small puppets. This may seem surprising given how much sophisticated cartoon animation and computer graphics they are accustomed to seeing on television. But puppets have an appeal all of their own. They are like dolls or toys. Children accept them as extensions of themselves, as friends.

Many people assume that puppets simply provide light entertainment for children, such as Punch and Judy shows. Yet in some countries, puppetry is taken far more seriously. In Japan, it takes years of apprenticeship to be allowed to operate one limb of a Bunraku puppet – and the plays the puppeteers present are mainly for adults.

Puppets can be highly sophisticated. The famous Muppets manage to appeal to all age groups. The wit of the scripts, the clever characterizations, the appealing design and the sheer skill of the puppeteers almost make the audience forget they are watching puppets.

Various children's theatre practitioners have used a mixture of characters played by puppets and by real actors. In productions by the Open Hand Company of Leeds and the Polka Theatre, puppets very often play important roles. In Polka's production of *The Odyssey*, large monsters were successfully created using huge rod puppets operated by several people. These puppets impressed because of their size and their horrific appearance. And when Open Hand adapted Roald Dahl's *Fantastic Mr Fox*, it made absolute sense for the trio of farmers to be played by actors and the foxes and the chickens to be played by puppets.

I first used shadow puppets in *Meg and Mog Show* because there were certain scenes that I knew I couldn't stage in any other way. For instance, on their quest, Meg, Mog and Owl fly to various locations. Flight was possible using shadow puppets. When they arrive at the zoo, simple animal shadow puppets such as an elephant waving his trunk indicated to the audience that the journey had been successful. The delighted shrieks of recognition of the silhouette shapes was remarkable.

In *The Old Man of Lochnagar*, I needed to show the audience that the 'heathercraft' were flying over the Scottish highlands, spraying the heather with purple dye. This was clearly impossible to stage naturalistically and shadow puppets provided the ideal answer. Also, the three manic Haggis characters are shrunk by a magic potion and become puppets. The children found this funny as well as magical.

In *Rupert and the Green Dragon*, Wise Owl and the Squirrels, who help Rupert on his quest to ensure a sunny day for Edward Trunk's birthday, were played by puppets, operated from behind a tree. They needed to be smaller than the other characters and their role in the plot did not involve them travelling. Also, I introduced a Snowbird who leads Rupert through the snow. This puppet was operated by three people. Long rods enabled the Snowbird to 'fly' high. The actors wore 'blacks' and the scene was played against black curtains. Snow fell. Only the bird was visible and it looked very effective.

In the second half of *The BFG*, the Big Friendly Giant is played by a giant puppet. The design of this was relatively simple, but many people thought its operation was more sophisticated and assumed the whole thing was animatronic. It can be fun to use puppet versions of the characters played by actors, as long as there is a logical reason for this. In the final scene of *The BFG*, all the human characters we have seen earlier reappear as puppets, enabling the actor playing the BFG to look enormous in comparison.

Magic within the Plot

Achieving the impossible by magic is intrinsically theatrical. It follows that a story with magic as part of the plot can make good children's theatre. Spells, transformations, growings and shrinkings can be used for good, as when the Fairy Godmother magically provides Cinderella with her ballgown and coach, or they can be used for evil, as when the malicious fairy turns the Prince into a frog. Stories new and old are full of magic beanstalks, magic potions, magic lamps, magic rings, magic carpets, magic mirrors or magic paintbrushes. Witches and wizards, fairies and magicians can all be useful.

It is important that the magic is actually seen to work. In the theatre there are all sorts of tricks and clever staging and lighting effects we can use, but it can be useful to employ the services of a professional magician or illusionist. I found this when working on *The Witches*, where it was essential to convincingly transform Boy into a mouse and, even more problematic, to transform a dozen or more witches into mice at the end. We used several specially created magical illusions, but it is interesting that the disappearance of all the witches was achieved relatively simply, partly by distracting the audience from looking in the right place at the right time.

Colourful Look on Stage

Children love colour. Most of them know their colours long before they can read or count. Very young children will understand and be mystified when I turn a blue handkerchief into a red one, but if I make four cards disappear from a stack of ten, they are indifferent. Children's publishers know that the books that sell best for young children are rich with colourful illustrations. So a bold and bright use of colour works well in the theatre.

Colourful sets, props and costumes can provide instant appeal and focus. When looking for subject matter, playwrights could do a lot worse than finding ideas that lend themselves to colourful presentation. The pictures we make on stage should be comparable with the bright illustrations characteristic of children's books. It can be helpful to find exciting locations and characters, with interesting visual possibilities.

Most of my plays require this colourful look. Even *Save the Human*, in which we used black and white cartoon slides as backgrounds, had colourful props. And although the style of the play dictated that the actors should wear simple tracksuits the designer made each one a different bright primary colour. This contrasted with the black and white backgrounds and looked 'special'.

Having said that, I remember two remarkable plays that had little or no set and that were played in 'black boxes'. The actors wore simple, dark rehearsal costume. At the Royal Court the actors who later became Theatre Machine, who specialized in physical theatre, performed a play in which there was a very funny sequence involving a magic invisible wall. You could only pass through by saying the password; anyone who didn't know the password bumped into the invisible wall. And *Squeak* at the Unicorn, was all about a squeak, which transferred itself from various objects like a revolving door or somebody's shoe. The audience loved this idea. There was no colour to attract the eye but the imaginative content was so high that it didn't matter. These plays stick out in my mind because they are the exceptions to the rule that most plays for children benefit from bright, colourful design.

Lighting

The power of lighting on stage was really brought home to me when I directed *Flibberty and the Penguin* for Whirligig. The first performance was at the Civic Theatre, Darlington at 9.45 in the morning. As the production team sat down in the back of the stalls a full house of very excited children were making an incredible din. Many of them were fighting and throwing things.

Flibberty and the Penguin is a reasonably gentle play about a young penguin who has lost his parents. He is helped in his quest to find them by a friendly goblin called Flibberty. I suddenly started worrying that the content would not be strong enough to maintain this audience's attention. Eventually the house lights dimmed. A huge roar echoed through the auditorium. It seemed intimidating, not encouraging. The short overture began but was virtually drowned by the whoops and cheers of the audience. The curtain rose on a darkened stage. This only increased the noise from the children, for whom darkness became a free zone. But then the magic happened. It is a moment I will never forget. The first lighting cue was given. A slow fade to suggest dawn. The cyclorama began to glow. The light shone through the cut cloth and borders, causing silhouette shapes of tree branches and leaves. A pretty, yet not extraordinary effect. Just one cue. Suddenly the whole auditorium went quiet. Quiet apart from one sound. I realized it was the sound of gasping. These tough, boisterous, over-excited children had been becalmed. The magic of theatre.

Lighting can also create suddenlies and atmosphere as well as a variety of visual images. For instance, it can be a good idea to locate a night-time scene between two scenes in day-time. To suggest the passage of time a lighting cue can help maintain visual interest.

Children enjoy special lighting effects: 'gobos' which can project shapes on to the stage or create the look of dappled light coming through the trees; strobe lights for exciting chases; and special lanterns which revolve or zigzag or corkscrew in a fascinating way, used to accompany magic spells.

In certain circumstances, ultra-violet light can create memorable sequences. The actors wear 'blacks' against a black background, and the ultra-violet light only picks up the ultra-violet painted objects that are carried across the stage. Or the costumes can be treated to pick up the light. This device is very useful for underwater scenes, or flying scenes in the sky or through outer space. By using a cyclorama curved round the back of the stage it is possible with lighting to change completely the colour of the background for different scenes. This effect in itself is very theatrical.

Sound

It is only in recent years that theatre sound has become electronically sophisticated. In Ronald Harwood's play, *The Dresser*, it was great fun to watch the stage crew create the sounds of the storm for a production of *King Lear* in the days when you didn't simply turn on a tape recorder. The huge thunder sheet echoed and the vast box of rattling pebbles created the heavy rain. The sound effects were atmospheric rather than realistic, just as the style of acting was declamatory rather than naturalistic. With the advent of television, audiences possibly expect more realism and this is now possible.

Amplified sound has also improved vastly. I always remember seeing pantomimes at the London Palladium in the early sixties. Then there were a certain number of general coverage microphones ranged across the front of the stage. One or two stand mikes were used to amplify the voices of the singers at the side of the stage. A solitary radio mike was given to the top-of-the-bill star, who was often a pop singer or comedian, whose projection skills were limited. It was always fun to watch the star playing a scene with other actors, who gradually crept in closer and closer, hoping that their voices, too, might be picked up by the radio mike. The sound quality of these shows was rather garish and unsubtle.

Nowadays, many children's plays, particularly those performed in large theatres, have radio mikes for all the actors and sophisticated sound equipment. Tape or digital recordings are often used for the sound effects. It would be a mistake to think that radio mikes are used simply because actors can no longer project their voices, although to some extent this may be true. I believe that because the volume knob on the television is so easily controlled, many of us have lost the ability to listen. We expect things to be louder and to be clearer. Children are no exception. So the playwright and/or director should use sophisticated sound techniques if possible.

In several of my plays, the Big Ones are the human beings whose actions affect or dominate the lives of the characters in the play. They provide a major threat in *The Gingerbread Man* and *The Plotters of Cabbage Patch Corner*. We never see them, but they cast shadows on the set, and we can hear their voices. And because we are identifying with the small creatures on stage, their voices can be effectively amplified to suggest their size and power. The voice of a giant could similarly boom through the auditorium, and even when he arrives on stage, his voice should be large, in proportion to his size.

In a similar way, simple sound effects like door slams can be made into suddenlies. Increased volume gives them extra significance. The use of echo can help create a sense of scale, and also help to create atmosphere, for example in a spooky scene set in a darkened wood. General background atmospheres such as birdsong to suggest the countryside, waves lapping to suggest the sea, or traffic noises to suggest the city, can play underneath scenes or introduce scenes, as long as they are not distracting. In *The Ideal Gnome Expedition*, the realistic, heightened, traffic noises that frighten the gnomes are recognizable to the audience and help the whole idea of playing a fantasy situation within the real world.

Sound effects can set the scene. This can be particularly useful when the scene is not going to be fully realized in the design. For example in *The Witches*, there was a short scene on board ship, in which Grandmother and Boy discussed the nature of witches while on their way to England. A simple ship's rail was enough to set the scene, but it was enhanced by the sound of a ship's hooter followed by seagull cries.

The storm scene in a present-day production of *King Lear* would most likely involve highly realistic claps of thunder, rushing wind and driving rain. It is a good idea, in a children's play, to use dramatic scenes such as a storm to add the maximum theatricality.

I have often used specially contrived sound effects, such as whooshes for magic spells. Some have added humour to the play. For instance in *More Adventures of Noddy*, Tubby Bear puts fizzy lemonade into the petrol tank of Noddy's car. The car develops hiccups and, when Noddy tries to start the car, there is a combination of engine-revving and metallic 'hics' which the audience found very funny.

In *The See-Saw Tree*, the Big Ones are a gang of workmen who come to cut down the tree. They are never seen but are very much the villains of the piece. The threat they pose is enhanced greatly by the sound effects of their voices, their vehicles rumbling towards the tree, the savage sound of their chain saw and the sound of crashing branches.

It would be a mistake to think that all children's plays need sophisticated, realistic sound effects. I have seen very effective children's plays in which the characters create their own sound effects from everyday objects or improvised percussion instruments. This is arguably more imaginative than the use of batteries of sound gear. But the importance of sound of any kind in a children's play should not be forgotten when planning a production.

Music

Songs and incidental music should help keep the story moving. If there are songs, the music and lyrics need to be accessible to the audience. They need not be overtly catchy, but the use of tuneful melody and bouncy rhythms is possibly more effective than more discordant, sophisticated harmonies. The songs should ideally reinforce character and situation and, where possible, drive the plot forward. Themes can be composed for each character to aid identification and, in the case of a baddie, to help encourage the audience to react. By the end of the song we should be a little further into the plot. Superfluous songs tend to hold things up and lose the audience's attention.

When there are no songs, incidental music can be used for linking the scenes, for covering scene changes and for focusing the audience's attention to let them know that something is about to happen. A musical overture can calm an excited audience and be the bridge to the opening scene. Underscoring, common in films, can create an atmosphere of joy, tension, danger or excitement. A sad scene can be enhanced by gentle music accompanying the emotional content.

Music can effectively accompany action scenes where dialogue would be superfluous, but it would seem somewhat empty to act them out in silence.

In plays set in foreign lands, the music can be a crucial aid in establishing a characteristically local flavour. The use of sounds and instruments from the appropriate country immediately sets the tone.

Most of my own productions have been able to afford only one musician. In the early days we used a piano. Now there is a whole range of electronic keyboards and synthesizers which can create different musical sounds to give variety. Although I have occasionally had the luxury of a small group of musicians, I would be unlikely to use a large orchestra as this could unbalance the production. I have found that many sequences in my plays are best accompanied rather like a silent film. The action on stage must be followed carefully and echoed by the musician. After a certain number of performances, the music will probably have settled into a regular pattern, but because of possible audience participation there must always be a certain amount of leeway, even improvisation.

Mime and Movement

It is worth remembering that a children's play should never be too wordy. There need to be the occasional breaks; moments when mime, dance, movement or unspoken action carries the story forward.

Children are intrigued by the body's mobility and virtuosity. They enjoy acrobats. They might not enjoy a performance consisting solely of mime, but the use of movement as an integral part of the production can be very effective. This gives the audience a rest from the spoken word and is a natural invitation for musical accompaniment.

Climaxes and Cliffhangers

The structure of any play is important; in a children's play, structure is crucial. A basic sense of good storytelling is required. The story must build as situations are established and problems encountered and overcome. There will be a series of mini-climaxes, developing towards a major climax, which resolves the situation and ties up the ends. A sense of completeness is then achieved, which is satisfying and logical. In this way the structure helps maintain the interest of the audience and attains a sense of growing excitement and involvement. If a play is written in two acts, it can be useful to create a cliffhanger at the end of Act One, giving the audience something to discuss and look forward to after the interval.

Justice and Fairness

> In the traditional fairy-tale, the hero is rewarded and the evil person meets his well-deserved fate, thus satisfying the child's deep need for justice to prevail. How else can a child hope that justice will be done to him, who so often feels unfairly treated? And how else can he convince himself that he must act correctly when he is so sorely tempted to give in to the asocial proddings of his desires?
>
> Bruno Bettelheim, *The Uses of Enchantment*

As children immediately respond to unfairness or anti-social behaviour, many good children's plays will exploit this in order to involve the audience in the struggle for right to prevail. In many plays this leads to a just resolution. But the playwright should find ways of concluding the story clearly and thoughtfully with the hope that such a story may never need to happen again. Hope rather than despair, a chink of light in the darkness, should temper a story about the cruelty of human nature or the waywardness of fate.

In some plays, particularly those for older children, a happy ending would be impossible. A play about Anne Frank can hardly end happily, but Bernard Kops, in *Dreams of Anne Frank*, manages to end on an upbeat by giving the last speech to Anne's father, who speaks directly to the audience, expressing his pride in his daughter's achievement in leaving us a book which will teach us something of the horror of the Holocaust. Yet he would willingly swap the book for the return of his daughter.

Taboos

It is worth concluding this list of possible ingredients for a children's play by asking the question, 'Are there any subjects that are unsuitable?' We should not set out to frighten or disturb the audience for the sake of it. We should always consider the age range to which the play is aimed. We must all have a sense of responsibility and treat sensitive issues carefully. It would be foolish to target a play about a nuclear holocaust to an audience of three-year-olds. But there are few areas that are totally out of bounds, save those where children are incited to violence or intolerance. And we should not necessarily be influenced by extreme political correctness.

When I embarked on an adaptation of *Noddy*, I was naturally aware of the concerns of certain educationalists over some aspects of Enid Blyton's creation. I agreed that her use of golliwogs as baddies was not appropriate today. Indeed, in recent editions of the books, they have been turned into goblins. I felt that, had she been writing today, Enid Blyton would have introduced more female characters who were instigators rather than passive participants. This is why I promoted Tessie Bear, giving her almost as many big moments as Noddy. But I couldn't take seriously the American criticism of the name Big Ears; I couldn't believe that people with big ears could be offended. And the concerns about Noddy and Big Ears' relationship to me seemed ridiculous. Big Ears is clearly an avuncular figure who helps Noddy; there is no ulterior motive.

A German company once showed interest in producing my play *The See-Saw Tree*. Germany is well known as a 'Green' country, and plays on environmental issues are popular there. But the producer would only do the play if I changed the scene in which Rabbit dies. Death, he said, was not a suitable subject for inclusion in a children's play. I pointed out that it was an important moment in the play. Rabbit tries to save the tree from destruction by biting the electric cable for the chain-saw, which has just been turned on in preparation for the destruction of the tree. The sudden electric shock that kills Rabbit is really the climax of the play, highlighting the struggle of the animals to keep their home.

The moment is similar to the death of Seagull in *The Selfish Shellfish*. The seriousness of the moment makes the audience think, and I have seen children shedding tears at the loss of a friendly character. I don't believe any child was traumatized by the moment. The structure of the play made it possible for the actor playing Rabbit (and Seagull) to revive in order to resume his role as narrator. No child was left with the image of a dead rabbit littering the stage. It reinforced the 'play-within-a-play' device, in which the actors are seen to assume the roles they play. This to some extent softens the death scene. The German producer was not convinced. The play has never been seen there.

In an earlier play, *Hijack Over Hygenia*, one of the fantasy characters is Auntie Septic, a matronly nurse in the shape of an anti-septic spray. She gives her all – literally – in the struggle against the Measlygerms. By the end of the battle she has lost all her anti-septic spray and is quite empty. This logically means that she dies. The other characters mourn her loss and revere her as a heroine, without whom the Kingdom of Hygenia would have been overthrown. I cannot see that this idea is unacceptable. I'm sure that children understand, in their own way, as much about the idea of death as adults. It is the unknown. Sooner or later we all have to face up to the death of a loved one or a friend and our own mortality. As long as it is sensitively handled, it is perfectly acceptable to use death in a children's play.

If I had to choose one word to sum up all the elements that appeal to children, that word would be *theatrical*. Theatricality, the use of all the facilities a theatre can offer, can lead to a magical experience. The basic ingredients outlined in this section are not hard and fast rules, rather a palette of possibilities, a knowledge of which will help pave the way to writing original plays and adaptations, leading to a show that really works with the audience.

Part 3   Writing Original Plays

The Craft of Writing an Original Play

When I'm asked 'Where do your ideas for original plays come from?' my usual reply is 'Sheer panic.' Ideas come from various sources. I might go and talk to children in a school. I might look around a toy shop. I might delve among the shelves of a secondhand bookshop. Very often a spark of an idea will come into my head and, over a period of days or weeks, develop into something more substantial.

I am not one of those writers who has ideas flowing out of every pore and who can't wait to get to the typewriter to share them. On the contrary, the actual writing part is not something I look forward to. I have been very fortunate in that most of my plays have been commissioned by theatre companies so I work to the dreaded deadline. I find it hard work coming up with ideas, but I enjoy it once it is done.

Writing a Synopsis

There is a difference between the creation of the play and the writing of the play. The creation, whether it be original or adaptation, can involve a lot of development and change and thinking and inventing. But the writing of the play must follow a logical progression, which dictates and gives it a structure.

While I think it is wonderful to start off with a blank piece of paper and write a story, I am not sure that that is the best way to write a children's play. I believe the structure of the play is so important that it is essential to have the whole thing mapped out first, in the form of a synopsis. It may well be that changes take place during the actual writing, or that other ideas suddenly occur which are better and more workable, but I would never start writing the play until I had this very detailed plan in front of me. Therefore, I would advise the first-time playwright to start within the rigorous structure of a synopsis. This will not only help in the long run, but also provide you with something concrete to show others for comment.

The working synopsis might run to fifteen or twenty pages. It can be read by prospective producers, director, designer and other members of the production team and, once it has been approved and comments registered, it becomes the working guide to the script. From the working synopsis, prospective producers and other interested parties can get a complete idea of the scale of the production, the number of actors needed and how the play works.

A synopsis breaks down as follows:

- introduction – making important general points (not *always* necessary)
- list of characters – with a note on doubling if relevant
- an indication of musical and sound requirements
- design – costume and set (this may be an overall note or broken down into scenes if appropriate
- synopsis of the action, scene by scene

Bear in mind that you may not need *all* of these sections in *every* synopsis. If there are no general points to be made then do not waste time with an introduction. Likewise, if your ideas for costume and set run throughout the play or are split between Acts One and Two, then a scene by scene breakdown is irrelevant.

Nine steps towards a synopsis

Step 1. Theme (world or microcosm)
Step 2   Characters
Step 3. Story
Step 4. Structure
Step 5. Action
Step 6. Language
Step 7. Songs
Step 8. Theatrical Magic
Step 9. Clarity

Step 1. Theme (world or microcosm)

Whether the theme is rooted in fantasy or based on reality, the first thing to look for is the world or microcosm in which the play will take place. Look for a world that children will relate to, understand or find interesting. Obvious ones are inhabited by dinosaurs, toys, animals or creatures from outer space. Do you want to write a modern story or give your play an historical setting. Find a world that will be visually exciting and colourful, or a magical world where extraordinary things can happen. Consider myths and legends set in far off lands. Talk to children, read children's books, look in toy shops; think back to your own childhood, the games you played and the stories your treasured.

Remember that the location of a children's play can often be more imaginative and inventive than for an adult play. It is fun to focus on one contained area which becomes a microcosm of the real world. I have used a rock pool and a garden, and I have seen plays set in a human brain or a toy cupboard. Try inventing a community with one common feature like my own Papertown, in which buildings and people are all made of paper.

Step 2. Characters

Ideas for characters should spring naturally from the world you have chosen to explore. Insects in a garden; cavemen or dinosaurs in a prehistoric landscape; aliens in outer space; toys in a toy cupboard. Try to find a variety of characters who will offer possibilities when you come to create a story-line. Some characters will help you get the story going; others will surface later, once the story has started to take shape. In a children's play consider the following:

● **Characters will often tend to be larger than life**
Look for colourful, quirky, funny, eccentric, imaginative characters. Even characters with conventional occupations need not be mundane. In *Flibberty and the Penguin* there are two conductors – a bus conductor and an orchestral conductor. The fact that they are both conductors causes confusion in the story. But individually they are

more than ordinary conductors. Mr Maestro is so musical that he always sings instead of speaks, and can only understand you if you sing to him. The Bus Conductor is also the Bus Driver and, to remind him which job is which, wears a reversible hat and uses two voices.

● **Some characters will lend themselves to becoming protagonists**
They will instigate the story. Things will happen to them. Maybe they are looking for something. These characters may be larger than life but will become the 'norm', with whom the audience will journey through the play. They could be children to whom the audience will swiftly relate, like Dorothy in *The Wizard of Oz*. These characters will be sympathetic so that, however fantasy-based the situation may be, the audience will identify with them and root for their success.

● **Some characters will provide conflict**
They will be flies in the ointment, who try to foil the protagonists and endanger a happy or satisfying resolution to the play. Captain Hook in *Peter Pan* is the classic example.

● **Some characters will learn something**
As the action proceeds their attitudes will change. They will grow.

● **Some characters will inject humour**
They must be integrated into the plot, but their main function is to provide comedy.

● **Some characters may be oracles**
A fount of wisdom to whom the others turn for advice can introduce an atmosphere of authority and mystery.

● **Characters will often have one predominant characteristic that motivates them**
Such a characteristic will give them individuality and lead to ideas in the story-line.

● **Characters can be created from verbal puns**
I have often found this an enjoyable and profitable exercise. In *The Selfish Shellfish* puns were particularly helpful. I chose Mussel as one of the shellfish. The name immediately suggested he was strong, full

of 'muscle'. His strength was used several times in the play, and added to the irony of his being rendered unconscious by the storm. Suddenly the physically strongest character becomes helpless and the others have to come to his aid.

Urchin is, of course, a sea urchin. But the pun suggested to me that the character should be a cheeky child. The children in the audience may not know the word 'urchin', but no matter. In the planning stages it gave me a concrete image of the character, which made it live and breathe in my mind. Besides, 'urchin' is a nice word.

Similarly H.C. is a Hermit Crab, the selfish shellfish of the title. The phrase suggests, in human terms, a lonely recluse, and this describes H.C.'s character.

● **Characters need not be human beings**
Animals, toys and inanimate objects all make good characters and some plays usefully employ a combination of them. The garden gnomes (inanimate) in *The Ideal Gnome Expedition* become involved with Chips, a street-wise cat (animal), as well as a clockwork duck (toy). There is also a fierce Securidog (animal) and a tar-whacking machine called Wacker (inanimate).

All these characters exist in the real world. But by bringing inanimate objects to life and giving animals human feelings, the story takes on a fantasy life of its own. In such a play, where most or all of the characters are animals or fantasy creatures, it is important to remember that they will only work if they have highly pronounced human characteristics. They must think and in many ways behave as human beings. But the children's playwright has the fun of exploring human characteristics within the framework of a non-human world.

● **Each character should be easily distinguishable from the others**
Look for variety. Make sure your characters are a good mix. Will they look different from each other? Different shapes? Different sizes? Different colours? Will they offer possibilities for idiosyncratic movement? Do they suggest different ways of speaking? Such variety in your characters will help lead to a richer story-line.

- Characters, human or fantasy, depicting a family relationship will appeal to children

For instance, a cheeky child cocking a snook at authority, in the form of a parent or elder, can be guaranteed to give amusement.

- When creating a balanced mix of characters it is important to consider the male/female ratio

It is often said that in the theatre there are more good roles for men than women. In children's plays this is no longer true. At the risk of stating the obvious, we must ensure that female characters instigate plot development as much as male characters.

- Some characters make good narrators

It is sometimes profitable to have a direct link with the audience, a character who tells the story, either as an outsider or as a protagonist who steps in and out of the action.

Step 3.   Story

Just as a good storybook makes the child want to turn over the page to find out what happens next, so the playwright must aim to carry the attention of the audience through the twists and turns of the plot towards a satisfying conclusion.

Having established the 'world' you want to explore and some of the characters who populate it, it's time to carve out a story-line. Is it to be a quest to find something? What sort of problems have to be resolved? What do the characters want? Do they have a dream? Is it a happy world threatened by change? Does the arrival of somebody new on the scene suggest possibilities?

It is a good idea to think backwards. In other words, decide how the play is going to end before working out how the conclusion is reached, and what hurdles have to be negotiated before a successful resolution. The invention of one major threat can provide a useful through-line for the play.

Sometimes, in the belief that conflict is a vital part of any play, I start by thinking of life and death situations. All my plays have a hard reality, with elements of life and death in them. This is important because it gives a scale of tragic possibilities and that enhances the excitement. What is the worst possible thing that could happen to the characters in the world I have imagined?

In *The Papertown Paperchase*, the threatened destruction of Papertown by invaders from the Land of Fire is their worst fear. In *Hijack over Hygenia*, the cleanest kingdom in the world suffers the worst possible disruption when germs start to invade the people's hygienic, disease-free lives.

The characters will not all co-exist in a happy, carefree state. The world we have created cannot be too simplistic. There must be a certain amount of internal conflict as well. They will have squabbles and differences of opinion. Like any community, sharing their lives with others will cause tension and problems. When constructing the story-line, it is important to consider the day to day problems of the community, to establish relationships and thus provide a believable background for the main through-line.

I believe that a children's play needs to end with a feeling of triumph or success over adversity. Ends need to be tied up. The audience should leave the theatre on a positive note, even when the content of the play has been challenging or depressing. Whatever problems the characters encounter, the audience should be drawn into sharing their concerns. The story needs to move logically to a satisfying conclusion.

Step 4. Structure

Sorting out the structure of the play is often the most time-consuming activity. I often use a very large piece of paper, on which I try out the sequence of events from beginning to end. This way, I can view the development of the story in one glance. It is rather like making a chart. Sometimes I will have certain ideas or plot developments written on separate slips of paper which can be arranged and then re-arranged on the chart. Gradually a shape begins to emerge.

Look at the best way of introducing new characters, trying not to give too much information too soon. Some characters may well be saved for quite late entrances, to change the direction of the story.

Look for suddenlies at this stage. Consider changes of fortune, or moments of intense happiness suddenly changed into moments of danger. Look for different atmospheres, moments for tension, cliffhangers, particularly one with which to end the first half. Look at the locations, trying to envisage practically how a designer might achieve the necessary changes of scene. Avoid long delays on stage while the set is changing. Sometimes a fully staged scene might have to be followed by a simpler scene to enable a scene change to take place during it. Even if the play is taking place on one basic set, it is a good idea not to reveal everything all in one go. Keep a few surprises up your sleeve.

Very often the invented 'world' will yield visual ideas that contribute to the actual story-line. It was fun when working on *The Selfish Shellfish* to imagine the various pieces of debris which might find themselves washed up by the sea in the rock pool. After every tide Mussel has to clear the rock pool of old sweet-wrappings, corks and bottle-tops. And an old tin can and flip-flop are used as important props in the story.

As the ideas develop, it is important to chart the development of each character. How does he or she change as the story proceeds? What special characteristic can be employed to help or hinder the action? Try to differentiate between the contributions of each character. How will each character react to a new problem? Does each character have enough to do? If you know in advance how many actors are available it is worth checking at every turn how the doubling will work. Will an actor have enough time to change between appearances?

If you have decided to use audience participation, it is best to work out how it can be incorporated into the story at this structuring stage rather than later. Is the audience to be involved in any decision making? If so, make sure the scene is carefully constructed so that the audience knows exactly what it needs to do.

Is the audience to be incorporated into the action? Will there be any set pieces in which, for instance, it actively contributes to the successful resolution of a problem? In *The Selfish Shellfish*, the audience fools the Great Slick into thinking a storm is coming.

It is often a mistake to include too much participation too early in the play. Once the children realize that they are being encouraged to participate, they may well want to participate too much. They may voice their opinions or shout warnings in places you have not anticipated. It is best to use audience participation sparingly, and only when there is a real purpose to it.

Step 5.   Action

> There's nothing more terrifying or gratifying than sitting among 500 eight-to-ten-year-olds who are instantly reviewing my play. I was shaken to the core when during an early preview of *The Portrait, the Wind, the Chair* at Seattle Children's theatre, a young audience member sitting next to me shouted, 'This is so boring!' Her outburst over, she turned her attention back to the play. At the end, after the clapping, I braved an inquiry. 'So you didn't like it,' I started. She looked at me as if I were from another planet. 'But you said it was boring.' She replied, 'No, it was fabulous. Only that boring part was boring.' In other words, that boring part where the playwright had resorted to narrative because she couldn't figure out the exposition. Oh, I thought, best not let that happen again.
>
> Y. York, playwright

As the structure of the play begins to come together, it is advisable to check the balance between the amount of action and amount of dialogue happening on stage. Are the characters doing too much talking? Are there enough things for them physically to do? Think of the visual possibilities. Perhaps you could use chases. Perhaps the characters have to cross a stream or climb over a fence. Perhaps they could build a house. What props can they make use of? Can physical skills such as acrobatics or stilt-walking be employed? Are there any magical transformations? Might slow-motion be used somewhere? Maybe the characters have to escape from somewhere. Maybe they appear to fly. Are there opportunities for exciting visual images, such as an incoming tide? Will the lighting designer and the sound designer have enough interesting moments to work on? Maybe it would be a good idea to have a couple of sections where no speech is necessary. Is mime appropriate?

Above all, keep the action flowing. Find enough suddenlies to keep the audience interested and alert. Make them eager to know what happens next.

Step 6. Language

It is worth, at this stage, thinking of the style of speech each character might employ. Aim for a variety of styles. Will some characters adopt colloquial speech and others speak more formally? Might a character's language be oily, posh, expansive or clipped? Do accents, foreign or regional, suggest themselves? Could any characters use jargon or technical language? For instance, Red Admiral in *The Plotters of Cabbage Patch Corner* uses pompous nautical phraseology. Might a character speak in rhyme? Might another get words muddled up or use spoonerisms? Is there an opportunity to invent a nonsense language? For example, robots could 'bleep' or cavemen could 'ug', and the audience would enjoy translating. Is there room for a mute character, whose only language is mime, which the audience are invited to interpret? Will characters' movement affect their language? A hopping character might speak in a staccato fashion. A slithering creature might speak languorously. Might a character have a repeated catchphrase?

Step 7. Songs

Now is the time to decide whether your play should have songs. Go through the story looking for suitable subjects for songs, making sure they are reasonably well spaced throughout the play.

Some songs may introduce and set up characters. Others may develop the action. Some of the most effective songs will become a substitute for dialogue, covering a whole slice of action. All songs should be relevant as well as fun.

A song can also be useful to express fervent hope, almost like a prayer. Such feelings are sometimes difficult to express in dialogue. Avoid songs that are too reflective or romantic. Nothing too sentimental in the lyrics or music is advisable. Use rhythm and a foot-tapping beat, but avoid being too simplistic or relentlessly rum-te-tum.

In a play about a quest, it is appropriate to have a song announcing the beginning of the quest, expressing hopes that it will be successful. It is important that the actors do not simply stand there and sing the lines. The playwright should give adequate room for preparations to be taking place, or the beginnings of the quest to be seen. Thus the song becomes an action song rather than a statement of what is about to happen.

A song which, almost anthem-like, sums up the overall attitude of the characters might be appropriate.

Audience-participation songs can be effective, particularly for younger audiences. They should not be too complex, and should have a relevance to the plot. In *The Ideal Gnome Expedition*, the audience help teach the gnomes about road safety by singing a song, taught to them by Chips the Cat, called *Use Your Eyes and Ears*. This involves movements as well as words. In the same play, the clockwork duck is given a name by the audience, who then shout out the name at relevant moments during the song.

A song of celebration might effect a triumphant, joyful ending to the play. The audience could be encouraged to join in.

Step 8. Theatrical Magic

It is now worth checking whether your play will use exciting theatrical techniques to tell the story. Some of these have already been mentioned. Are there opportunities for lighting and sound? Will the set and costumes be visually exciting? Is there any possible use of scale, such as big characters on miniature sets or vice versa? Are there any magical transformations? Can puppetry be employed? Do any characters come to life? Are there enough theatrical surprises and changes of mood?

Step 9. Clarity

Finally, check through the story-line and make sure it is logical and clear. Will the audience understand the ideas in the play and the way in which those ideas develop? Does it make sense? Are all the ends tied up successfully? Is there a satisfactory resolution?

To illustrate how these nine steps can lead to the synopsis of the play, I have retraced the development of two of my own plays as examples. I have chosen *The Gingerbread Man* and *The See-Saw Tree* because they are two very different types of play.

Steps towards a synopsis for *The Gingerbread Man*

In 1976, I was invited to write a play to be produced at Christmas at the Towngate Theatre, Basildon. This theatre had no flying facilities and limited wing space. The seating capacity was quite small, so the brief was to write a play for only six actors on one basic set. I agreed to the commission without having any specific ideas.

A few months before production I had a phone call from the theatre asking for the title of the play. There was to be a summer carnival for which the theatre would provide a travelling float advertising the Christmas play. They needed to know what the play would be about. At this point I still had no ideas, and suggested I ring back in a couple of days' time, but the theatre insisted I tell them there and then because they had a meeting that evening to discuss the carnival. I closed my eyes seeking inspiration and, without knowing why, suddenly said 'The Gingerbread Man'. 'Fine,' said the voice, and put the phone down. I realized I had lumbered myself with a title without having a clue as to the content of the play. When I started work, I decided that I did not want to re-tell the nursery story of *The Gingerbread Man*, in which the Gingerbread Man runs away and, trying to cross a river, is eventually eaten by a cunning fox. I wanted something more original, a totally new idea, using a gingerbread man as a central character.

Step 1. Theme (world or microcosm)

I imagined a newly baked Gingerbread Man. Where would he logically be found? Some years previously I had thought that a Welsh dresser, with its worktop and shelves, would make an exciting environment for a play. *The Gingerbread Man* gave me a good excuse to use it.

Giant plates, a rolling pin, a teapot, a portable radio – all the items one might expect to find on a dresser – immediately offered possibilities. Here was a world, set in the corner of a kitchen, that must have existed for quite a long time. Perhaps there would be characters living on the dresser for whom this would be the full extent of their world. To escape it would mean dropping on to the kitchen floor. The worktop would be the stage floor and a shelf or shelves would offer different levels on which action could take place, different locations which could be reached without having to change the set.

A newly baked Gingerbread Man would not understand the rules of behaviour of his new home and would presumably have to learn them. The long-standing residents of the dresser might well find him a handful. Maybe by the end of the play he would have proved himself to be a valuable citizen and be finally welcomed aboard. And who had baked him? Presumably the human people in whose kitchen the dresser was situated. Maybe they could provide a useful outside threat.

Thus the world of the Welsh dresser became the starting point. I welcomed the confines of the geography and characters this world would suggest, realizing that it would fulfil the brief of one basic set. All the characters (except obviously the human beings) would live on or possibly behind the dresser and the story-line could only use characters and objects which would normally be found on the worktop and shelves of a kitchen dresser. The idea had immediate visual possibilities including the use of appealing giant props, all of which would be recognizable to children as objects they would find in their own homes.

Step 2. Characters

For the next few weeks I found myself studying the kitchens of my friends and relatives and looking in kitchen shops searching for ideas for characters. I already had the main one, but who would he be most likely to meet?

Salt and Pepper were the most obvious. Salt and pepper pots are familiar to all children and would certainly 'live' on a dresser. A common variety of salt pot has blue and white horizontal stripes. Salt comes from the sea. Sailors wear blue and white. Salt, I decided, would be a frustrated sailor who had never seen the sea. He could talk in hearty nautical language. He could be good at tying knots, which might come in useful. He would see the dresser as a ship and this could increase the richness of his language, calling his friends shipmates, calling out 'Ahoy there!' or welcoming the Gingerbread Man 'aboard'. I immediately saw him as a friendly character who would give the newly baked Gingerbread Man the benefit of the doubt.

This would contrast well with Pepper, who could (using the pun) be rather hot-tempered and impulsive. I saw her as a shapely red pepper-mill, which would contrast with the rather squat shape of Salt. The shapeliness suggested Pepper would be female, which would be a good combination with a male Salt. All children know that pepper makes you sneeze, so it was a fairly obvious thought that the character could, by twisting her grinder, produce little peppercorns which could be used in defence against attack of some kind. I decided that she would be less welcoming to the Gingerbread Man, and would probably find Salt's enthusiasm rather annoying. She would be a practical character, saying what she felt, impetuous and sometimes insensitive.

Next, I wanted to find a character who might be living on the dresser, but not immediately visible. This could provide a surprise value. Maybe this character could be a loner, someone of whom the other characters were wary. Maybe the top shelf of the dresser would be a good place for this character to live, away from the events that would take place on the worktop. Many people keep decorative teapots on the top shelves of their dressers and some look like little cottages. Such a teapot would be an ideal home for somebody. Eventually I thought of the idea of a tea bag. Again, a tea bag is something children would be familiar with. Suppose a tea bag – I immediately thought of her as female – had been the last one in her packet and had managed to escape to a teapot seldom used by the human beings (whom I immediately thought of as Big Ones). Here she could be safe. I began to think of her as a cantankerous, elderly hermit, who would not welcome visitors on her shelf. 'She keeps herself to her shelf and her shelf to herself.' This could provide a threat should the Gingerbread Man have cause to go up there.

Other objects on the top shelf might include a honey pot and a row of herb jars. The idea of herbs having magical properties made me think that the tea bag might be a witchy kind of character, who knew the individual properties of the herbs and might even use them for magic potions. I decided to call her the Old Bag, which seemed a nice pun for this cantankerous character.

In most kitchens a clock can be found. I thought that a cuckoo living inside a cuckoo-clock could be a useful character. He might not actually live on the dresser, but alongside it. He could visit the dresser regularly, particularly at night when the Big Ones would be upstairs asleep. I realized that this was cheating somewhat, because he was not part of the dresser, but the more I started thinking, the more attracted to him I became. In fact, as things turned out, Cuckoo provides the mainspring of the plot, because he loses his voice and is desperately worried that the Big Ones, realizing that he no longer works properly, will throw him in the dustbin.

Having such a problem could, I realized, give the Gingerbread Man an opportunity to be helpful, to try to find a cure for Cuckoo's sore throat. Cuckoo-clocks are usually made in Switzerland, which would mean that Cuckoo would have a French or a German accent. Being Swiss, he could perhaps yodel instead of sing; his yodelling would be adversely affected if he had a sore throat. I also thought it might be fun to involve the audience by teaching them to yodel, which is an amusing sound to make. Also, the fact that he would be a bird would add to the variety of characters on the dresser.

Finally, I decided to find another character who would be a threat to life on the dresser, a character who maybe did not actually live there. He could arrive towards the end of the first half as a total surprise and suddenly change the course of events. A villainous, scavenging mouse fitted the bill. He could live in the skirting board behind the dresser, scrabble up to the back of the worktop and gnaw his way through, arriving behind a plate. The noise of his scrabblings would be theatrically interesting. But what sort of mouse should he be?

I wanted him to be funny as well as frightening, and decided that he should be a tough guy, who wasn't really tough. He would present an image of macho bravado, imagining himself as a gangster straight from an American film, but in fact he would be rather cowardly. Realizing that a mouse invading a dresser would probably be hungry and searching for food led me to the thought that he might be unusually keen on sweet rather than savoury food. A mouse who doesn't like cheese but prefers something like a gingerbread man. This could provide another life or death situation in the play.

Sleek the Mouse had another function in the play – to elicit reaction from the Big Ones should they ever see him. A mouse in the kitchen is something human beings get very upset about. If they found him, perhaps they would try to get rid of him by putting down poison – yet another threat for the dresser folk.

The Big Ones had gradually become rather important characters in the play. But I knew it would be wrong ever to see them because of the problem of scale. To the characters on the dresser they would be giants. But their voices could certainly be heard booming from above, and their presence in the kitchen could thus be felt. Not only that, life on the dresser would be in many ways subject to the actions of the Big Ones. If they were in the kitchen, the dresser folk would automatically freeze.

The Big Ones would have no idea of all the activity that took place on the dresser when they were not around. This could be useful as far as the Gingerbread Man himself was concerned, because, when he first 'arrived' he would not understand that when the Big Ones walked into the kitchen he had to freeze. This would provide a tension between him and the others. And, of course, Sleek the Mouse would not be bound by the same rules. Being an outsider, he might well be seen by the Big Ones.

Steps 3 & 4. Story and Structure

The parameters were set. I had my 'world'. I had my characters. Now came the interesting part, structuring a story for them.

It seemed appropriate to set the play at night-time when the Big

Ones would be safely out of the way. I imagined that every night the dresser would come to life. The residents would have meetings and parties. Maybe the play should all take place during one night (observing the unity of time dating back to Greek drama). This would allow the play to flow continuously.

Maybe the play should start at midnight when all is still. Cuckoo could be the first to appear, cuckooing the time. If he suddenly realized he had a sore throat and failed to cuckoo twelve times clearly, this could immediately set up a problem to be solved. If he had lost his voice, his first reaction would be to visit his friends on the dresser to seek advice. Salt and Pepper could be his first port of call.

He would have to wake them up. To make such a sequence interesting I decided that the Big Ones had propped a letter in its envelope between Salt and Pepper, using them as a letter rack. This would cause a bit of aggravation. Indeed, it helped set up Salt's character straight away, because, feeling the envelope leaning against him, he could have a nightmare imagining that the wind-blown sails on his ship had collapsed on him.

The discovery of the Gingerbread Man was an important moment to work out. Presumably this would be a diversion, temporarily taking attention away from Cuckoo's lost voice. I felt it was a good idea if Salt and Pepper didn't know exactly what the Gingerbread Man was when they found him. The audience would be able to tell them.

But I had to find a reason why the Gingerbread Man didn't come to life immediately. Indeed, what would make him come to life? I decided that the Big Ones had baked him that day, but had not finished him off. He would have no face and Salt, Pepper and Cuckoo would have to provide him with one. The audience could suggest suitable objects for mouth, eyes and nose. And finally to make him come to life, it seemed appropriate that Pepper should make him sneeze.

I decided that a sense of danger rather than sheer delight should be the immediate reaction to the Gingerbread Man's waking. He should behave in an anarchic manner, excited to be alive, nearly toppling plates and rushing around shouting at the top of his voice. The others would be fearful that the Big Ones would wake up. Having a radio on the dresser, which the Gingerbread Man could explore and eventually turn on, blaring out loud music, would help this. Then the Big Ones could be woken and come down to see what was going on. Such interruptions by the Big Ones would be very useful as suddenlies.

To introduce the Old Bag, I needed a reason for the Gingerbread Man to climb up and visit the top shelf. Cuckoo's lost voice provided the answer. Cuckoo needed something to make his voice better. The audience could be asked to suggest something soothing and health-giving. I reckoned rightly, as it happily turned out, that if the honey pot on the top shelf was visible, the audience would suggest honey, prompting the Gingerbread Man to go and find some. The others could then warn him of the unpleasant Old Bag who might try to stop him taking any.

The quest to find the honey should not be made too easy. Just climbing up to the top shelf could provide a visually interesting problem to solve. I wondered how Salt would cope practically with such a problem, and came up with the idea that he would create a sort of capstan, using a piece of string and the rolling pin. By tying one end of the string to the Gingerbread Man, looping it over a hook on the shelf above, then tying the other end round the rolling pin, it would be possible to heave the Gingerbread Man upwards, by rolling the rolling pin in seaman-like fashion.

The transfer of the action to the top shelf suggested a complete change of atmosphere. It would be rather sinister up there. The Gingerbread Man would try to steal the honey, but would be caught by the Old Bag, who could emerge from her teapot and stalk him. This could lead to pantomime-style audience participation, with the audience desperately warning the Gingerbread Man of the danger. Also, I realized that the scene between the Gingerbread Man and the Old Bag could establish her unpleasantness. The Old Bag not wanting to help Cuckoo because he was so noisy, getting cross with the Gingerbread Man for trespassing and trying to steal her honey, and generally behaving in an unfair, confrontational way. But at the same time it could be seen that she was behaving in this way because she was lonely and perhaps the Gingerbread Man could try to be her friend – even if, at first, the reason for this would be the ulterior motive of wanting the honey for Cuckoo. At this point, the Old Bag could show off her health-giving herbs, planting a later clue for a possible solution to Cuckoo's problem, should the honey not work.

A nice moral dilemma presented itself now. Should the Gingerbread Man steal some honey? Was Cuckoo's need so great that the theft would be morally defensible? I decided it probably was, and even thought of the possibility of the Gingerbread Man asking the audience whether he should take it. In performance, the audience, albeit somewhat nervously, usually agree that he should steal it. What I liked about the situation, and the earlier ones in which the audience became part of the play, was that they were being forced to be involved and help make decisions.

Another useful idea came concerning the honey. Supposing, once the Gingerbread Man had stolen some, it became contaminated with poison. This could lead to Cuckoo eating some and becoming really ill. This would be a very strong end to the first half of the play. To achieve that, Sleek the Mouse could make his appearance, meet the Gingerbread Man and chase him, in order to eat him. Such a sequence could build to a noisy climax, culminating in the arrival of the Big Ones, who could spot the Mouse, put down the poison (which could fall on to the honey), and then go back to bed. Cuckoo could then emerge, happily anticipating his honey remedy, and start to eat what the audience would know was poisoned. Hopefully they would shout out an impassioned warning. Curtain. End of Act One. A nice cliffhanger for the interval.

In the second half I had several strands to resolve. First, Cuckoo, having eaten some poison, would collapse. The Gingerbread Man could then remember the Old Bag's ability to use her herbs to cure diseases, and enlist her help. This could be hampered by the arrival of Sleek the Mouse on the top shelf, still chasing the Gingerbread Man. The Old Bag could be terrified of the Mouse, who would try to nibble her perforations. She would be heroically saved by the Gingerbread Man, to whom she would obviously be very grateful. Her rescue could involve her being helped to the worktop below where she would have to confront the other dresser folk and eventually make her peace with them. Not only that, she could then help Cuckoo get his voice back by making a magic herbal potion.

But there was also the question of Sleek the Mouse. How could he be logically disposed of and his threat vanquished? First of all, I thought it would be fun to trick him into the Old Bag's teapot and to shut him in. Then a plan could be worked out to catch him and finally force him behind the dresser, blocking off his means of access with a giant plate. It seemed to me that this sequence could involve the whole audience, who would take great delight in tricking Sleek.

Maybe the dresser folk could invent a special mousetrap. Salt's nautical know-how came in useful here. Using an up-turned mug, with string tied to its handle and looped over the cup hook on the shelf above, it was possible to raise the mug enough for Sleek to go underneath and be caught. As bait, put under the mug to lure Sleek towards it, I thought it might be an idea to ask the audience for a sweet, so that, again, they would directly participate in his capture. This led to them also shouting and screaming like the Big Ones did earlier, in order to make Sleek freeze long enough for the mug to be dropped over him. This sequence would hopefully galvanize the whole audience into a state of excitement. Pepper could also prove useful in this sequence, by scattering peppercorns all round the edge of the worktop, to prevent Sleek escaping into the audience and terrorizing them.

With Sleek out of the way, it would be possible to see Cuckoo's recovery, thanks to the Old Bag, and the Old Bag's finding of friendship, thanks to the Gingerbread Man. All this, I realized, needed a time lapse. Everyone would go to sleep until eight o'clock in the morning, when the Big Ones would come down for breakfast. At this point, everyone would hope that Cuckoo would emerge from his clock and call his eight cuckoos with a perfectly clear voice. Thus all would end happily.

But what about the Gingerbread Man? There was a basic problem here. Gingerbread men are normally baked in order to be eaten. The solution came in the Big Ones' realization that the Gingerbread Man, lying on the worktop where they had left him, would have been made germy by the Mouse scampering all over him. A final frisson was possible here, because the Big Ones could decide not to eat him, but rather to throw him in the dustbin. Then the final resolution could be that they like his face and, forgetting that they did not actually give it to him, decide that he is attractive enough to become a sort of decoration for the top shelf. The Old Bag would be delighted by that.

Step 5. Action

As I worked towards the synopsis stage, I hoped that the story developed logically and that structurally it had enough highs and lows in the right places to give variety, tension and excitement. I tried to make sure that the development from incident to incident never became too wordy. The use of giant props helped enormously. The envelope, the plates, the rolling pin. Everything was used physically to achieve something, leading to action sequences. The characters were often doing things rather than simply talking about them. Making the Gingerbread Man's face, the Gingerbread Man exploring and dancing to the music of the radio, the Old Bag stalking the Gingerbread Man, Sleek chasing the Gingerbread Man, throwing down the herbs to make the potion, scuttling back to first positions whenever the Big Ones arrive, getting Sleek into the teapot, helping the Old Bag down from the top shelf, sliding the giant plates. These action sequences would provide visual interest and variety.

Step 6. Language

I felt that there would be enough variety of speech and language to maintain interest. Salt's nautical bluster, Pepper's unpredictable directness, Sleek's pseudo-gangster language – eventually embellished with spoonerisms – Cuckoo's German accent and word orders and the Old Bag's colourful, crotchety mysteriousness all contrast with the Gingerbread Man's 'normality'. He is the one the audience must identify with. He is much less of a 'character' than the others, although the fact that he is a gingerbread man obviously gives him an individuality of another kind. Finally, the booming voices of the Big Ones give yet another contrast.

Step 7. Songs

Several ideas for songs had presented themselves while thinking of the story. I tried to make sure that each song led somewhere rather than simply echoing a situation. For instance, Cuckoo's opening song, which would incorporate his yodelling, would explain the problem he was having with his voice and demonstrate it, getting worse as the song progressed. By the end of it, he would have virtually no singing or 'cuckoo-calling' voice at all.

When Salt invents his capstan to lift the Gingerbread Man up to the top shelf, I wanted the song to be a nautical shanty-style, and to see the Gingerbread Man ascend during the song. At the beginning of the song he would be on the worktop; by the end of the song he would be on the top shelf. During the song *The Power of the Leaf*, sung by the Old Bag to explain her ability to tell fortunes (tea leaves), it would be possible actually to have her tell the Gingerbread Man's fortune within the song, leading us forward rather than keeping us standing still.

In the song *Herbal Remedy*, in which the Old Bag would describe the properties of her herbs, she would also be collecting them from the herb jars, assisted by the others, and then mixing them in an egg cup. By the end of the song the potion would be ready to be drunk by Cuckoo.

Pepper could sing a song called *Hot Stuff*, telling us how she can make people sneeze. Not only that, during the song she would be distributing pepper along the edge of the dresser ready to help catch Sleek.

One or two songs would incorporate action development rather less, but hopefully ways could be found to make them interesting. For example, the title song, *The Gingerbread Man*, simply announces his arrival and acts as a 'welcome to the dresser' song. But in the staging it is possible to show how the other characters are reluctant to accept him fully, because of his anarchic bounciness, but eventually succumb completely to his exuberant innocence and 'happy to be alive' warmth. By the end of the song everybody unequivocally celebrates his arrival.

The *Beware of the Old Bag* song could consist of warnings about the unpleasantness of the Old Bag, but it could be staged in such a way that the dresser folk play out the danger, surprising and scaring the Gingerbread Man, and themselves sometimes. There is the possibility for an audience-participation song, yodelling along with Cuckoo and the others in celebration when his voice has returned.

Step 8.   Theatrical Magic

There were no problems as far as the possibilities of theatrical magic were concerned. The giant-scale dresser and the potential for visually interesting costumes were immediately recognizable. All the giant props would be appealing, particularly when used in the plot. There were opportunities for interesting lighting: moonlight as though shining through a window, the sudden brightness when the Big Ones entered the kitchen and turned on the light, the transition from one area to another, particularly from the worktop to the top shelf and the isolating of the clock when Cuckoo popped out. There was also the possibility of shadows being cast by the Big Ones.

The use of sound was limited, but was potentially effective whenever the Big Ones entered the kitchen. Their booming voices and the noise of footsteps down the stairs or the door opening or closing could all heighten the tension. Also the noise of Sleek scratching and scrabbling his way through the back of the dresser could be effective.

Other theatrical possibilities included the hands of the clock being practical, so that the audience could see the hands going round. In the time-lapse sequence as we approach eight o'clock, the lighting could slowly brighten as dawn approaches. The throwing down of poison on to the worktop by the Big Ones could be made quite spectacular by releasing glittery poison from above, falling slowly and threateningly on to the honey below.

Step 9.   Clarity

All the time, as I worked towards the synopsis stage, I was trying to ensure that every step of the plot would be clear to the audience. I hoped that the domestic location would present no problems, and that the characters and their development would prove logical and theatrically satisfying. I hoped that there were enough moments for the audience to share, both in pleasure and in fearful anticipation, and that they would enjoy engineering the come-uppance of Sleek, while at the same time finding the character entertaining.

Now I was ready to write the synopsis.

Synopsis for *The Gingerbread Man*

Design

The action of the play takes place on a kitchen dresser. The characters are all but inches high; therefore the set is magnified. It is one structure, which remains throughout the play.

The stage surface is the 'top' of the dresser, in other words the working surface. The edge of the stage can therefore be the edge of the dresser. Positioned, say 12 or 15 feet up stage, is the back of the dresser, incorporating one practical shelf, and hopefully the beginnings of another (non-practical) shelf. Naturally, at stage surface level there is a 'shelf-like area', under the practical shelf above.

On the 'lower' shelf are two plates standing upright, one of which is practical in that it slides to one side to reveal a hole in the wooden back of the dresser, through which Sleek the Mouse enters; the other is practical in that it is used in the action to put things on. There is also a practical mug. There are several hooks along the edge of the shelf. There is also a length of string, which could be in a tin, or just the remains of an opened parcel. Also a sugar bowl, with several practical lumps of sugar. And an eggcup. A gaily coloured pocket transistor radio can either be suspended from another hook, or stand horizontal on the top surface.

On the 'upper' (practical) shelf is a cottage-style teapot. It has a practical front door. Next to it are various herb jars, which never move, but could have lids. There is a pot of honey. Other larger jars could be visible (probably painted or simply the front façades).

Beside the shelved part of the dresser, probably attached to it, is a cuckoo clock, with a practical door. Cuckoo should be able to reach from his cuckooing podium to the dresser working surface, perhaps by swinging on the short end of the pendulum or by having a pendulum with rungs, like a ladder. But as two characters have to make the return journey – i.e. from dresser to clock – it may be more feasible to make the 'podium' a sort of balcony, reachable by stepping up from the working surface.

On the working surface itself sits a rolling pin. A tea-cloth is somewhere handy.

Other dresser clutter could be visible – non-practical fixed 'dresser dressing'. This could extend to a non-practical top shelf, which could extend into the flies; or the very top of the dresser could be visible.

The set is backed by black tabs, and hopefully a floor cloth, with the dresser surface painted on; this should have black surrounds extending from the surface edges to the wings, thus truly defining the working area.

If possible, a front cloth could be used instead of tabs. This would have the show's title and possibly a Gingerbread Man motif, plus a design of the dresser (on its own or as part of a kitchen scene). This could help establish the large-scale set.

Characters

Monsieur le Cuckoo – the Swiss-made cuckoo in the cuckoo clock. He wears lederhosen.

Salt – a salt cellar, based design-wise on the blue and white horizontal striped variety, thus making him look like a sailor, and indeed that's how he sees himself.

Pepper – a well-groomed, svelte, elegant female pepper-mill.

The Gingerbread Man – who looks like what he is!

The Old Bag – an elderly, short-tempered tea bag, who lives on the shelf, inside a cottage-style teapot.

Sleek the Mouse – an American gangster-style villain. Not as smooth as he'd like to appear.

The Voices of the Big Ones – these can either be pre-recorded or doubled by other members of the cast. They are the voices of the family who own the house in whose kitchen and on whose dresser the action takes place.

Songs

Act One

1. Cuckoo's Song – Frog in the throat/yodel (Cuckoo)
2. Dresser Waltz (Salt, Pepper, Cuckoo)
3. The Gingerbread Man (Salt, Pepper, Cuckoo, Gingerbread Man)
4. The Old Bag – Beware Song (Salt, Pepper, Cuckoo, Gingerbread Man)
5. Yo Heave Ho – Shanty (Salt, Pepper, Cuckoo, Gingerbread Man)
6. Fortune Telling Song (Old Bag)
7. Sleek the Mouse Song (Sleek the Mouse)

Act 2

7A. Reprise of Yo Heave Ho (Salt, Pepper, Gingerbread Man)
8. Remedy Recipe Song (Old Bag, Salt, Pepper, Gingerbread Man)
9. Hot Stuff! (Pepper)
10. Hopeful Song (Salt, Pepper, Gingerbread Man, Old Bag)
10A. Reprise of Cuckoo's Song with audience-participation yodelling (Cuckoo, Salt, Pepper, Gingerbread Man, Old Bag)
11. Celebration Song (All except Sleek)
11A. Reprise of The Gingerbread Man (All except Sleek)

Synopsis

Act One

It is midnight. We hear the ticking of the clock as the lights come up to reveal the kitchen dresser. The light should be moonlight, but enough for us to see the dresser well. Salt and Pepper are in their positions, backs to the audience, an envelope between them.

From his clock door, Monsieur le Cuckoo enters, clears his throat and starts off on his 12-cuckoo-call. With difficulty he keeps count, and towards the end becomes disturbed by a frog in his throat. He finishes, but instead of returning inside, practises a few scales, which sound husky. He sings a song which explains he is Swiss-made, from the mountains, and how he loves to yodel – but as he comes to the yodelling chorus, he cannot do it.

He locks his door (Monsieur le Cuckoo is always meticulous) and sets off for the other side of the dresser where he starts talking in a hoarse whisper to Salt. At first Salt can't hear him, but finally jumps in alarm, is kissed on both cheeks by Cuckoo, recovers, and, with difficulty, listens. Then he, Salt, whispers to Pepper, forgetting that he needn't whisper. Pepper expresses impatience, aggravated by the envelope leaning against her – the Big Ones always use her and Salt as a letter rack. She unfeelingly blurts out that if Cuckoo can't cuckoo properly, he is obviously a candidate for the Dustbin – the ultimate threat and danger to the dresser folk. Salt suggests a holiday by his beloved sea; that would surely bring Cuckoo's voice back. Pepper points out that Salt has never been to the sea – the old sauce-boat was the nearest he got to it, and that ended up cracked and in the Dustbin.

A row is developing and Salt calms them all by suggesting they get on with their customary midnight party. They sing and dance a song, *The Dresser Waltz*, which Salt could accompany on the squeeze box. The song ends abruptly because Pepper is bored with the staid tempo of a waltz. Suddenly, however, their attention is drawn to something unusual.

Behind the rolling pin, on which Salt has been sitting, they find, lying flat out, a new creature.

This is the Gingerbread Man, as the audience will probably inform them. He has probably just been made by the Big Ones. They decide to lift him up to see whether he can talk. This leads to a lot of fun as he nearly topples over, etc. He has his back to the audience, which means that Cuckoo, Salt and Pepper can finish him off, with eyes, nose (currants) and mouth (lemon peel perhaps). Finally, with the aid of Pepper, he is made to sneeze, which wakes him up. He exuberantly leaps about as the others introduce themselves and tell him where he is. He looks around and finds the transistor radio.

The others don't think he should touch it, but he fiddles, and rock music blares out. He starts gyrating and singing a song – *The Gingerbread Man*. Pepper is thrilled by the rhythm compared with the waltz she danced before, and eventually Salt and Cuckoo join in too. The Gingerbread Man turns up the volume; everyone is really enjoying themselves. Then:

Suddenly – a loud noise followed by a violent lighting change, in which all the lights go on to a blinding full. All react to this. All except the Gingerbread Man realize it is the Big Ones and make a dash to return to their positions – Cuckoo back to the clock, Salt and Pepper to their positions with the envelope between them. In the midst of the scurry they forget the Gingerbread Man, who stands transfixed. Salt calls to him to lie down, which he does, just as the Big Ones' voices are heard, and their giant shadows are cast over the set. They have been disturbed by the radio, which they thought they had turned off. It clicks off.

As the Big Ones prepare to leave, Monsieur le Cuckoo pops out of his door, and gives a terrible croaking 'cuckoo' to signify one o'clock. He curls up with embarrassment as he goes in again. The Big Ones comment on the awful noise and think possibly the Cuckoo is past it – Dustbin perhaps? They exit, turning off the 'floodlight'. Quiet.

Cuckoo is first to emerge from his door, in a terrible state – he has heard what the Big Ones said. He, Salt, Pepper and Gingerbread Man meet up again, and they explain to Gingerbread Man about the Big Ones, and in fact are a little cross with him for playing the radio so loud. Cuckoo can't help bringing up his throat problem again. Gingerbread Man wants to help him, especially as he unwittingly disturbed the Big Ones and brought the party to an end. He offers to get something for Cuckoo's bad throat, and then perhaps they can carry on the party more quietly, by which time the Big Ones will be asleep.

The offer is accepted, and they consider what might be good for a sore throat. The audience will probably shout out 'honey' (if the pot is visibly marked on the top shelf), so the Gingerbread Man will get some of that. But he is warned about the Old Bag (song), the tea bag who lives alone in the teapot. She doesn't like anybody, and if she catches anyone on 'her' shelf, she looms up on them like a ghost. The dresser folk have even suspected her of being a witch who wills evil things, e.g. when the rabbit-shaped jelly mould, which was rather noisy, got rusty and was thrown in the Dustbin, some folk thought the Old Bag was to blame.

At the end of this song, the Gingerbread Man pretends to be the ghost-like tea bag. He hides under a tea-cloth and tries jokingly to frighten everybody.

Then he sets off on his 'honey' quest. But the problem is, how to reach the shelf? He tries a pile of sugar lumps, but they collapse.

Finally Salt suggests a nautical solution. Using a piece of string, to which the Gingerbread Man is tied with a nautical knot, he throws the other end over a cup-hook in the edge of the shelf. Then, using the rolling pin as a capstan, helped by the others, and all singing a Yo Heave Ho-type shanty, Salt hoists the Gingerbread Man aloft, until he reaches the shelf and gingerly sets off towards the honey. Meanwhile, the others relax. Cuckoo returns to his clock and Salt and Pepper sit on the rolling pin, backs to the audience.

Up on the shelf, as the Gingerbread Man searches for the honey, the door of the teapot surreptitiously opens and the Old Bag peeps out. Audience participation as she menacingly stalks him. Panto-like 'she's behind you' shouts, ending with them bumping into each other back to back.

The Gingerbread Man is forced to converse with the Old Bag, who accuses him of trespassing. He tells her he wants some honey for Cuckoo's throat, but she won't co-operate – she's always hated that noise every hour. If his throat is sore, she can get a bit of peace. It turns out she dislikes everybody, mainly because she never sees anyone. She is really rather lonely. The Gingerbread Man is sure people would like her given the chance – for instance, the audience.

But she conducts a survey based on 'Who likes tea?' and probably finds that the majority of the audience (children) *don't* like tea.

She offers to tell the Gingerbread Man's fortune – tea leaves have always been used to do that – in the 'Fortune Telling' song, in which she warns him of 'Trouble which will help conquer other troubles.' Not sure of what she means, he prepares to leave, asking again for some honey. She refuses again, and goes back inside her house.

He considers what to do, and, probably encouraged by the audience, tentatively advances on the honey, and then steals a chunk. He goes to the edge of the shelf and calls down to Salt and Pepper, who eventually react. They fetch a plate and 'catch' the honey, thrown down by the Gingerbread Man.

At this point the Old Bag re-emerges. The audience warns the Gingerbread Man, who swiftly puts his string harness on again and is lowered by Salt and Pepper. The Old Bag shouts warnings at him. Stealing deserves punishment. Anyway, he won't be there much longer – he'll probably be eaten tomorrow.

She retreats, but the Gingerbread Man has heard. And Salt and Pepper cannot deny the truth of the Old Bag's statement. He is temporarily, naturally, upset that he is going to be eaten, but bravely says he must make the most of the next few hours.

Placing the plate with the honey on it near the cuckoo clock, the Gingerbread Man goes to the clock door and knocks. The sick Cuckoo pops his head out, and is very pleased to hear that a remedy has been found. He gratefully and effusively thanks the Gingerbread Man in true continental fashion. He will come out for his honey very soon – after he has croaked the imminent two o'clock call.

As he returns towards Salt and Pepper, who are relaxing on the rolling pin again, the Gingerbread Man hears a noise, a rustling, scraping sound. He tracks it down to behind a plate (one of the vertically displayed ones) on the side of the 'shelf' on stage level. Tentatively he slides the plate to one side. Enter, sniffing hungrily,

Sleek the Mouse. He sings his song while the Gingerbread Man watches, half-hidden behind the plate.

The shifty, seedy Mouse continues his search for the tasty food he can smell. The over-trusting Gingerbread Man approaches to introduce himself. Sleek reacts, realizing that this is the juicy meal he smelt. He starts cornering the Gingerbread Man, who senses danger and makes towards Salt and Pepper, who join in the scene by trying to ward off the Mouse. Pepper tries shaking pepper in his path, which makes him sneeze. The chase should be amusing as well as dramatic, building to a climax when:

Suddenly, the noise of the Big Ones is heard, and the glaring lights come up. Salt, Pepper and Gingerbread Man realize in time what is up and freeze back in their positions; but Sleek is caught unawares and stands in the centre of the dresser unable to escape. The Big Ones spot him and one shrieks while the other shoo shoos. Eventually he comes to his senses and dashes for cover on the side opposite his hole.

We hear the Big Ones decide to put poison down to get rid of the verminous creature. Seeing the plate (with Cuckoo's honey on it), they decide to put the poison on it. From the flies floats down the poison (glitter, say) onto the plate.

At they leave, Cuckoo emerges and sadly croaks two o'clock. After another disparaging comment about the Cuckoo's voice, the Big Ones go and the light reverts to normal.

Salt, Pepper and Gingerbread Man all remain frozen after this panic, and the Mouse is hidden. Only Cuckoo moves. He is unaware of all the Mouse saga, and, happily seeing the plate with his honey on it, approaches it.

The audience, realizing he is going towards a plate of poison, scream out a warning. As he reaches the plate, the curtain falls.

Interval

Act Two

The act opens where Act One ended. Cuckoo bends down and eats some of the honey poison. The Gingerbread Man sees him just too late, and rushes over, followed by Salt and Pepper. At first Cuckoo expresses pleasure in his throat feeling better, thanks to the honey. He does some happy 'cuckoos'; but very soon they become painful and he clutches his stomach. The others lay him down and cover him with the tea-cloth to keep him warm.

Salt and Pepper realize that the only person who can help in this critical situation is the Old Bag. She could provide a remedy. The Gingerbread Man calls up to the teapot above. But no response. He decides to go up again, in spite of his fear that the Mouse may attack again.

To an urgent reprise of the 'Heave-ho' song, the Gingerbread Man is again hoisted to the shelf above. He approaches the teapot and knocks on the door. Suddenly, the Old Bag opens up. She has not forgiven him for stealing the honey. He explains his mission and begs her to prepare a remedy for Cuckoo. She refuses, even though he takes her to the edge of the shelf and shows her the prostrate, poisoned Cuckoo below. He mentions the Mouse, at which point, though she doesn't really believe the story, the Old Bag becomes nervous. She hates mice; they try to chew her perforations. Suddenly Sleek the Mouse emerges, on this shelf, from the herb jars. He has clearly climbed up the back of the dresser. Panic as Sleek chases both the Gingerbread Man and the Old Bag, who, petrified, is precariously positioned on the edge of the shelf. This is seen by Salt and Pepper, who, realizing the Old Bag's potential value to Cuckoo, grab the tea-cloth and hold it beneath, like firemen waiting for people to jump from a burning building. (If necessary, the Gingerbread Man may have to join them to strengthen the team.) Eventually the Old Bag is forced to jump, is caught in the tea-cloth below, and taken care of. The Gingerbread Man hides temporarily and the Mouse demands the audience's help. If not, he will come down and pinch their sweets.

Finally, the Gingerbread Man manages to edge near the teapot door, during several attacks upon his person. Finally, Sleek 'charges', the Gingerbread Man manages to open the door, Sleek dashes inside, and the Gingerbread Man shuts the door, and pulls an object over to keep the door shut.

Down below, the Old Bag is thanking Salt and Pepper for saving her life. They point out that the least she can do is help poor Cuckoo. She agrees, and, in a song, calls out the ingredients, which Salt and Pepper shout up to the Gingerbread Man, who throws them down. The Old Bag mixes them in a cup. By the end of the song the brew is ready; some is given to Cuckoo, who is then helped to his clock, where the Old Bag will sit with him. She thinks he will recover, hopefully in time for the eight o'clock call – the first the Big Ones will hear in the morning. Salt and Pepper are relieved, but suddenly reminded by the Gingerbread Man – still on the shelf above – that there is another problem: how to get rid of Sleek the Mouse.

After discussion an elaborate plan is worked out which involves the audience's involvement and participation. Basically the idea is to lure Sleek to a strategic point over which an upturned mug will already be hoisted from its handle (the opposite lip still touching the 'floor') by Salt, using the string. When he is in position, the audience will shout the noises of the Big Ones (some shrieks and some 'shoo shoos') to make him freeze in panic as he did when the real Big Ones came in. Then the mug can be lowered on to him, pushed, with him inside, to the corner of the dresser, then upturned manually just sufficient to get him to escape through his hole behind the plate. Then the plate can be slid back and he will be kept out.

To lure him to the correct spot a sweet is requested from someone in the audience, and placed in the relevant place as bait. The Gingerbread Man directs the audience in a rehearsal while Salt sets up the mug trap.

A final refinement is added as, to prevent Sleek from going to the audience as he threatened, Pepper surrounds the top of the dresser with pepper, singing the *Hot Stuff* song.

All is set. The Gingerbread Man quietly opens the teapot door and hides. Sleek comes out and threatens the audience, then goes through his hole on that shelf, which the Gingerbread Man immediately seals off. Sleek re-emerges down below and advances on the audience, but comes in contact with the pepper and sneezes violently. He tries this a couple of times, then picks up the scent of the sweet. The audience directs him to it. He reaches the spot and greedily attacks the sweet. The audience shout their Big Ones' noises and he freezes in panic. Salt lowers the mug. He and Pepper push it to the corner, then release the string and use it to help the Gingerbread Man down from above. Then the three of them release the Mouse; he scuttles away down his hole and the plate is slid back. Victory!

Hearing the celebration, the Old Bag comes out of the clock and is told the good news of Sleek's defeat. She says Cuckoo is better. All sing a time-passing 'hoping for the best' song, at the end of which all are asleep.

Time-lapse music until a lighting change, plus, hopefully, the hands of the clock moving round, tells us it is nearly eight o'clock. The clock door opens and Cuckoo emerges for a practice. He can do it again! He sings his yodelling song with delight, which wakes the others up. They join in with pleasure at his recovery. It becomes an audience-participation song (the equivalent of a song sheet) in which all the audience learn to yodel.

As this ends, a loud noise heralds the arrival of the Big Ones, and as the lights glare the dresser folk return to their places, as they started off, except that the Old Bag hides behind the rolling pin with the Gingerbread Man.

The voices of the Big Ones register pleasure that there is no sign of the Mouse. Cuckoo pops out and performs to perfection his eight o'clock call. The Big Ones are delighted. He is not past it after all. He beams with relief, forgetting to go back inside.

'Do you want to eat the Gingerbread Man for breakfast?' asks one Big One. The Gingerbread Man's head emerges nervously from behind the rolling pin. But it is decided that the Mouse probably trod all over him and left germs, so he won't be eaten. Relief. 'Throw him in the dustbin then?' inquires a Big One, creating even more concern on the Gingerbread Man's face, and the Old Bag's too, for she has ventured to peep over the rolling pin also. But the other Big One likes the look of the Gingerbread Man and decides to keep him – he can stand on the shelf by the teapot, as a sort of decoration.

The Big Ones leave the kitchen to go to work, and the dresser folk celebrate. The Old Bag says, as the Gingerbread Man will now share her shelf, he can call her teapot his home whenever he likes, and she will no longer be lonely. Her fortune telling was right, too – all the Mouse trouble led to the conquering of other troubles.

All sing a celebratory song, which develops into a reprise of *The Gingerbread Man* song.

The End

Subsequent changes to the synopsis

My synopsis was fairly detailed, and as I had really mapped out the whole play in my mind before setting to work, not too many changes were made.

1. Monsieur le Cuckoo became Herr Von Cuckoo, mainly, I think, because I felt that the German accent and word order would be more interesting than the French. In the build up to the Gingerbread Man's visit to the top shelf, I decided not to have the characters tell him quite so much about the Old Bag. Instead, some of these details were incorporated into a scene in the second half.
2. Towards the end of Act One, just before Sleek the Mouse arrives, I decided that Salt, Pepper and the Gingerbread Man should go to sleep. This makes it more effective when Sleek's rustling, scraping sounds are heard. The Gingerbread Man is woken up by them.
3. When the Big Ones put poison down for Sleek, I decided it was too obvious for them simply to decide to use the very plate on which Cuckoo's honey has been left. Instead, they simply pour it down and it happens to fall on the honey.
4. In Act Two, I decided that the Gingerbread Man, rather than Salt and Pepper, should realize that the only person who can help Cuckoo is the Old Bag. This makes the Gingerbread Man the instigator,

which, at this point of the play, shows how important he has become on the dresser.

5. The ending seemed somewhat perfunctory. I strengthened it by using the hours leading up to Cuckoo's important reappearance at 8 a.m. The dresser folk tidy their worktop and sing a song of hope that all will resolve happily. There is then a time-lapse tick-tock until Cuckoo wakes up in full voice and the Big Ones decide to keep him.

Steps towards a synopsis for *The See-Saw Tree*

In 1985, Stephen Barry, Artistic Director of the Redgrave Theatre, Farnham, invited me to write a children's play for the following year. There were no restrictions on subject matter, but a maximum of eight characters was suggested, possibly on one basic set. There are no flying facilities at the Redgrave. The play might have to fit on top of an evening show.

Step 1. Theme (world or microcosm)

I started looking around for ideas and, as luck would have it, received a letter from a new ecological organization called Common Ground, who had heard of my plays, *The Selfish Shellfish* and *Dinosaurs and All That Rubbish*, both of which have an environmental theme. They wondered if I might write something which would tie in with their objective, 'To reassert the importance of our everyday contact with nature and the natural world, and in particular in making links between the conservation of landscape and nature and the Arts.' A subsequent letter informed me that, 'During the next three years we hope to organize a programme of events, exhibitions, etc. to heighten public awareness and creative caring for trees and woods by stressing the importance of their cultural and spiritual value.'

I started thinking about trees and conservation. Immediately I could see that a tree could be a microcosm. Many different creatures would live on it, interrelating with one another, facing daily domestic problems, dependent upon the tree for their home and survival. If the tree were threatened, life for the community of birds, animals and insects would be disrupted. A life and death problem. To look at such a problem from the point of view of the creatures, under threat from the actions of human beings – the Big Ones – struck me as a very strong idea. But it was also important to link in with Common Ground's objectives to stress the importance of trees to the lives of human beings.

Maybe the threat to a special tree should be discussed by the community before its future would be decided. Perhaps the Parish Council of a rural village might be considering the redevelopment of a piece of land on which sat a tree of historical significance. The necessity to involve the audience of children emotionally led me to suppose that the Parish Council might hold a public meeting to discuss the issue. Suppose the audience became the parishioners at the meeting. Suppose they were invited to hear various arguments and then vote on what action the Council should take.

I decided that 'serious' audience participation of this kind was perfectly possible, but it seemed a little obvious simply to ask the children if they thought it was a good thing to conserve a tree. Somehow both the pros and cons had to be carefully structured to make possible a real moral dilemma. Also I needed to find a reason why the action of the play should transfer to the tree.

The main narrative, I was sure, should involve the tree creatures and the problems they face when threatened with the loss of their home. It suddenly struck me that it might be possible to make the audience vote in favour of the redevelopment of the land by not immediately mentioning the existence of the tree. Suppose the Council's idea was to clear the land in order to make a car park for the local supermarket, part of which would be used to create a children's playground, where children could be safely left to enjoy themselves while their parents did the shopping. The idea of a children's playground would naturally appeal to the children in the audience, who would probably vote in favour. From then on, the idea would be, using a play-within-a-play, to change the children's minds, encouraging them to vote in favour of saving the tree, even if it meant losing the children's playground. The final scene would involve voting, and hopefully lead to a celebration that the tree would live on.

Indeed, it might be suggested that the tree should become part of the children's playground. Maybe, in years gone by, the tree had been used by local children for that very purpose. Maybe they had placed a plank across a lower branch to create a see-saw. This idea gave me the title for the play – *The See-Saw Tree*.

Step 2.   Characters

At this stage in the thought process I was more concerned with the Parish Council meeting structure than the action which would take place on the tree itself. There would be a Chairperson, a Treasurer and Secretary, plus the local supermarket owner who wanted to improve facilities for his customers, plus the whiz-kid entrepreneur who would set up the children's playground, complete with pinball-tables and fruit machines. I decided that local villagers might be planted in the audience to add contributions from the floor. This would give the children the feeling of a real meeting at which their views were going to be considered seriously. Now I needed a way to turn the argument. A local villager who would represent the interests of the tree. A kind of Friends of the Earth activist, who would ask embarrassing questions of the supermarket owner and entrepreneur, wheedling out of them confirmation that the clearing of the land would involve the destruction of one particular oak tree of great local historical significance. This character could explain his position by telling the story of *The See-Saw Tree*, leading us into the play-within-a-play, in which the predicament of the tree creatures would be explored. Then the action would return to the public meeting. Hopefully his story would sway the audience to change their minds and vote to preserve the tree.

Next I began thinking about the tree community. Which animals and birds would provide a good character mix? How would they learn about the possible destruction of their tree? How might they try to fight for their survival? Whereabouts on the tree should the action focus? Maybe there would be mileage in setting some of the play at the foot of the tree, with the trunk in evidence, allowing a character such as a rabbit to set off along the ground or under the ground to check the situation. Further up the tree, there could be a network of branches and 'homes' – a nest, perhaps, a squirrel's drey, a hollow for an owl, plus various levels which would be theatrically interesting.

In other plays I have used the Big Ones as a threat to such a community. In this play it was obvious that the contractors employed to clear the land with their destructive machines would be possible bringers of potential doom, their voices booming out and their chainsaws roaring menacingly.

I'm not an expert in natural history, so I consulted books about trees. It became apparent that an oak tree would be the most appropriate choice. Many books described the creatures who co-exist on an oak tree, and schoolteachers told me that they often did projects with their children about this very subject.

Steps 3 & 4.   Story and Structure

One of the books I came across was fuller and more academic than the rest: *Oak Watch* by Jim Flegg. It is a marvellous study of the life and activity in an oak tree throughout the various seasons: its inhabitants, visitors, food chain, how it copes with different weather conditions and storm damage. But the most fascinating aspect was that the author treated the oak tree as a microcosm. He focused on the interdependence of the creatures and even talked about a 'cast' and 'supporting characters'. Jim Flegg was clearly the man for me. I wrote to him and he kindly agreed to meet me.

Jim was a huge help. Quite apart from his amazing knowledge about the life of an oak tree, he proved willing to depart from his academic approach, and answer my questions about the 'human' characteristics displayed by various creatures. In other words, I wanted to know about the hierarchy in the tree and how the various creatures might react to one another. Was there a natural leader? How might certain creatures annoy others? Did any of them present dangers to one another? Such anthropomorphic musings might well have been irritating to a scientist, but Jim entered fully into the spirit of the idea and came up with some fascinating information. From my conversations with him the list of characters narrowed and I began to imagine the daily life of the tree, the happiness and the frustrations, all of which would be thrown into disarray as soon as the tree-folk learnt about and lived through their common danger. Squirrel would be an aggressive hoarder of nuts, a home-lover, who would fight to protect his 'castle'. Jay would be a flashy, talkative bird, who might not actually live in the tree, but would arrive looking for food or nesting material, a rather dishonest creature, who would happily steal. In the play he becomes a travelling salesman, a bit of a spiv, colourful and opportunist, offering his wares to the other creatures. He is also practical and good in a crisis.

Owl, said Jim, would definitely be top in the pecking order. Biologically it is true that she could eat virtually anything on the tree. She would be the natural leader in the fight to save the tree, using her ability to hear well and to fly silently. She would stand no nonsense from the other creatures, and could even be used to frighten the human beings with her rather spooky hooting. Her night-hunting might mean that she is not at home when news of the crisis breaks, which could be useful.

Cuckoo, I learnt, would not be a permanent resident of the tree, but would be a rather unpopular bird, feared by the others, arriving as a summer visitor, like a tourist, coming all the way from Africa simply to find a nest in which to lay an egg. Then, leaving her offspring to be brought up by the put-upon foster parent, she would go back to foreign climes. In human terms, she might well have a foreign accent. As a calculating, exploitative bird, she could well add to the domestic problems of the tree community.

Jim told me that bats were clubbable, nocturnally active creatures, which immediately suggested that, in human terms, every night Bat would go down to the local disco. He would not be a particularly popular member of the tree community, partly because of his smell and also because he might well claim the best spot to 'hang out' during the day – Owl's hollow would be particularly desirable. His ability to use radar to sense approaching objects could well be useful. He would also be particularly vulnerable to the loss of his home and, in an emergency, would be a strong member of the team. I began imagining him as a rather 'hip' character, enjoying his wild parties and listening to loud disco music through large headphones. I imagined him returning the worse for wear from his night out, annoying the other tree residents with his unsociable behaviour.

It seemed a good idea for one of the characters to be laying eggs, particularly so that Cuckoo could try to leave an egg in her nest. Mistlethrush seemed a good bet. Jim described her as a rather disruptive, strident bird with an unpleasant, unmelodic song. Apparently her nest is always very untidy, and bits and pieces of nesting material often drop down to other areas of the tree. Mistlethrush would be a devoted mother, whose main concern if the tree were under threat would be for her eggs.

Jim agreed that Rabbit could be very useful to the tree folk. He would be very well informed, because of his burrow network, and he could penetrate into other areas of the wood. He would have every reason to dislike the Big Ones, who would often disrupt his burrow with new buildings. He would be wary of Owl for obvious reasons, but would probably know Squirrel and be able to communicate with him. Jim told me an extraordinary fact – it would be possible for Owl to lift Rabbit up into the tree. That proved very useful in the story.

We also discussed a more ordinary, drab little bird. At first it was to be a treecreeper, but eventually we decided on a dunnock. This bird would know all areas of the tree and spend a lot of time 'cleaning' it. She would keep her ear to the ground and take messages to other characters. A hard worker, a kind of caretaker, Dunnock could be the type of character who people take for granted. But in a crisis she could come into her own, defiantly determined to save her home.

Armed with my copious notes, I next started working out possible patterns of behaviour involving the characteristics of each of the characters. Dunnock would clean out Squirrel's drey, carry messages and would help Mistlethrush in labour. Jay would try to sell things to the others and steal acorns from the indignant Squirrel. Cuckoo would arrive and try to lay her egg in Mistlethrush's nest. Owl would stop various domestic squabbles and lead the resistance against the tree's destruction. She would have a running battle with Bat, who would return from his night at the disco, invading the peace of the tree. Rabbit would bring news of the developing destruction of adjacent areas. All the characters would be galvanized into activity once their tree was threatened.

I suddenly became aware that the links between the human community and the animal community could be made stronger by linking the characteristics of both. In other words, each actor would play a human being at the Council Meeting and then become one of the tree creatures. Suppose in the initial Council Meeting scene they established themselves in such a way that their animal counterparts could have similar traits. Thus Owl became Miss Wise, the strong Chairperson of the Meeting. Squirrel became Mr Storer, the Treasurer, looking after the money with as much devotion as Squirrel looked after his nuts. Dunnock became Mrs Dunnock, the Secretary of the Parish Council, keeping a low profile, but being efficient and helpful. Jay, the travelling salesman, became Mr Jay, the supermarket owner. Mistlethrush became Mrs Thrush, an outspoken local resident, who takes public service seriously and speaks from the floor of the meeting. Cuckoo became Mrs Cook, an outsider, not a local person, but one who drove to the village each week to do her supermarket shop. Bat became Mr Batty, the whiz-kid entrepreneur. And Rabbit became Mr Bunn, a local concerned conservationist.

I knew that the children in the audience might not pick up the links between the human and animal characters, but it helped me to give a solid framework to the play. It also helped clarify the importance of the issue to both communities.

Step 5. Action

The play suggested many opportunities for action: the various journeys up and down the tree, the dramatic evacuation, the suddenlies provided by various arrivals of the Big Ones with their machinery, the hatching of Mistlethrush's eggs, the various celebrations and moments of protest, the bickering over acorns between Jay and Squirrel, and the frantic activity leading to the dénouement.

Two important elements of the play were late additions to the developing story-line. First was the idea of using a white cross painted on the tree trunk, the Big Ones' sign that this tree was due to be felled. This proved useful, not just as a symbol, but in a practical way. First of all, when Rabbit discovers the white cross, the paint still wet, he immediately senses that something is wrong. He wants the other characters to see it too to discuss what it means. Later in the play he realizes that other trees are being felled, all of which have the white cross painted on them. He realizes that the only way of saving the tree is to remove the white cross. Using some of Jay's cleaning products, Dunnock and Owl make the journey down to the ground and frantically scrub off the white cross. The plan works. The tree is spared. The tree folk enjoy a victory celebration. But their joy is cut short as the Big Ones discover that they have made a mistake and that the tree must come down. Structurally this apparent victory gives the opportunity for joy followed immediately by further impending doom. This leads to the evacuation and the final, futile, defiant song of protest before the Big Ones move in with the chainsaw.

Secondly, it became clear that the play-within-a-play needed a really dramatic climax in order to point the very real danger home, before coming back to the Council Meeting and the final vote. I decided that Rabbit, echoing his activist human role, should make one last desperate stand. He should try to bite through the electric cable of the chainsaw, but be electrocuted. His death, the ultimate sacrifice, would be a sobering moment with which to end. It would then be possible not to witness the final destruction of the tree, but to leave the ending open, to pave the way for the final vote. I knew that the death would have a powerful effect on the audience, because Rabbit would inevitably be a likeable character. However, as I didn't want the audience to go away with the lingering image of a dead rabbit, I decided that Rabbit should be seen to revive and once again become Mr Bunn addressing the Council Meeting.

Step 6. Language

The range of characters offered good opportunities for individual movement and also language. The groovy Bat, the spivvish Jay, the foreign Cuckoo, the 'loud' Mistlethrush and the formal Owl were all idiosyncratic enough to give them distinct manners of speech.

Step 7. Songs

I decided the play should not be a musical, but there were certain opportunities for songs which proved irresistible. Mistlethrush, with her somewhat out-of-tune voice, practises the lullaby she will sing once her eggs have hatched. She also sings a song to welcome the spring. Both are in character and amusing because of their stridency. I gave Bat a funky number called *Hanging On*, which he could sing trance-like as he arrived back from the disco. The song could also be used to celebrate the temporary reprieve of the tree. A desperate song of protest, in which the characters plead for their home, was effective in its simple sincerity. And the final song of celebration once the audience had voted to save the tree was a joyful antidote to the dramatic death of the Rabbit. The songs were treated as natural extensions of the action.

Step 8. Theatrical Magic

My desire for 'theatrical magic' seemed to be granted in abundance by the structure of *The See-Saw Tree*. The public meeting itself proved highly theatrical, as well as the 'dissolve' into the story set on the tree. This obviously involved a change of scale, seeing all the tree creatures against the vast setting of the tree trunk and the 'bowl' of the tree above. The voices and mechanical noises of the Big Ones were accompanied by lighting effects of car headlamps and torches, plus smoke and red light to suggest the burning of adjacent trees. This provided a highly theatrical image against which the evacuation of the tree took place.

Step 9. Clarity

Before writing the synopsis, I checked through for clarity. I knew it would be important that the Parish Council meeting should be very firmly controlled and that the questions put to the audience should be very clearly expressed. The use of Mr Bunn as a narrator to get us in and out of the play-within-a-play would hopefully be logical and understandable. The development of the story, particularly the transfer from the domestic bickering sequences to the coming together of the characters against a universal threat, seemed to be clear, but I knew that the scene changes would have to be swiftly effected in order to keep the continuity of thought.

Now I was ready to write the synopsis.

Synopsis for *The See-Saw Tree*

Design

The play takes place in three locations:

1) A Village Hall. This could be represented by nothing more than a table and chairs, against tabs or plain backing.

2) The Bottom of an Oak Tree, i.e. the base of the trunk. The scale will be quite large, bearing in mind the characters in the play live on the Tree. Various knobs and root-formations sprout from the bottom, which might be used as 'seats'. If possible, the entrance to Rabbit's burrow should be incorporated. Ivy climbing the Tree could afford masking for scaffolding or ladder-like rungs, down and up which characters can climb.

3) Further up the Oak Tree. This will be the basic set, on which most of the play takes place. It will hopefully include various levels, dominated by, at stage level, the 'hollow', the home of Owl. This should incorporate a closed-off section which could be like a hut, complete with door; however, it might be more appropriate, and less fantasy-oriented, to have a portion partitioned off by a leafy equivalent of a bead curtain. Owl's hollow becomes the main acting area, at which meetings of the tree community take place. Other important locations are a hole in the trunk in which Squirrel has his drey, an upper level for Mistlethrush's nest, and a branch from which Bat can 'hang'. (For practical reasons, it is not necessary for the

actor to hang by his legs, as it were. As long as he can support himself on his arms, with his legs in the air, and his head thus pointing downwards, the illusion should be acceptable.) Branches should provide walkways between the locations, or the set could be stylized, using scaffolding and steps. However, the set should certainly bear a token resemblance to an oak tree, and the use of levels is important when seeing the characters visit one another.

The costumes need not be realistic in any way. There will not be very much time for the actors to change from their human roles to their animal roles. Maybe half-masks could be of use, or basic identification factors. In other words, we should not be disguising the fact that actors, indeed the human characters in the play, are playing the parts of the tree inhabitants.

Characters

Each actor plays two parts, the human role linked with the animal role:

Actor 1: **Miss Wise** – The Chairperson of the Parish Council. Solid, fair and authoritative. **Owl** – the leader of the oak tree community.

Actor 2: **Mrs Dunnock** – Secretary of the Parish Council. Keeps a low profile. Efficient, helpful, knowledgeable, but unshowy. **Dunnock** – a rather drab, hardworking bird, willing to perform menial tree tasks, cleaning, taking messages, etc.

Actor 3: **Mr Storer** – Businesslike, financially oriented Treasurer of the Parish Council. **Squirrel** – Home-loving, conservative, occasionally excitable member of the tree community.

Actor 4: **Mr Jay** – rather flashy supermarket owner, smarmy businessman, ingratiating. **Jay** – a flash itinerant member of the tree community, popping in and out almost as a travelling salesman, on the lookout for a good opportunity.

Actor 5: **Mrs Thrush** – a fairly outspoken woman, who takes public service seriously and loudly espouses a cause. **Mistlethrush** – a strident member of the tree community, builder of untidy nests, not afraid to be outspoken.

Actor 6: **Mrs Cook** – not a local person, but not afraid to put her views. Might be regarded as somewhat common by the residents. **Cuckoo** – an itinerant visitor to the tree, a colourful character from Africa, whose sole motive for visiting is to dump her eggs in some unsuspecting bird's nest.

Actor 7: **Mr Bunn** – a concerned conservationist. Outspoken. **Rabbit** – a member of the animals' underground movement. Resistance leader. Practical.

Actor 8: **Mr Batty** – entrepreneur, whiz-kid smooth operator. **Bat** – hi-tech way-out member of the tree community. His radar comes in useful. He has big headphones connected to a Walkman-style 'radio'.

Songs

Act One

1. Spring Song (discordant, unaccompanied, short song for Mistlethrush).
2. Possible short 'funky' song for Bat as he sings along with his Walkman (title, 'Hanging on'?)

Act Two

1. Protest song (possible title, 'Save Our Tree') for Owl, Squirrel, Bat, Jay, Dunnock, Rabbit, Cuckoo and Mistlethrush.
2. Final celebratory song (All).

Synopsis

Act One

The play opens as a public meeting, with the houselights up. Members of the Committee arrive with the audience. Some sit on the platform, some sit with the audience. Mrs Dunnock sweeps the stage, and brings coffee for the Committee members. As the show begins, she rings a bell for attention.

Miss Wise introduces the meeting. A local farmer has died and left a field, now a wasteland used as an unsightly tip, to the Parish Council. The Council wishes to sell the land to Mr Jay, the owner of the adjoining supermarket. He announces his plan to convert it to a children's playground, for the benefit of his customers. The meeting (the audience) is invited to vote on this idea. It is then revealed that Mr Batty will be given the concession to operate the children's playground on a commercial basis, complete with a building housing video games, pinball machines, etc. Mr Bunn criticizes the plan, because it will involve the cutting down of trees, including a particularly historic oak tree, known to previous generations as the See-Saw Tree – children used to see-saw on a plank balanced over a strong low horizontal branch. As he voices his conservationist views, the lighting changes to isolate him, and we hear the sound of a creaking see-saw. Meanwhile, the other actors vanish to prepare for the play. Mr Bunn asks us to see the tree as a community as rich as the village itself, and asks us to look at the situation from the point of view of the inhabitants of the tree. He asks us to imagine a scenario of what might happen to those inhabitants, should the tree be cut down. As he talks, he dons his costume (Rabbit), and leads us into the play-within-a-play.

Lighting reveals the base of the trunk of the oak tree. It is dawn. Sound effects of birdsong.

On the tree trunk is painted a white cross. Rabbit looks at it, and reacts concerned. He calls up to Dunnock, who is cleaning the tree. She peers down through the foliage. Rabbit asks Dunnock to take a message to Squirrel to come down and meet him. It is urgent. Dunnock, grumbling at being interrupted in her work, reluctantly agrees, and disappears.

Suddenly noises in the distance. Machinery, vehicles moving, maybe voices. Rabbit reacts to the noises, concerned, and enters his burrow. Perhaps headlights momentarily light up the tree as he vanishes.

The noises recede. Squirrel descends the tree, grumbling to himself about being sent for, but he sees no sign of Rabbit. He peers down the burrow, and calls. No reply. He calls up to Dunnock, complaining that he has been called out on a false alarm. But then he sees the white cross on the tree trunk, and reacts concerned. He climbs up the tree again, telling off Dunnock on the way.

Dunnock, annoyed that she has been told off by Squirrel, climbs down and calls down Rabbit's burrow. She is surprised when Rabbit enters from off stage, having come up through another entrance to the burrow. He is even more agitated and is concerned to find that Squirrel is not there. He asks Dunnock to go up again and tell Squirrel it is most urgent that he come down. Dunnock starts to climb, grumbling.

Rabbit waits, as the scene changes to the main set, halfway up the tree. Rabbit disappears with the tree trunk, which is either revolved or flown. We see Dunnock climb up to Squirrel's drey, wake him and give the message. Squirrel once again descends, complaining that his work has been interrupted. He is doing his acorn tally, keeping a count of his stores. He asks Dunnock to clean the entrance to his drey, but insists that she should not touch any acorns. He descends out of sight.

Dunnock starts cleaning the drey entrance. Bits of rubbish fall from above, accompanied by strident birdsong. Dunnock complains to Mistlethrush, above, who is building her messy nest. Mistlethrush is excited. She explains she cannot help herself, because it is time to prepare for egg laying. Dunnock clears up the rubbish.

Jay arrives, making an early start, wheeling and dealing. He tries to 'sell' food or nesting material to Mistlethrush, who is too busy to be interested. Jay uses acorns as currency. He approaches Squirrel's drey, but finds that Squirrel is out. Dunnock, who is finishing off her cleaning, doesn't know when he'll be back. Behind her back, Jay takes the opportunity to steal some acorns.

Dunnock moves on to Owl's hollow, to start work there. Meanwhile, Squirrel returns and calls to Owl. Dunnock says that Owl is still hunting – she is cleaning the hollow in Owl's absence. Squirrel says it is a matter of great urgency, and asks Dunnock to let him know the moment Owl returns.

Squirrel goes home and is very cross to discover some acorns gone. He catches Jay in the act. A row breaks out.

Mistlethrush angrily calls down for quiet. She is trying to concentrate on laying. It is a very painful process.

Squirrel threateningly forces Jay away from the drey, towards Owl's hollow. Both are suddenly surprised by Owl, calling for quiet. Owl has returned, tired, from a rather unsuccessful hunting trip. Jay tentatively tries to barter with Owl, offering her goods, but he cannot provide Owl with a tasty mouse or even caterpillars, and is chased away. Owl wants to rest, and thanks Dunnock for her work. Dunnock decides to go and assist Mistlethrush in her labours.

Squirrel tells Owl that Rabbit needs a meeting urgently. Something is seriously wrong. Owl, tired, says 'later'. Squirrel, concerned, decides to go down to see Rabbit again. He descends the tree.

Jay returns to steal more acorns, but is interrupted by Bat, returning from the Battery Disco – he jigs around to the music coming through his headphones from the radio. Jay offers Bat some goods, maybe electronic spare parts. He has to shout, because Bat is wearing the headphones. Owl is woken by the noise, and Bat is told off. Owl finds Bat disagreeably smelly. Bat grudgingly goes to his perch, and settles to sleep, complaining that he is uncomfortable there and would far rather have Owl's hollow. Owl, too, returns to sleep. Meanwhile, Jay takes the opportunity to invade Squirrel's drey once more. The scene changes back to the base of the tree trunk. This is accompanied by the sound of a mechanical digger.

Squirrel descends the tree. He is agitated to find no sign of Rabbit. He calls down the burrow, and Rabbit suddenly appears, muddy and in a nervous state. He reports that the Big Ones have arrived in the field, and have started clearing land, digging in some places and filling in rabbit burrows in others. The other end of his burrow has been filled in and completely destroyed. It is now an emergency situation. Owl must help – she will know what to do. He begs Squirrel to make Owl come. Squirrel says that Owl will be unwilling to budge, but remembers how last year, when the flood waters came, Owl lifted Rabbit and several of his friends and relations to safety in the tree until the danger of the flood had passed. Maybe Owl could lift Rabbit up for the meeting. Rabbit agrees. They briefly discuss the white cross again. Rabbit will investigate the Big Ones further, but he will return very soon to be picked up by Owl. He departs, overground, not underground. Squirrel starts to ascend the tree.

The scene changes back to halfway up the tree. The scene change is accompanied by sound effects of more digging and clearing and general sounds of menacing activity.

The sound effects fade away as the scene begins. Owl and Bat are both asleep. Jay is happily feeding. He jumps with fright at a sudden noisy interruption from Mistlethrush squawking happily because she has successfully laid her eggs. She thanks Dunnock for her help. Owl and Bat both wake up and angrily call for quiet. They return to sleep. Dunnock offers to fetch some food for Mistlethrush, while she sits on the nest.

Squirrel returns and wakes Owl yet again, plus alerting all the others. Owl is at first furious, but when Squirrel explains about the Big Ones' arrival and the destruction of Rabbit's burrow, she accepts the urgency and agrees to bring Rabbit up for a meeting. She disappears behind the tree, ready to fly down.

Bat takes the opportunity to invade Owl's hollow. Meanwhile, Squirrel returns to his drey, does a quick acorn count, and emerges to row with the thieving Jay once again. Squirrel aims acorns at Jay, throwing them towards Mistlethrush's nest. Mistlethrush complains about the dangerous behaviour, as does Dunnock, because she has to clear them up. Squirrel realizes that other things more important than squabbling are happening, and calms everyone down. Squirrel and Jay discuss 'home'. Squirrel loves his home, whereas Jay is the type to travel round living out of a suitcase.

Owl and Rabbit arrive. Rabbit suffers from vertigo. Bat is forced to evacuate the hollow, or at least to evacuate the inner sanctum. Owl tells Dunnock to alert all the residents for a meeting. She rings a bell. All assemble except Mistlethrush, who is reluctant to leave the eggs in her nest. She is eventually persuaded that the situation is urgent enough, and carefully covers her eggs before leaving.

Rabbit is invited to speak. He tells of the arrival of the Big Ones in the field. Big machinery. Sharp metal. Some of his friends and relations who were in their burrow have already been buried alive by the activity of the Big Ones. Others are keeping watch on the situation. All want to know what is going on. Owl, while recognizing that the situation could be serious, cannot fully understand what the Big Ones might be up to. Squirrel mentions the white cross on the tree. Rabbit says that other trees have been similarly painted.

General discussion – does this mean danger? Owl chairs the meeting.

Sudden interruption. The arrival of Cuckoo, who hasn't been seen for the best part of a year. Mistlethrush gets hysterical, remembering what happened last year – Cuckoo laid an egg in her nest and she was forced to bring up Cuckoo's child. A fight breaks out. General row. The domestic bickering is brought to a sudden halt by the noise in the distance of a chainsaw. Bat uses his radar to discover that a tree that was on the other side of the field at dawn is no longer there – he is getting no echo sounding from it. Owl realizes with horror that the Big Ones have started to cut down trees in order to clear the land.

The noise intensifies as the tree folk look concerned.

Interval

Act Two
The act opens with the savage noise of the chainsaw, and a tree falling.

In the hollow, the tree folk urgently discuss the situation. Dunnock has prepared acorn coffee for everybody. Owl invites suggestions as to what they should do. Their home is in danger. They are in danger. Varying opinions. Cuckoo is not as concerned as the others, because she doesn't live there. However, if she cannot lay her egg there, it would be inconvenient. The meeting echoes the human Committee meeting at the beginning of Act One.

Rabbit has the practical idea that the white cross could mean that the tree is to be felled. Perhaps if they were to remove the white cross? It is agreed that Dunnock will go down to clean it off. Rabbit will be taken down by Owl to help, and then to liaise with his friends and relations.

Suddenly, the noise of the chainsaw once again, slightly nearer this time, goads everyone into action. Dunnock, Rabbit and Owl prepare to leave.

The scene changes once again to the base of the tree trunk as the chainsaw noise increases in intensity. As the lights come up, Dunnock is busily scrubbing out the white cross. Owl and Rabbit emerge from behind the tree. Rabbit helps Dunnock. Owl prepares to leave.

But suddenly a bright light flashes across the tree trunk. The Big Ones' searchlight. Owl and Dunnock hide. Rabbit is caught by the light and plays dead. We hear the voices of the Big Ones. They find it odd that this tree has no cross on it. Maybe they should fell it anyway. They consider taking Rabbit to be eaten.

Suddenly, Owl hoots menacingly from behind the tree. This makes the Big Ones nervous. They decide to move on.

(Optional: It would be possible to put in an audience-participation section where they are encouraged to make frightening noises – owls' hoots, jays' chatters and mistlethrushes' rattles. However, I feel that this may well divert from the main intention at this point.)

Owl points out that it is only a matter of time before the Big Ones realize their mistake. They will return. Rabbit leaves to reconnoitre. Owl and Dunnock prepare to go back up the tree.

As the scene changes, more menacing chainsaw noises.

Back in the hollow, Bat is tracking the Big Ones' progress on his radar. Dunnock and Owl return. Further discussion. Nobody wants to leave the tree, but maybe they will have to.

Suddenly, the tree folk smell something. Smoke begins to appear. Owl realizes that the Big Ones are burning the trees they have felled.

The situation is even more serious. Evacuation immediately is essential. They decide to go down to the base of the trunk. Domestic bickering is forgotten as all pull together for the benefit of the community. Squirrel and Jay agree to pool their food resources. All form a chain to pass acorns out from Squirrel's drey and drop them down to the bottom of the tree. Mistlethrush is desperately worried about her eggs. Cuckoo generously offers to help her. They take the eggs with them, keeping them warmly wrapped.

As the smoke increases, Bat announces that his radar suggests the men are returning. Another tree is heard to fall.

Panic. Then orderly evacuation begins.

More menacing sound effects of burning logs and chainsaws and men. Meanwhile, the scene changes back to the base of the tree.

The tree folk descend, collect their acorns, and bravely take up positions in front of the trunk, forming a chain, in a vain attempt to protect their home.

Rabbit returns, announcing the devastation of all the trees in the field except this one. His burrow is also in ruins. Noise of approaching men and machinery interrupt him.

Exciting lighting effects as the glinting reflection of the chainsaw lights up the protesting tree folk. The threatening voices of the Big Ones about to strike. All sing a protest song, during which the chainsaw is turned on, and the noise increases. In desperation, Owl leaps forward and tries to attack. Similarly Jay and Cuckoo. But in vain. They mime being beaten back. The noise of the chainsaw increases in intensity. The cable/flex of the chainsaw swings into view, as the Big Ones start lopping some upper branches. Branches crash down from above, including Bat's perch, Owl's 'doorstep', plus remnants of Mistlethrush's nest. The tree folk react.

Suddenly, Rabbit, in a last desperate attempt to save the tree, starts chewing through the cable of the chainsaw.

The noise stops. A flash indicates a fuse having blown. Rabbit dies. The others look on aghast. Song?

Rabbit, alone in a pin spot, comes to life and removes his Rabbit identification factors, returning to his Mr Bunn character.

Meanwhile, in the darkness around him, the scene is changing back to the village hall public meeting.

Mr Bunn finishes off his story.

He points out that if this meeting agrees to the proposals, the tree will indeed be cut down. The work of three minutes will destroy the work of 300 years.

Miss Wise puts the vote to the meeting (audience). Hopefully the audience vote against the proposals.

Other suggestions are then put forward, a compromise. It is agreed that a children's playground can still be created on the site, but that the tree will remain, and that indeed a plank will be provided once again to make a see-saw, thus returning the tree to its previous employment.

A final song and dance, probably a celebratory song of trees/life/ fertility, etc. The audience is encouraged to join in.

Final sound effect, as the characters freeze – the creak of a see-saw, suggesting that the tree has been returned to its original employment.

The End

Subsequent changes to the synopsis

Although the structure remained intact, I introduced more suddenly interruptions from the Big Ones and took Owl down to see the white cross and to meet Rabbit. This gave more strength to her leadership later, because she had witnessed the threat for herself.

I also felt that Act Two needed another big dramatic reversal of fortune, so made the tree folk truly believe that once the white cross was removed from the tree the danger had passed. They enjoyed a celebratory song and dance before the Big Ones suddenly returned and decided their plan was marked wrongly and that the tree must indeed be cut down. This obviously created more panic leading to the evacuation.

The Writing of the Play

A children's play must be tight. It should never feel too long. The ideal length for a children's play should not exceed two hours including the interval. It may well be that a shorter length is preferable. This has something to do with the attention span of the child, but it has more to do with a determination to keep the interest and involvement of the audience.

So keep the play flowing. Make sure before you start writing that you have, in your synopsis, clearly established the progress of the story, the development of the characters, the transition from scene to scene, the climaxes and moods and exactly how you are hoping the audience will respond.

I write plays very quickly. I allocate a period of time during which I can devote myself totally to writing, breathe deeply and take a run at it. The virtue of this approach is that the structure of the whole play stays firmly in the mind and I can't get side-tracked or find myself getting repetitive. I allow myself to be sucked into the play, almost getting swept along in the action.

I always have a mental picture of the play and try to visualize it happening on stage as I write. I write fairly full stage directions, clearly explaining the setting and trying to paint the picture for the reader. The play, as much as the synopsis, often has to be a selling document. It has to grab the imagination of the reader. So try to put on paper everything that to you, the creator, seems exciting and imaginative.

Perhaps it is because of my background as an actor that I always speak the dialogue in my head as I'm writing it. I try to put myself in the place of each character and imagine how they will speak and how they will react in each situation. As I write, I aim for clarity of expression, but this does not necessarily mean that I try to make the language too simple. I'm constantly aware of the fact that unless the children understand what is happening, I will lose their attention, which will lead to boredom.

A avoid long wordy conversations or long individual speeches. Even if there is a considerable amount of information to impart, it is possible to break it up with interjections from other characters. If narration is required, I try to keep it short or sometimes divide it between several characters.

Most plays will break down into scenes or sections. I always find it useful to concentrate on each section in sequence. Before writing a section, I think hard about it, making sure I am certain what the intention is, what exactly happens, and who is involved. Then I try not to stray from these basic guidelines. The synopsis is vital in this process.

If you are intending to use audience participation, don't leave it to chance. Try to imagine exactly what the audience is thinking and write them in as a character. A magazine article about my work once queried this approach. The writer thought I was being rather arrogant in predicting how the audience would respond, but this is all part of the job. It may seem like manipulation, and in a way it is. I need to be sure whose side the audience is on, whether they will instinctively want to join in at certain points, and whether their contribution will enhance the scene. If the characterization and situations are well thought out in advance, it is likely that the audience will react as expected, particularly when they sense an injustice.

Constantly monitor the play for changes of pace, suddenlies and clarity of story-line. If a scene seems to be going on too long, or appears to ramble, find ways of simplifying it. Enjoy your characters and the way they speak. If appropriate, use alliteration and internal rhymes to make the lines fun to say and fun to hear. Don't be afraid of incorporating scenes with little or no dialogue, as long as you make sure their purpose can be clearly acted out. And if you feel that incidental music or sound effects can enhance the scenes, write them in.

To be honest, I couldn't do draft after draft – it would bore me rigid. However, some playwrights prefer to re-draft several times. When you finish your first draft, it is often a good idea to put it on one side for a while and have a rest from it; at a later date return to it, and any inconsistencies or longeurs will stick out like sore thumbs. It might even be a good idea to ask some friends to read it aloud and hear the play come to life off the page for the first time.

Part 4   Adaptation

From Page to Stage:
Adapting a Children's Book

As I became reasonably established as a children's playwright, so commissions came in or people telephoned showing interest in me adapting well-known books into children's plays. I have been fortunate to adapt work by Roald Dahl, Enid Blyton, Helen Nicoll and Jan Pieńkowski, Edward Lear, Michael Foreman and others.

Some of the plays suggested themselves without any prodding or commercial pressure. For example, one evening I read a bedtime story to my younger daughter. It was the first time I had read it, and as I read I visualized the whole thing on stage. It was incredibly theatrical and eminently stageable – which is quite unusual for a book. It had its own sense of pace and rhythm and climax which totally fitted a one-act play. I promptly took the book downstairs and wrote a letter to the author, Michael Foreman.

A few weeks later, a school requested me to write a play for a large number of children and an orchestra and a choir. Michael Foreman gave me the go-ahead to adapt *Dinosaurs and All That Rubbish*. The basic adaptation was quite easy as I didn't have to restructure or reorder the events at all. I wrote lyrics for the songs and put some of the third-person narrative into dialogue.

When a producer has an idea whereby a book or television series will be adapted into a theatre show, the reasons are often commercial; the producer sees this property as something that will make money. But just because a story works in one medium does not automatically mean that it will work on stage. For example, there might be a television series in which the characters, made of plasticine, can do extraordinary things with their bodies that actors can't do. Children know and love these characters. To translate them – as children know them – to the stage would be very difficult. I would possibly decide not to accept such a commission.

I am primarily interested in a story that will work well on stage; not just a title that will bring people in. I am always very careful about making sure that I can do the original story justice before accepting any commission. Therefore, one of the initial steps to consider is whether the property is going to be straightforward or impossible to adapt.

Once I was invited to adapt Terry Jones' splendid book, *Erik the Viking*. This is epic fantasy in the grand style involving characters climbing vast mountains, encountering huge birds' nests with giant eggs and having adventures on sea and land. To me it lent itself to the big screen far more than to the stage. It might have been possible to envisage an imaginative, minimalist production, but the producer wanted a fully staged production in large theatres. I reluctantly declined the commission. It didn't feel right for me. However, a few years later, *Erik the Viking* did take the stage, in a highly enjoyable production mounted by Peter Duncan.

Sometimes the episodic nature of children's books and indeed television series can prove problematic. In particular, stories for small children may be very short and perfectly rounded. The ideas expressed in those stories may well be small ones – delightful but small. Creating a coherent plot through-line which progresses using these ideas is impossible because you would simply be starting the idea, going up a little hill, coming down the hill, stopping, going up another little hill, coming down, stopping and so on. The mountain would never be climbed – you would never get further than the foothills. The job would be to carve or create a story-line from all those stories. That is not impossible, but it is not necessarily easy.

When I have found a book that I am interested in adapting, I find it fascinating trying to enter the mind of the writer to understand what he or she was really getting at, to analyse the ingredients that make his or her book so popular, and to translate them to another medium. Being faithful to the book does not mean a slavish adherence to every twist of plot; it does not mean that the playwright is prohibited from inventing dialogue or even new characters. What it does mean is that the spirit of the book must be observed and that the basic story must remain, otherwise why do it in the first place? The very qualities that make a book worth adapting are what should be kept at all costs.

A student who wanted to write a play for children once asked me if it was better to attempt an original play or to adapt an existing story. It was an impossible question to answer. To write an original play might ultimately be more satisfying because the imaginative content is all one's own, but it is not cheating to adapt. The characters and situations may be handed to us on a plate, but there is still the necessity to craft and structure the material into a satisfying theatrical experience. As both amateur and professional theatre companies want to attract full houses, very often a familiar title is the best way to achieve this. For someone writing his or her first play for children, an adaptation might well be the ideal way to start. If so, choose a book to adapt that you like and admire and that you can remain faithful to.

If you have read the previous chapter on writing original plays, you will already be aware of the importance I place on putting together a synopsis before attempting to write the play (see pp. 65–76). The synopsis is as vital to an adaptation as it is to an original play.

The following four-step process will help you when embarking on an adaptation.

Four steps towards a synopsis

Step 1. Finding a story and assessing its suitability
Step 2. Gutting the book
      a. Précis of the story
      b. Notes on character, location and theatrical moments
Step 3. Problem solving – how to conquer the difficulties of putting it on stage and basic first notes towards a working synopsis
Step 4. Writing a synopsis

Step I.   Finding a story and assessing its suitability

Look around for a story which fires your imagination and which you can, however vaguely, visualize on stage. Now, in order to confirm its suitability for adaptation, I suggest you use the following checklist of ingredients.

1. Story
2. Theme (fantasy within reality, fairy-tale, myth/legend, old wine in new bottles, anthropomorphic, contemporary, quest, toys/inanimate objects, worlds)
3. Characters
4. Life and Death Situations
5. Language and Silence
6. Suddenlies
7. Humour
8. Audience Participation
9. Scale
10. Puppetry
11. Magic within the Plot
12. Colourful Look on Stage
13. Lighting
14. Sound
15. Music
16. Climaxes and Cliffhangers
17. Justice and Fairness
18. Taboos

If you need to refresh your memory, a full description of this checklist is in Part Two, pp. 38–61.

You might find it a useful exercise to look at your favourite children's play and subject it to the ingredients checklist, examining how the various elements are fused together. A play like *Peter Pan*, not surprisingly, scores very highly.

Now consider your proposed story; read it carefully several times and make notes against the headings. If your story scores well feel confident to proceed.

Step 2.   Gutting the book

a. Précis of the story

Now is the time to examine the book in detail. It is necessary to take it to pieces, to explore how the story develops, to break down the story into sections and to see what makes it work. This is a way of getting to know the book inside out and finding out how the author's mind works. When the problem of adapting the book for the stage comes to be tackled, the internal logic of the story should be so imprinted upon your mind that you can experiment with changing the order of events or leaving out certain sections without damaging the basic idea.

When using this process I go through the book making notes, following the story. I then sometimes make notes on these notes, shortening further, to try to get the basic story into as few words as possible.

b. Notes on characters, locations and theatrical moments

List the characters. How many are there? How important are they in the story? If cast numbers might be limited, is any doubling possible? Are there any characters who do not seem totally necessary to the main story? Trace through all the entrances and exits of the characters in the story. Try to imagine certain scenes from the book acted out on stage. Look out for useful dialogue, which might be usable straight from the book.

Examine the main relationships in the book. Do they develop interestingly and dramatically? Is there a useful amount of conflict?

Look for the essential locations in the story. Are there some that are more important than others? Are there some scenes which could be transferred to an existing location? Is there a way of using one location to represent others?

What you want to avoid is a succession of mini-scenes: that could not only get very boring, but the scene changes may end up taking too long. The play shouldn't be jumping around in place and/or time in such a way as to become confusing. Keep the action flowing.

Now, go through the book looking for moments that are intrinsically theatrical and that you can keep in mind for use later on. Note how they are spaced within the narrative.

Is there a natural place in the story for an interval? Is there a moment of high tension which would be a suitable cliffhanger to leave the audience looking forward to the second half?

Step 3.   Problem solving – how to conquer the difficulties of putting it on stage and basic first notes towards a working synopsis

Carving out a structure for the play is, for me, the most challenging and often the most enjoyable stage. Problems can vary from condensing the material into a proper shape through to finding a way to stage certain scenes. It is helpful to know the limitations you are working under: for example, cast numbers, the type of theatre space, and the budget for sets and costumes. Could the actors play more than one part? Might some settings be less elaborate than others? Will the scenes be able to follow each other without too complicated a scene change?

Once you have solved most of the problems posed, you are ready to commit your ideas to paper.

Step 4.   Writing a Synopsis

Unless a simple basic idea is enough to achieve a green light, the first stage is to come up with a synopsis for the producer to consider. In many ways this is often the most difficult part of the process, more difficult than the eventual writing of the script. I believe it is necessary to have the complete structure worked out before putting pen to paper. In a children's play the structure is paramount. The through-line and clarity of the story cannot be left to chance. I find that the synopsis stage of the work takes far longer than the actual writing of the play but I try never to put pen to paper until it is watertight. Obviously, in the writing process, new ideas may occur or develop, but unless the structure is set, there will always be the danger of the play veering off into irrelevant areas and straying from the main through-line.

However well-considered your synopsis may be, there will always be new ideas or changes made when writing the script or producing the play. It is instructive to look back at the synopsis afterwards and see how it has evolved.

As a example of the four-step process, I have chosen Roald Dahl's *The BFG*, which I was invited by Clarion Productions to adapt in 1990. The book, published in 1982, had already become an established classic. It was a bestseller and was one of the most popular books borrowed from libraries.

Steps towards a synopsis for *The BFG*

Step 1. Finding a story and assessing its suitability

Here is my ingredient checklist for *The BFG*. (If you are not familiar with Roald Dahl's novel, it would be useful to read it first and come back to this chapter. You might perhaps want to work through the checklist yourself first before comparing it to the one set out below.)

1. Story
Very strong. Sophie snatched from her orphanage by Giant – luckily friendly – taken to Giant Country from where other giants make child-eating raids – Sophie and Big Friendly Giant friendship develops – plan to save the children involving the Queen of England – triumphant ending.

2. Theme
● Fantasy Within Reality – yes. Child-snatching very real, though Giant is fantasy – 'reality' of Sophie's raw deal as orphan – Buckingham Palace scenes suggest reality, though given fantasy treatment.
● Fairy-tale – yes, in part. Use of Giants – good defeats evil – triumph of child over great adversity – use of Queen, albeit a 'real' Queen.
● Myth/Legend – not really, although the Giants give the story a timeless feel.
● Old Wine In New Bottles – very much so. Combination of orphan, Giants, Queen, all traditional elements of story-telling, but served up fresh.

- Anthropomorphic – no.
- Contemporary – in spite of the fantasy/giant theme, the story feels modern. Sophie's sparkiness – scenes in Buckingham Palace may not actually name the Queen as Elizabeth II, yet we automatically 'see' her in the role – heads of Army and Air Force, plus use of helicopters add to modern feel – the dreams that the BFG creates to give children a happy time feel modern – dreams about teachers, the President of the United States, annoying parents, modern fantasy inventions (car running on toothpaste), etc. – telephone call made by Queen to King of Sweden.
- Quest – yes. Sophie and BFG's quest to save the children of England involves a dangerous journey, avoiding Giants, breaking into Buckingham Palace, etc. Strong through-line of determined attempt to achieve success against huge odds.
- Toys/Inanimate Objects – no, not as characters.
- Worlds – yes, although the whole story does not take place in one fantasy world. Giant Country is a world of its own – in a way, Buckingham Palace is, too – both of them are 'foreign' to Sophie, through whose eyes we see them.

3. Characters
Very strong. Sophie, the child protagonist with whom the reader identifies – the BFG, a vegetarian among child-eaters, gentle and, by the end, heroic – both are misfits in their own environments and, though totally different from each other, become bonded very touchingly – the terrifying, bullying brutish Giants with splendid names like Childchewer, Fleshlumpeater and Bloodbottler – the Queen amusing yet not sent up – Mary, her chatty, gossipy maid – the wickedly stereotyped heads of the Army and Air Force, frightfully British and rather dense – Mrs Clonkers, the over-the-top, unpleasant woman in charge of the orphanage – Dahl's subversive nature showing itself in the teacher and the parents in the dreams – very rich variety of strong characters.

4. Life and Death Situations
Yes. Sophie being snatched from her bed fearful of her fate – the giants' child-eating raids – the threat to both Sophie and the BFG

from the other Giants when they suspect he is harbouring her – the quest to stop the Giants from eating the children of England.

5. Language and Silence
Splendid special Giant language using invented words – reminiscent of Edward Lear's nonsense – constant humour possible from such language – very funny dialogue in Buckingham Palace scenes, particularly the Queen and Mary scene and the heads of the Army and Air Force; opportunities for silent sequences include the BFG leaping over fields and mountains, carrying Sophie back to Giant Country – the Giants setting off on child-eating raids – the BFG taking Sophie on a dream-collecting expedition to Dream Country – the journey to Buckingham Palace.

6. Suddenlies
The story is full of them. The snatch – the first appearances of the Giants – the Fleshlumpeater invading the BFG's cave – Sophie's discovery in the Queen's bedroom – the book constantly makes the reader want to turn the page to find out what happens next – the shifts from location to location – the development of the relationship between Sophie and the BFG, etc.

7. Humour
A remarkable amount considering the basic theme of the story is child-eating. The BFG's language – the snozzcumber and frobscottle sequences – the whizzpopping – the subversive nature of the dreams – the child-eating itself has a certain black humour – the Buckingham Palace scenes – the way the Palace staff have to cope with the arrival of a Giant – serving him breakfast on a table made of grand piano, grandfather clocks and a table-tennis table – the reaction of the heads of the Army and Air Force to the presence of the BFG.

8. Audience Participation
Possible. Warnings to Sophie of oncoming danger, etc. – yet somehow the strength of the story and the fact that it is aimed at an audience slightly older than that most receptive to participation makes me instinctively feel it would be wrong in an adaptation.

9. Scale

Vitally important to the story. The fact that Sophie is a little girl and the BFG is a 22-foot-high Giant is crucial – also the enormous size of the other Giants – undoubtedly a plus in story terms, but could be very difficult to stage.

10. Puppetry

Opportunities, perhaps, in coping with the scale problem. Maybe shadow poppets could be used for the various journeys – could Sophie be a puppet? – could the BFG and the other giants be huge puppets? – the main problem is that both Sophie and the BFG are vital through-characters – somehow it feels wrong for one of them to be a puppet.

11. Magic within the Plot

Not in the form of tricks or magical transformations. But the BFG's dream bottles, which light up, displaying their swirling contents, could appear magical – the story is somehow stronger without magic – the reality of the situation is so immediate and involving.

12. Colourful Look on Stage

Yes. Particularly in Dream Country and Buckingham Palace – the orphanage and Giant Country do not suggest a lot of bright colour, but the locations themselves are intrinsically interesting and offer good design possibilities – again, the combination of fantasy and reality will offer great scope to the designer.

13. Lighting

Great possibilities in all the different locations. Different atmospheres for the snatch, the journeys, the cave, Giant Country, Dream Country, Buckingham Palace, etc. – the lighting can be quite sophisticated.

14. Sound

Some opportunities. Booming giant footsteps – howling wind sounds during the BFG's journeys over vast distances – humour from the amplified whizzpoppers – the roar of helicopter engines – the opportunities for sinister echoes and amplified voices in Giant Country.

15. Music
Yes. Opportunities for incidental music, electronic sounds to create mysterious moods, atmospheres, etc. – regal music and fanfares in Buckingham Palace – exciting music to accompany the journeys – strange haunting music for the dream-catching sequences as well as the scenes where the BFG shows Sophie some of the dreams – possible opportunities for songs – a whizzpopper song – a song of the child-eating Giants – a song in the Palace – yet somehow the story does not immediately suggest a musical which might dilute the strength of the story, maybe even trivialize it somewhat.

16. Climaxes and Cliffhangers
Plenty of dramatic opportunities from the snatch onwards. The life and death situations mean that the tension and eventual resolution of desperate situations have their own in-built climaxes – possible cliffhanger, although not a real one, is the setting off on the quest to enlist the Queen's help – leave the audience wondering if the quest will succeed.

17. Justice and Fairness.
Yes. Sophie's situation as an orphan, unfairly treated by Mrs Clonkers, gives her immediate appeal – she is unfairly snatched by the BFG, who in turn is treated unfairly by the other Giants – the Giants' child-eating activities are clearly unjust and must be stopped – they satisfactorily get their come-uppance at the end – both the BFG and Sophie are given happy endings, thanks to the Queen.

18. Taboos
The black and somewhat anarchic story-line may not be offensive in a book, but will it work on stage? Can we get away with child-eating, cannibalism? How can it be staged? Will we get away with the whizzpopping? Is breaking wind in the imagination, as one reads the book, made unacceptable if portrayed on stage complete with booming sound effects? Probably OK if treated imaginatively, somehow translating the fantasy elements into theatrical moments.

The checklist exercise suggests that *The BFG* is eminently suitable for theatrical adaptation – on a scale of ten it scores at least eight. There will be many problems to solve in order to present it faithfully, but on this evidence it is certainly worth going on to the next stage.

Step 2. Gutting the book

a. Précis of the story

Here is the story of *The BFG* in a nutshell.

Sophie in orphanage dormitory, night-time. Sees Giant from window. He snatches her and carries her off to Giant Country.

BFG's cave. She is frightened. He is nervous. But luckily he will not eat her – unlike other Giants, whom he shows her from the cave.

As they get to know each other, the BFG mentions dream blowing. Encourages her to eat horrible snozzcumbers.

Bloodbottler arrives, suspicious that the BFG has a child in his cave. Sophie nearly eaten.

Sophie revived with frobscottle causing whizzpoppers.

BFG takes Sophie dream-catching, but is bullied by the other Giants.

Dream-catching in Dream Country – dreams caught in net and stored in bottles. Including a trogglehumper – a nightmare.

Back in Giant Country, BFG gets his revenge on the sleeping Fleshlumpeater by blowing him the trogglehumper. Fleshlumpeater roars in fright, thinking Jack of beanstalk fame is attacking him. Other Giants disturbed and attack him.

BFG shows sample dreams to Sophie.

Giants set off for England to eat children.

Sophie/BFG plan to save the children. BFG reluctant, persuaded by Sophie to mix a special dream for the Queen to convince her of the child-eating problem.

Dream mixed. Off to England. London. Buckingham Palace.
BFG puts Sophie in Queen's bedroom window. Blows dream to the Queen. Queen has nasty dream.

Mary the maid arrives next morning. Newspaper report of child-eating activity. Queen has dreamt it. Sophie is revealed. Persuades Queen that the BFG is here and that help is needed.

Queen gives Sophie benefit of doubt. BFG welcomed to Palace.

Eats breakfast in ballroom.

Queen checks information by phoning King of Sweden.

Queen calls in heads of Army and Air Force. Plan to use helicopters to catch the Giants.

Giants, back in Giant Country, caught, brought back to huge pit in Regent's Park Zoo and fed snozzcumbers.

BFG given his own house and Sophie invited to live in a cottage next door.

BFG revealed as author of the book.

This is very basic, but the outline highlights signposts in the story. The detail is still in the memory or in the more detailed notes.

b. Notes on characters, locations and theatrical moments

The BFG offers a rich mix of characters, from Sophie (with whom the audience is bound to identify) to the outrageous cannibal Giants, from the Big Friendly Giant himself to the Queen of England. The development of the Sophie/BFG relationship offers great possibilities. Sophie starts off fearful of the BFG and he is quite shy of her. By the end of the story they have formed an affectionate bond and a working partnership strong enough to save the children of the world.

The locations are pleasingly varied, including the orphanage, Giant Country, the BFG's magical cave, the Queen's bedroom and the ballroom at Buckingham Palace. To represent all of them natur- alistically may prove problematic.

There are several big moments which cry out to be dramatized. For example, the snatch of Sophie, the first arrival of the Giants, the dream-catching and the capture of the Giants by the Army and Air Force. Other intrinsically theatrical ideas include the glowing dream bottles, the frobscottle drink (with bubbles going down instead of up), the fantasy dreams and the entertaining of the BFG by the Queen (including whizzpoppers in front of Her Majesty).

Step 3. Problem solving – how to conquer the difficulties of putting it on stage and basic first notes towards a synopsis

With *The BFG*, I had huge difficulty in working out how the book could be staged. It had all the right ingredients but for a time I was reluctant to adapt it. I was very worried that children would be disappointed as the book is a huge favourite. *The BFG* is about a 22-foot-tall giant and a little girl, and I knew that children would be expecting a real giant; in fact, real giants. Although this might be possible with imaginative puppetry, creating the real character of the BFG, with all his warmth and humour, really needed an actor. I turned down the job twice, saying that I didn't feel it could be done. It was obvious to me that children were going to be disappointed if they didn't see a real giant and the little girl.

The producers persuaded me to think again, and one fine morning while I was having breakfast in a Bristol hotel contemplating another meeting about the *The BFG*, convinced that I would be turning the commission down for a third time, a sudden thought occurred to me. What would happen if I went into a school and worked on *The BFG* with a class of children? I would approach them saying, 'Today we're going to do *The BFG*.' The children would play act and use their imagination. Somehow we would tell the story. I reckoned there would probably be a bossy little girl who'd say, 'I am going to be Sophie,' and then she'd look at me being the tallest person in the room and say, 'You can be the BFG.' Then I thought she might well pick up a doll and say, 'No, this will be Sophie! I'm still Sophie but this is Sophie too.'

Then I thought, suppose *in the play* that the actress playing Sophie manipulated a miniature version of herself. Suppose that *The BFG* was the girl's favourite story and she was acting it out with her friends. They could play Giants. Maybe the girl's father could play the BFG, and her mother could play the Queen.

But where would the play take place? The producers wanted to tour to major theatres and to use large sets. I realized that the play could take place at a child's birthday party. Maybe a magician fails to arrive and the children have to make their own entertainment. The birthday girl would be Sophie. The action could take place in a room, perhaps Sophie's bedroom, or even a bedroom combined with a large attic room at the top of a house.

Next came the ideas of how the fantasy within the story could be achieved. Maybe the giants could wear masks, and other characters find bits and pieces of costume and props in a dressing-up chest. If the giants were going to be played by normal-size actors, maybe the children they eat could be represented by dolls and soft toys which would be in the room. Maybe Sophie's bed could be used for the Queen. The attic room could be used for most of the scenes. What about the BFG's cave? Perhaps a bookcase could open out revealing the cave. In other words, perhaps we could develop the fantasy from this ordinary room.

What about the orphanage scene? How would we achieve the BFG snatching Sophie from her bed? Well, if Sophie was the narrator, using a doll or puppet as her miniature self, maybe there could be a doll's house from which the BFG could snatch the doll.

By now I knew I had virtually cracked it.

But I was concerned about the Buckingham Palace scenes. It would be far more theatrical if we could go to a realistic representation of Buckingham Palace, particularly the Ballroom, where the BFG is entertained by the Queen. But this posed another problem. If the actor playing the BFG was going to be human-size, how could he share the same stage as human characters like the Queen and the heads of the Army and Air Force? Back to the scale problem. The answer came when I realized that in many ways Dahl's story breaks into two halves. In the first half there is one human being (Sophie) within a world of giants. In the second half there is one Giant (the BFG) in a world of human beings. Why not change the scale? In other words, in the first half use human beings to play Giants and a small puppet to play the human being; in the second half use human beings to play human beings and one huge puppet to play the Giant. Not only would that 'work', but it would provide a real *coup de théâtre* when suddenly the attic room would change completely into the Palace Ballroom. This, I felt, would take the audience by surprise. Not only that, rather than improvising the costumes from the dressing-up chest, suddenly we would see the real thing – the Queen complete with ballgown and tiara (plus corgi, perhaps!), the heads of the Army and Air Force in complete uniforms and the butler and maids in proper costumes too.

The question of how to stage the journeys was solved by imagining a large window in the room, above a platform or dais. This could be back-lit, making the BFG silhouette-shaped. Thus he could, in slow motion, make a stylized running journey between Giant Country and England.

I liked this basic idea because, just as Roald Dahl had created a fantasy story from a realistic beginning, so, in the stage version, we would start off 'real', and let the fantasy gradually take over. Because the cave could be realistic, even though it was revealed within the room, all the dream bottles could have swirling lights and fulfil every child's expectation. Furthermore, in the Buckingham Palace scene, the audience would actually be able to see a Giant. (This turned out to be 14 feet high, resembling the actor playing the part and constructed to look much like the illustration in the book of the BFG eating breakfast. The puppet could be operated by the actor playing the BFG whose voice was amplified by a radio mike.) I now felt that the audience need not have their expectations dashed.

The notes towards a working synopsis ended up being written on the back of a leaflet which I found in the foyer of my Bristol hotel. By the time I got to Bath for the meeting an hour later, it was all worked out in my mind how *The BFG* could be adapted. I agreed with the producers to go ahead to the next stage and produce a working synopsis. This is how it turned out.

Synopsis for *The BFG*

Introduction

Its subject matter makes the adaptation of *The BFG* necessarily a theatrical non-naturalistic version, but because the book is so popular and well known it must, through invention and surprise, avoid leaving the audience disappointed. The aim should be to let the audience share the problems and enjoy the way they are solved, then turn the tables by developing the initial convention and, as the world of the imagination takes over, surprise the audience by changing the physical scale.

So, in the first act, a family and their friends act out the story as a play-within-a-play, but in the second act the story takes over for real. This will necessitate ingenuity of design and the use of quite sophisticated theatrical techniques in the way of lighting, puppetry, music and sound.

Characters

The eight members of the cast will act as a team, doubling and trebling, working as puppeteers and probably helping narrate the story. The basic division of roles will be as follows:

Father/BFG
Mother/Queen/Giant/Dream character
Daughter/Sophie
Son/Fleshlumpeater/Mr Tibbs/Dream character (NB this actor should
    be tall, could be understudy BFG)
Party Guest (M)/Bloodbottler/Head of Air Force/Dream character
Party Guest(M)/Giant/Head of Army/Dream character
Party Guest (F)/Giant/Mary/Dream character
Party Guest (F)/Giant/Dream character/
    possibly Queen of Sweden/Maid

The musical director is unlikely to be able to be one of the above. Incidental music (as well as possible songs) plus musical sound effects will keep him/her fully occupied. A combination of Clavinova-type electric piano plus synthesizer is probably best.

A sound tape will probably be necessary, hopefully operated by a sound engineer. It might be advisable to consider a basic touring sound rig, especially for the larger venues.

Settings

Act One
Takes place in a large attic playroom, an exciting room with colourful toys on shelves, a rocking horse, a doll's house, a small

(toy?) grand piano, musical instruments – toy trumpet, horn, fishing net, a puppet booth, toy helicopters, a dressing-up chest plus a rail of clothes, masks, wigs, crown, etc. There is a chest of drawers and a grandfather clock, a door to the landing, and perhaps a door leading to a small dressing-room or large cupboard. A bed.

A major feature of the room should be an area which becomes a 'stage'; curtains part to reveal a window, but as the play progresses, other 'scenery' will be revealed, rather like the inner stage of Shakespeare's Globe. In might be good to have a platform in front of the curtain, like a small thrust stage; this could even be a table-tennis table. To one side should be bookshelves (which will revolve to become the BFG's bottle-shelves). A strobe effect could appear to come from a toy projector.

SCENE 1 (Playroom) The family and party guests decide to entertain themselves telling the story of the BFG.

SCENE 2 (Playroom) The snatch of Sophie.

SCENE 3 (Playroom) Running to Giant Country.

SCENE 4 (Playroom) The BFG's cave.

SCENE 5 (Playroom) Dream Country (dream collecting).

SCENE 6 (Playroom) The BFG's cave.

SCENE 7 (Playroom) Running to England and arrival at Buckingham Palace.

Act Two

SCENE 1 (Playroom) The Queen's bedroom.

SCENE 2 (*Transformation*) The ballroom. This scene is in 'giant' scale. Using recognizable objects from the Playroom, the BFG is seated high on a chest of drawers resting on a grand piano; his table is made of a table-tennis table resting on a clock, piles of books, etc. The spacious, airy, light-filled ballroom should be a complete and surprising contrast to the Playroom.

SCENE 3 Shadow puppet sequence requiring a screen. Helicopters capture the Giants and drop them into a pit. A major segment, not 'improvised'.

SCENE 4 For final end-tying scene, it may be best to return to the

Playroom, and briefly see the actors once again as the family and friends of Act One, Scene 1.

Synopsis

Act One

SCENE 1

As the houselights fade, giant booming footsteps echo throughout the theatre.

Lights up on the Playroom. Screams as Daughter and her birthday party guests react to the footsteps. Enter elder Brother – 'It's only me.' Groans. He wishes his sister happy birthday as friends play (puppet booth? table-tennis? rocking-horse?).

They are waiting for the party entertainer, but Mother and Father arrive and announce he cannot come. Initial disappointment fades when it is suggested they should all make up their own entertainment and act out Daughter's favourite story – the BFG.

All prepare, opening the dressing-up chest, moving furniture, etc.

Daughter puts on night-dress to become Sophie, then takes a puppet/doll, which becomes Sophie too. The doll's house is brought forward.

An introductory fanfare from the piano. Sophie starts to narrate the story, placing the doll inside the doll's house, which becomes the orphanage.

SCENE 2: The Snatch of Sophie

Father, as the BFG, acts to narration. He blows a dream into an imagined house, then approaches the 'orphanage'. Because Sophie has seen him, he snatches her (the doll).

SCENE 3: Running to Giant Country

Carrying the Sophie doll, the BFG runs, on the spot, on the platform stage. The curtains part and either with strobe and changing coloured lights on the window, or using moving backgrounds manipulated by the cast (trees, etc), the BFG speeds towards Giant Country. Sophie narrates as necessary.

SCENE 4: The BFG's Cave

The BFG takes Sophie doll into his cave (Sophie narrating and attaching a rod to the doll, so that she can manipulate it as a puppet). An area of the Playroom becomes the cave, bookshelves revolving to reveal rows and rows of colourful, glowing bottles and jars.

Putting the Sophie doll on a table or on his shoulder, the BFG talks to her. He explains he snatched her because she had seen him, and he doesn't want publicity. Sophie is worried he will eat her. The BFG denies this. Noises from outside the cave; the other Giants. 'These giants would eat you,' says the BFG, and lets Sophie peep out of the cave.

On the platform, cast members play the Giants, looking menacing and hungry. Lighting effect should cast their giant shadows up above. The BFG identifies some Giants individually, and tells Sophie what kind of humans they like to eat, and that they make nightly human raids. They mustn't know she is there.

Back in the Cave, the BFG introduces himself (possible title song), explaining why he is different from the other Giants and why Sophie is safe with him.

Sophie asks what the BFG eats if not humans. He introduces the vile vegetable, the snozzcumber, a large, gnarled veg. like a giant's club.

As Sophie tries eating it, Bloodbottler and Fleshlumpeater (two of the Giants) burst into the cave and accuse the BFG of keeping a 'human bean' as a pet. Sophie (doll) hides 'in' snozzcumber (narrated by Sophie) as a row develops between the BFG and the Giants, who threaten and insult him. He persuades them that the taste of snozzcumber is a good substitute for the taste of humans. Blood-bottler tries it. Sophie narrates as the action goes into slow motion – Sophie (inside snozzcumber) finds herself inside the dreaded Giant's mouth, and then, thankfully, is spat out (mimed with doll) when Bloodbottler tastes the vile vegetable. A row breaks out between Bloodbottler and Fleshlumpeater. They club each other with the snozzcumber and eventually exit.

To help Sophie recover from the shock, the BFG offers her some frobscottle, a fizzy drink, the bubbles of which fizz downwards not upwards, causing (to Sophie's embarrassment, but the BFG's delight) noisy whizzpoppers. Possible song as BFG and Sophie doll are propelled in the air. (Maybe the BFG uses the bed as a trampoline?)

As they relax, Sophie says a little about her harsh life at the orphanage, which makes the BFG sad. But he cheers up when Sophie asks him what he was doing with a trumpet, poking it in bedroom windows. He explains his ability to give people dreams by blowing them in through their bedroom windows. He shows her the bottles and jars – these contain dreams. He collects them. He offers to take Sophie on a dream-collecting expedition. Taking a butterfly net and jars, they leave the cave, the BFG carrying the doll, and Sophie narrating, as the BFG tiptoes past the snoring Giants on the platform.

SCENE 5: Dream Country
The BFG and Sophie 'run' to Dream Country. Smoke effect fills the upstage area. Music. Coloured lighting effects on the smoke. Possible dream-catching song, as the BFG catches dreams both nasty and nice and transfers them from net to jar.

SCENE 6: The BFG's Cave
The BFG and Sophie, plus doll, return to the cave, where the BFG demonstrates dream samples for Sophie. One or two are set in school situations (as in the book) and are acted out by cast members on the platform stage. The final demonstration is the BFG telling how he once released a nightmare and blew it into Fleshlumpeater's head to terrify him; this too is acted out on the platform.

The fun is interrupted by the frightening sound of the Giants outside waking up. The BFG and Sophie peep outside. The Giants are seen on the platform resolving to go to England to steal and eat school-children. They set off.

Sophie decides she must do something to stop the Giants' cruel activity. The BFG thinks this is impossible. But when Sophie suggests the Queen of England might help, he agrees to mix a special dream warning the Queen of what is happening. Possible dream-mixing song as the dream is prepared.

SCENE 7: Running to England
Again using a strobe or magical colour-changing lighting effect, the BFG and Sophie doll set off. Perhaps we also see the Giants racing towards England.

Sophie announces their arrival at Buckingham Palace. The curtains part to reveal a backcloth or cut-out of the familiar frontage, lights twinkling from the windows.

Her narration is interrupted by Mother appearing and announcing an interval for tea. She brings on a birthday cake. The family and friends sing *Happy Birthday*, and 'Sophie' blows out the candles.

Blackout.

Interval

Act Two

SCENE 1
The family and guests prepare to carry on the story, positioning the bed in a prominent spot. Mother is inveigled into playing the Queen, dons dressing-gown and crown and goes to bed.

Sophie continues her narration, saying that the BFG and Sophie found the correct window of Buckingham Palace and the BFG blew the dream in, through his trumpet. We see a large-scale trumpet emerge through the curtains.

Sophie tells us she was deposited on the window ledge; she positions herself behind the curtains.

The Queen has a bad dream and calls out in her sleep. Mary, her maid, enters with a tea tray and the Queen tells her about her dream: Giants snatching children. Mary is amazed because the dream describes events on the front page of the newspaper. Suddenly, Mary, seeing the curtain move, drops the tray. Sophie is revealed (now, of course, played by the actress and not the doll). Mary is cross with Sophie, but the Queen, having dreamt about her, is eager to understand. And to learn if another part of her dream was true – that Sophie was put through her window by a giant.

Sophie calls the BFG to meet the Queen. The curtains part to reveal the BFG's huge head (giant scale) or an eye only, blinking. Mary then faints. The BFG's voice booms a greeting.

The Queen agrees to receive him – and Sophie – for breakfast. In the Ballroom.

SCENE 2: The Ballroom
Music over a transformation scene change. The Playroom recedes to become the Ballroom. It is suggested the window/curtains of the Playroom be retained to become the lofty door/archway into the Ballroom.

The BFG (actor in giant, fixed costume) is revealed sitting high up on a structure made of objects from the Playroom – a chest of drawers on a piano. His table is perhaps the table-tennis table balanced on the clock, piles of books, etc. (This is clearly a very solid piece of scenery.) Hopefully, although the BFG's head and face will not really be giant-size, his height (static, sitting) and giant costume (into which he fits his own actor's body) will create a satisfying picture.

Still to music, Mr Tibbs (the butler), a maid and Mary deliver breakfast, necessitating climbing a ladder to the 'table'. Meanwhile, Sophie and the Queen sit at a small table to the other side.

The BFG enjoys his food, but not coffee – he wants some frobscottle. Sophie warns him the results would be impolite. Whereupon the BFG does a whizzpopper; the Queen manages to retain her dignity. She prefers the bagpipes . . .

The Queen checks the BFG's story about child-eating giants by making a call to the Queen of Sweden, where the Giants rampaged the night before. (The Queen of Sweden is seen elsewhere on the set.)

Then a plan to defeat the Giants has to be made. The heads of the Army and Air Force arrive, having difficulty believing the story and in understanding the BFG, but eventually agree to use their resources to capture the Giants while they are asleep and bring them back to captivity. The BFG will lead them to Giant Country.

SCENE 3: A roar of helicopter engines leads into a shadow puppet sequence. This will necessitate a screen, possibly flown in for the purpose. It will probably need to be designed and directed by a puppetry expert; at this stage of the play we need to impress not 'improvise'.

The BFG leads a fleet of helicopters across the screen. Voice-over of the Head of the Air Force and a pilot expressing their amazement as they fly off the map. All disappear from the screen. Colour-change as the snores of the Giants are heard.

The helicopters reappear. Instructions are uttered. Sophie possibly narrates, as ropes are lowered from the helicopters to the bottom of the screen. We hear that the Giants are tied up as they sleep, then hoisted in the air. The ropes lift, revealing tied-up Giants. Then the helicopters set off across the screen, as the Giants, waking, are heard complaining they have been 'flushbunkled', etc.

SCENE 4: The Playroom
As the scene change takes place, Sophie narrates; she tells us a pit was dug for the Giants, who became a great public attraction. They were fed on specially grown snozzcumbers, except when the odd silly drunken human fell in the pit . . .

Back in the Playroom, the BFG is thanked by the Queen (now played by a puppet operated by Mother/Queen) on behalf of the whole world.

He says goodbye and starts to leave. Sophie (doll) wants to go with him. The Queen agrees to her having a holiday; then she is to return and live at the Palace.

The BFG with Sophie (doll) goes to the platform and prepares to 'run' home.

The others gather to wave goodbye – the Queen (holding Queen puppet), Mr Tibbs (plus Mr Tibbs puppet), the heads of the Army and the Air Force (with their puppets), Mary and Maid (with their puppets).

The BFG 'runs' in strobe/colourful lighting effects.

'Sophie' steps forward and starts the final narration, and then all the cast join in. She says that Sophie and the BFG wrote down their story, that now 'we' have acted it out – and thank you (the audience) who came to see it.

The End

Subsequent changes to the synopsis

It was decided that the stage within a stage beneath the window should not have curtains, which would look too contrived. Instead the curtains covered the window. This window was later used as the Queen's bedroom window, through which the BFG's giant-scale blowing trumpet was pushed when he blew a dream to the Queen. In the final scene of the play, we did return to the Playroom but we combined the two scales as we tied up the ends of the story. The children at the party and Mother manipulated rod puppets of their Buckingham Palace characters. The puppets waved a final farewell to the BFG who walked into the sunset as the light brightened through the window.

In Act One, Scene 1, the proposed opening giant booming footsteps were cut and transferred to just before the entrance of the elder Brother. In realistic terms, they were his footsteps coming up to the Playroom, but exaggerated to scare the other children. Also it put the idea of giants into the minds of the audience.

In Act One, Scene 2, the narration as the BFG sped towards Giant Country was in fact taken by all the actors, spoken almost with musical counterpoint. In Act One, Scene 4, and throughout the play, I decided not to use songs. The more I thought about it, the less appropriate songs seemed.

It is also worth mentioning that my idea in the synopsis of having two Giants burst into the cave and threaten the BFG worked well. In the book only one Giant comes in. It was possible to create a more threatening atmosphere with two.

Talking of Giants, we cheated a little in the original production by using specially made giant headdress helmets, rather than 'improvising' with masks from the dressing-up box. The actors kept their 'child at the party' costumes. The heads, plus stylized movement, were enough to convey the ferocity of the Giants.

It is worth noting that Sophie's narration, which features throughout the play, was done in the third person. Although she was Sophie, it worked better for her to describe the story at a slight distance, retaining her 'birthday child' image. This technique of narration, first seen by me in David Edgar's wonderful adaptation of *Nicholas Nickleby*, is very effective. In Act One, Scene 5, after the frobscottle interlude, I decided that the BFG and Sophie should go to sleep. After a time lapse, the BFG gets up to go to work. Sophie wakes and the BFG decides to confide in her about his dream catching, and then invites her to accompany him.

At the end of the scene, the BFG and Sophie leave the cave and, much as in the book, the other Giants bully the BFG. I had left this out of the synopsis, but decided to reinstate it.

In Act One, Scene 6, I chose two dreams to act out. The BFG invites Sophie to 'see' them. The other actors play the various roles. The American President dream I kept very much as in the book, but the one involving the teacher I changed and made a little more theatrical. A child possesses the ability magically to make the teacher dance. The headteacher enters and is scandalized, but he too is forced to dance in an ungainly fashion. Audiences loved this.

At the end of the first half, it seemed rather anticlimactic to have Mother suddenly announce tea. We simply did a big build to the arrival at Buckingham Palace. The whole of the back wall of the Playroom flew out revealing the familiar frontage of Buckingham Palace. This proved an effective end of act curtain.

Between Act Two, Scenes 1 and 2, the transformation into the Ballroom was a complicated technical affair, with parts of the Playroom revolving to become the wall of the Ballroom, plus the arrival of the giant BFG, which really needed a proper entrance. So we made this into a choreographed scene change, using the actors as servants at the Palace, led by Mr Tibbs, the butler, who acted as a sort of foreman, directing traffic. This became an interesting visual theatrical experience in its own right. But the idea only came at the technical rehearsal.

In Act Two, Scene 2, I decided (in time for the synopsis) to turn the King of Sweden into the Queen of Sweden. This was simply because I knew how many were in the cast, and an actress was more easily available than an actor.

As I wrote the play, and kept re-reading the synopsis as I worked, I was convinced that Act Two lacked a real climax of excitement. Although the shadow puppet sequence would be a new visual idea, somehow I felt we needed more.

I found the solution at the beginning of the following scene. Sophie narrates how the Giants are dropped into a pit and will be exhibited at London Zoo. As in the book, the BFG and Sophie go to have a look. I decided that perhaps Fleshlumpeater, the most unpleasant Giant, should somehow manage to grab Sophie and threaten to eat her. This would give a great moment of tension, a life or death situation, the heroine in danger, the Giant who loves her powerless to help . . . but how could she be rescued? I remembered that in the dream-catching sequence, the BFG had caught a couple of nice dreams, but also a trogglehumper – a nightmare. In the book, and indeed in the synopsis, the BFG describes to Sophie how he had once released a trogglehumper and blown it into Fleshlumpeater's head to give him a nasty turn.

I had always thought that this episode, which was told to Sophie but was not part of the action, didn't really fit into the structure of Act One, where I had originally placed it. I decided to transfer it to this crucial climax stage of Act Two. The BFG, fearing that Sophie is doomed, luckily has the trogglehumper in his suitcase, gets it out and blows it towards Fleshlumpeater, who suddenly has a terrifying nightmare about Jack of *Jack and the Beanstalk* fame coming to kill him. His nightmare leads him to wake up the other Giants, who start attacking him. The biter bit. This created a satisfactory climax and led into the final resolution.

The final scene of the play was changed considerably in the writing. In spite of my reluctance to change Roald Dahl's ending of the book, it seemed to me that to offer the BFG a house and Sophie a cottage near by was somehow dramatically unsatisfying. I thought it would be better if the BFG decided not to stay, but to go back to his familiar surroundings, the cave and Giant Country. This would give a bitter-sweet ending, a lump-in-the-throat feeling as he goes.

But I decided to temper this with the idea that Sophie should indeed be able to live at Buckingham Palace, and that the BFG should agree to return to see her once a year – on her birthday. This, of course, tied in with the birthday motif within which the play is framed.

I had changed the ending of *The BFG* and no-one complained. But after I had adapted another Roald Dahl book, *The Witches*, for the stage, I was amused to receive a letter from a child telling me off in no uncertain terms for having changed Mr Dahl's ending. Mr Dahl, said the child, would be very angry if he were still alive. The child had noticed that in the play the boy who has been transformed into a mouse is not changed back into his boy shape at the end. I wrote back informing the child that I had used Mr Dahl's ending exactly as he had written it. The child was confusing the ending of the book with the ending of the film version where the film-makers, presumably because they wanted a happy ending, decided that the mouse should be turned back into a boy. Roald Dahl hated this ending. For Dahl, the whole point of the ending was that the boy/mouse knew that his life expectancy was similar to that of his best friend, his elderly grandmother. This made him very happy – a bitter-sweet ending, maybe, but nonetheless a happy one.

Part 5   Directing and the Production Team

The Challenge

The director needs to invite each member of the team to share in the challenge, and make sure that they fully comprehend the nature of the challenge and understand how worthwhile and important the work is. The director should encourage each member to work with care and enthusiasm towards the first performance and become involved not just in their own specific area of expertise but in the whole production. As a result of this partnership, the whole team can share in the special pleasure generated by an audience of children thoroughly enjoying themselves. As long as there continues to be a strange and unjustified sort of embarrassment about being involved in a children's theatrical production, it is necessary for the director to establish this level of commitment in the production team, to inspire everybody to work to the highest possible level and to demonstrate the qualities that make it so exciting and demanding.

Section 1. Pre-Production

When gathering together the production team – designers of the set, costumes, lighting and sound, the music composer/director, the production manager and the stage management – the producer of an adult play will first and foremost be searching for talent and ability. The requirements for a children's play necessitate something more. The team needs to have a genuine commitment to working for and entertaining children.

Every member of the production team should have an appreciation of the child's world of humour, colour and imagination, and relish the chance to be part of it. Their attitude to the work should reflect a freshness of ideas as well as a level of excitement at the opportunity to produce high-quality work for children, especially at the thought that they have the chance to introduce a new generation to the unique experience of theatre-going. They should use their skills to ensure that this special audience is not disappointed and they should take a genuine interest in the response of the audience to the finished product.

Like every practitioner who endeavours to create quality plays for children, I make every effort to enthuse the experts who work with me, encouraging them to see the play as something special, giving them the opportunity to share in the creation of something arguably more interesting and rewarding than equivalent jobs in the adult theatre. When I interview prospective members of the team I have to make sure that they do not simply see this as another run-of-the-mill job. They must genuinely relish the opportunity of working for children. They must not be approaching the task grudgingly or wishing they were doing something for adults. They must take the job seriously and share my belief in the vital importance of the work.

One of the pleasures of my work with Whirligig Theatre, touring to major theatres throughout Britain, has been to extend this sense of enthusiasm to the technical crews working in each theatre we visit. In the early days it was very noticeable that many of these hardworking technicians had a lackadaisical attitude towards Whirligig's visit. 'It's only for kids' was often the motto. They didn't imagine it could be 'real theatre'. But many of them developed a respect for the work and suddenly found themselves experiencing a sense of wonderment at the delight they found in working on a quality children's production. Many realized that our productions asked them to be far more inventive and imaginative than many an adult production. They also enjoyed sharing with the company the uninhibited and joyful reactions to the play, understanding that children can be a truly rewarding audience who are entitled to the best we can offer.

Liaison between the members of the production team at regular pre-production meetings is essential to make sure that everybody is working towards the same goal. Here are some of the most common problems I have seen in both amateur and professional productions:

1. The actors are taken by surprise at the last minute by costumes that make it impossible to do what they rehearsed.
2. The designer has created a set that has forced the action too far upstage so that actors are too far away from the audience.
3. The scene changes are too long.
4. The choreographer has devised dance steps and intricate routines that are more suitable for an adult audience.
5. The music for songs is too loud, and the incidental music (if any) is not sympathetic to the action.
6. The use of lighting and sound is basic and unimaginative.

Sets and Costumes – Designer

Design is an integral part of a children's production. It demands considerably more invention and imagination than might be required for an adult play. Very often the designer will be called upon to create sets around fantasy ideas, interpreting them with an appreciation of colour and shape, yet making sure that the sets and costumes will be practical and 'work'. For example, it is no use designing a costume for a tar-whacking machine if the actor is unable to move in it. And the design of a giant flower pot is made more difficult when it must be lifted in order to trap three characters, but must also be able to support the weight of an actor when inverted, allow access through the hole and be transparent in one scene to enable the audience to see inside. Designers of plays needing traditional drawing rooms and characters in lounge suits may find the world of children's theatre something of a nightmare.

The designer needs to investigate ways of making the scene changes visually interesting and to avoid lengthy scene changes as some plays will demand several different locations. For instance, trucks can turn and become a new location. Red Admiral's cabbage in *The Plotters of Cabbage Patch Corner* turned to become Spider's Lair. *The Old Man of Lochnagar*'s cave turned to become the mountain top. In *The BFG*, a wardrobe opens up to reveal the BFG's cave. In some plays one-dimensional buildings or trees can be flown or trucked to suggest picture-book illustrations.

Understanding what will be acceptable to a child's imagination is necessary. A large, yellow, raked disc can become an island; a piece of material wafted by the actors can become the sea. Sometimes ideas can be taken from the way in which children play. For example, a cardboard box can become a boat; turned on its side, it can become a car or a wall. A table can become a house. Children enjoy such inventiveness on stage, as long as it is clear what is happening.

The designer needs an imaginative yet practical sense of scale when designing giant sets for small creatures or small sets for giants. The scale will never be exact. For example, in *The Selfish Shellfish*, the set must look like a rock pool. A whelk shell is the home of H.C., the Hermit Crab. This must not seem out of scale with the rock pool, yet must accommodate an actor inside.

When working on an adaptation of a book featuring well-known children's characters, such as Rupert Bear or Noddy, the designer has a responsibility to the original illustrator, particularly when the characters are visually recognizable to children.

Some plays will invite the designer to create a world of total fantasy. *The Owl and the Pussycat Went to See . . .* with its exotic Edward Lear characters and places offers considerable scope. But in other plays, where the fantasy is rooted in reality, the designer must be able to create an acceptably real world, to contrast with the fantastic events. For instance, in Roald Dahl's *The Witches* it is important that the hotel ballroom, dining-room, bedroom and kitchen are recognizably 'ordinary'. Similarly, the Welsh dresser in *The Gingerbread Man* needs to be a faithful representation – in giant scale – of an antique dresser, complete with plates, teapot, herb jars and honey pot. Only then can the activities of the fantasy characters be properly appreciated. And in *The See-Saw Tree*, the tree must be practicable enough for the actors to climb up and down its trunk and inhabit its 'bowl' and branches, but it must also look like a real tree.

Sometimes a more expressionist approach is possible. In *Save the Human*, we used cartoon backgrounds projected on to a screen. The cartoon settings were complemented by cut-outs of objects like a table, a television, a boat or a door. The style was inventive, yet the total effect was recognizably 'real'. In this play the actors presented themselves as actors in tracksuits, who 'became' the animal characters by putting on headdresses.

Over the years I have been fortunate enough to work with Susie Caulcutt who specializes in creating sets and costumes for different kinds of children's plays. She is able to enter the world of the child and her designs offer eye-catching pictures that enchant the audience and are at the same time practical and economical.

The choreographer and the costume designer should discuss how much movement is required of each character and how this might affect the costume. In the programme of one production I saw of *The BFG* the choreographer said how exciting it had been working with the actors on finding individual styles of movement for each of the Giants. But in the production itself, all the Giants seemed to move in exactly the same way. This was because they were all wearing heavily padded costumes which made movement extremely difficult. Clearly there had not been enough liaison between departments. I went backstage and asked one of the actresses if she had had a surprise when her Giant costume had arrived. She replied that she had been in tears for half an hour because everything she had learnt in rehearsal was now wasted.

If headdresses or masks are to be used, it is important to decide early on whether the actors' faces will be visible. Actors usually hate not being able to use their faces, and it is sometimes best to design a mask that does not completely encase the actor's head. Headdresses and masks should be available all through rehearsal and not delivered two days before the opening performance. They can completely change a performance if the actor is taken by surprise.

The costume designer will face considerable problems with fantasy characters. Designing, say, a butterfly or a tea bag is one thing, but remembering that a human body has to go inside it is another. The designer must also remember what the playwright's intention is. For example, the Red Admiral in *The Plotters of Cabbage Patch Corner* is both a butterfly and a retired naval officer. I have seen many productions of the play in which the character looks like a retired naval officer, but nothing like a butterfly. Other productions have emphasized the butterfly characteristics, with working wings and antennae, but the retired naval officer has gone out of the window. Similarly, I have seen productions of *The Gingerbread Man* in which the Old Bag looks nothing like a tea bag, simply a crotchety old lady. But I have also seen productions where the actress was encased in a wonderfully realistic-looking tea bag, which made it impossible for her to move. Compromise and balance must be patiently sought.

Choreographer/Movement Person

A choreographer of musical stage shows for adults, who is primarily concerned with devising dance steps and intricate routines for the cast and very often has the chorus performing complicated routines, all dancing in unison and ending each number with a punchy big finish, is not necessarily ideal for a children's production. The qualities of a children's theatre choreographer have much more to do with the development of acting than dancing skills. The cast is often made up of actors who can move rather than dancers who can act. The main question for the children's theatre choreographer is, 'Is everybody staying in character?'

In fact, the choreographer's role is more like a co-director, working out well in advance the aims of the play and the required movement style. The choreographer becomes involved with the overall style of the production, making sure that the musical staging becomes an extension of the dialogue and action rather than a number of separate self-contained routines. The choreographer collaborates with the director as much in the staging of scenes as in the musical numbers.

Since actors will be searching for a through-line in the characterizations, and will respond better to movement linked directly to that aim rather than to complicated dance steps simply for the sake of it, the choreographer needs to communicate in actors' language rather than dancers' language. For example, a scene might involve a chase sequence. A choreographer's sense of rhythm can greatly enhance the humour of the sequence in which characters pursue each other, just miss each other, bump into each other or mistake each other for someone else. The director can work out the logistics of the chase, but a choreographer can make it precise and stylish.

The individual movement of each character is a vital ingredient of a children's production, particularly where fantasy characters are involved. The way the characters move will affect the way the actors play their roles and add distinctiveness and clarity to their performance. The choreographer can also ensure 'clean', focused movement in silent mime sequences, ensuring clarity. For instance, the slow, languorous, slimy movements of Slug in *The Plotters of Cabbage Patch Corner* will contrast with the busy, 'hurry-scurry' movement of Ant. When both take part in the same song their 'steps' must be in character, even though they may be singing the same words. The Giants in *The BFG* need to move in exaggerated slow motion. This, together with slightly spaced-out speech, helps convey an impression of their enormous size. In one production I saw, the students playing toys each found one simple stylized movement.

The choreographer needs to liaise with the costume designer in the early stages of the production, explaining exactly what the actors are going to have to do in their costumes and making sure that the designer understands how the costume should 'work'. There may well have to be give and take in this area, but early consultations are vital. I have directed many of my own plays in happy association with the choreographer Sheila Falconer.

How the actor stands, sits, moves, is almost always the first clue an audience has to the character he or she represents and this visual impact is even more important for child audiences. It must be vivid, precise and above all, truthful. The actor must be 'quick'. By that I mean alive to the last nerve-end. I like to think that the work we do together is seamless, and that whether or not there is music, no-one can detect where my work begins or ends. It should begin at the beginning of the play and end at the end.

There are many ways a choreographer can enhance even the best and most wittily devised chase. For example, the split second when those involved come face to face. Standing still and making a funny face may be funny, but not exciting. What gives the 'buzz' is the suspended moment, which does not kill the animation, but is a hair-on-end state of peril, shown by a fully energized cessation of movement – perhaps one leg a-tip-toe, body half-turned, maintained for an improbable length of time. The burst of speed that follows is the release of tension into 'glee' for an audience. The timing and placing of energy is all. Think of the moment a cartoon character stays suspended in mid-air for several beats when he runs over a cliff top – before plummeting. I've learnt a lot from *Tom and Jerry*! Even in more conventional musicals, a choreographer will decide to keep a solo singer perfectly still, with just the odd movement of hand, foot, head or eye – all on the basis of text and character.

Sheila Falconer, choreographer

Composer/Musical Supervisor

Simplicity is often a virtue, but it would be misconceived and insulting to assume that a young audience can respond only to tinkly little baby-tunes. Similarly, an audience of children does not necessarily need to be musically bombarded by any current (adult-manipulated) 'pop' fashion, although that style may be absolutely ideal in certain situations. Many false assumptions are made by adults about the type of music that can be appreciated by children.

Peter Pontzen, composer/musical supervisor

It is crucial that a children's play with songs has a composer who appreciates the kind of music that children will respond to. This music tends to be rhythmic, tuneful and not too sophisticated. If there are any audience-participation songs, the tune must be relatively simple to enable the children to pick it up quickly. Children's theatre composers need to pay careful attention to the intentions of the lyrics and make sure the words are stressed clearly and effectively. They should be aware of the fact that the cast may comprise actors who sing rather than singers who act. The actors have been cast because of their ability to put over a song rather than to sing it with a beautiful operatic voice. Therefore, the musical range should not be too ambitious.

For many years I have allowed myself the indulgence of writing most of my own melodies for my own lyrics. I am not really a musician, but can just about write a comprehensible top line. Peter Pontzen has long been my musical supervisor, arranging the tunes, and sometimes having to make sense of my musical errors. He is totally committed to working for children and is particularly skilful in composing incidental music.

This works rather like film music, underscoring the action at appropriate points, increasing the tension or heightening the emotion. Very often the music accompanies the action like the music for a silent film, so that the length of a particular musical passage can vary from performance to performance depending on audience reaction. As a result the musicians must occasionally be able to improvise while watching the stage carefully to punctuate certain moments and reflect accurately the movements of the actors. Some musicians find this difficult to cope with, feeling more comfortable with a watertight score.

Before rehearsals begin, the composer/musical supervisor should work closely with the director, and in particular with the choreographer, discussing the role of the music from scene to scene. Music may be necessary to cover scene changes, and this should be carefully worked out, in order to retain the attention and interest of the audience. Very often the incidental music will be variations on the main song tunes or main themes. Occasionally, however, music may be composed especially for certain sequences.

When I write music, whether for a song or to underscore some action, a part of me always imagines itself as listener; the importance of this automatic identification is that it should help the result not only to be tailored to suit the dramatic material but to match the tastes and capacities of a good proportion of the potential audience. Beyond this simple precaution, it is unnecessary and undesirable to 'write down' to children: to do so would be as objectionable as 'talking down', a symptom of the condescension and disdain which is often unwittingly exhibited towards them.

Provided that a musician has sensitivity and an aptitude for 'following' when necessary in a song, or improvisation during the action, the opportunity to complement the play can be immense, enhancing the excitement and involvement of player and audience alike. Quite apart from musicianship and technical skill, there needs to be a commitment to the audience and to the emotional and narrative content of the play: a positive approach towards this type of work is essential.

Peter Pontzen

Sound Designer

The sound designer's contribution should not be underestimated. Sound can help create mood and atmosphere. The sound designer can have a great deal of fun, particularly when creating and recording sound effects.

I shall never forget the childlike hysteria in the rehearsal room of *The BFG* when Mike Furness, the sound designer, arrived to record whizzpoppers. The whole cast – and the director – spent half an hour blowing raspberries into the microphone. Big ones, small ones, fruity ones, 'polite' ones. It was all very silly and enjoyable. (Ironically, Mike didn't use any of them, but came up with splendid whizz-poppers in his studio at home.)

The sound effects in a children's play will very often be fantasy-oriented. The sound designer must create unlikely sounds, but make them totally believable. In *Noddy*, the bell on Noddy's hat was more difficult than we had expected. Real bells didn't sound like people's conception of real bells. In the end, tinkling on a glass proved the answer.

The sea-anemone in *The Selfish Shellfish* had to swallow an oil slick. In *Meg and Mog Show* it was necessary to create the sound of a stegosaurus munching and crunching Meg's vegetables, and a whole range of whooshing noises was created for magic spells or broom-sticks taking off. Sometimes a surreal, nightmare effect can be achieved using a combination of keyboard synthesizer sounds and recorded sound effects. For *The Witches*, Mike Furness devised an extraordinary cacophony of distorted clock chimes and alarm bells which complemented perfectly the bizarre transformation of all the witches into mice.

Creating 'real-life' sounds for the stage is sometimes not as simple as it sounds. In *The See-Saw Tree*, it was necessary to have all sorts of noises: vehicles, diggers, crackling fires and trees falling. All these sounds had to be menacing and exaggerated, particularly when heard from the animals' point of view. Similarly, the recording of the off-stage voices of the Big Ones needed a certain amount of echo, but also clarity. In the theatre it is sometimes difficult to hear words when you cannot see them being spoken.

The quality of the sound in theatre productions has improved greatly over the years. Radio mikes, one for each actor, are often employed, particularly in musical productions. The sophistication of radio mikes has increased in recent years, so that the sound need not be tinny, jarring or distorted. Float mikes along the front of the stage can also help audibility. Some people still wonder why microphones are necessary at all. Children, even when sitting absorbed in the production, will often shift their position, causing a rustling sound. It is extremely important that they hear what is going on, and amplified sound, particularly in a large auditorium, becomes a vital aid.

Lighting Designer

Many people's first theatre-going memories include the excitement of the lights going down, the intriguing pool of light on the front of the house tabs, followed by the lights coming up on a bright and colourful opening scene. In a children's production, the director must always bear in mind the theatrical potential of lighting and use it throughout the play to enhance the mood and atmosphere. Lighting create genuine theatrical magic.

A good sense of colour and the willingness to liaise with the set designer are essential. Before rehearsals start, the basic intentions should be discussed with the director and, using the set model, the lighting designer and the set designer should agree on the basic requirements. Working closely with the set designer and director, the lighting designer needs to define certain areas of the stage which will be used for certain scenes.

Variety of location can be very helpful in retaining attention, and keeping the stage visually alive is something in which the lighting designer should always assist. For instance, it is often effective to dip the lights slightly as a known 'baddie' enters, or to echo visually the footsteps of an off-stage giant. When a tight situation happily resolves itself, it is always effective for the lighting to increase, as though the sun has come out.

The lighting designer needs to enjoy using special effects. Mirror balls can create a night-time sky. Special rotating lanterns and flash boxes can enhance the atmosphere for magic spells. Strobe lighting can be used in small doses to create the look of a silent film or effectively light slow-motion sequences. (If you use strobe lighting you must put up a warning in the foyer as it promotes the symptoms of epilepsy.) Special lanterns can create underwater effects. Light shone through the smoke from smoke machines can create mysterious effects. Ultra-violet sequences against black backgrounds can be truly magical. Lighting a screen for shadow puppet sequences or the use of silhouette against the back of the set to suggest giants might be appropriate.

The lighting designer must take into account that even in the most atmospheric night scene, the audience needs to see the actors reasonably well. Avoid black-outs. Scene changes should take place in an interesting lighting state such as a blue wash. Follow-spots should be used sparingly for children. Inexperienced operators often move them jerkily, which distracts the audience.

From time to time, lighting plays a crucial part in the story-telling. For instance, in *The Gingerbread Man*, when the Big Ones enter the kitchen, they are not seen by the audience. We imagine them towering over the Welsh dresser. As they enter the kitchen they turn on the light. This provides a highly dramatic suddenly as the dresser folk scuttle to their usual positions and freeze before the Big Ones can see them. The lighting designer will have to find a balance between the amount of light (possibly moonlight) shining on the Welsh dresser during the previous scene, and the increased brightness caused by the kitchen light. This may also involve casting exciting shadows across the set. Indeed, I once saw a production where the Big Ones' shadows were clearly discernible as they talked. The convincing creation of such stage illusion is essential for the audience's comprehension of the plot.

At all costs the lighting designer should avoid a situation where there are only two lighting states – on and off. Shows have been known to arrange their get-ins only a couple of hours before the performance. There is no time to focus properly and rig the lighting, let alone plot it imaginatively.

The lighting designer should enjoy the challenge of giving his or her imagination a chance to shine – literally. It is true that budgets may be limited and that there may not be enough time to arrange lights in a sophisticated fashion, particularly in a touring production. But the colour and 'tricks' it is possible to use in children's theatre should be enough to whet the lighting designer's appetite.

Production Manager/Stage Management

If a production manager is to be employed, he or she will provide a vital role in co-ordinating the building of the set and the making of the costumes, and ensuring that the demands of the show are met. The production manager may advise on how to make the scene changes as swift as possible to avoid losing the audience's attention. He or she may also be very helpful in arranging for certain key props and costumes to be provided earlier than the dress rehearsal. Actors will need to work with them in advance.

In all areas of theatre the production manager is a key figure. In children's theatre he or she often needs to be even more efficient, making sure that all departments deliver on time, understanding how the set must work and co-ordinating everybody towards a smooth rehearsal period. Sometimes, sadly, set builders, prop makers and costume makers will not keep to their deadlines. But it is essential that certain key props and costumes are available during the rehearsal period, rather than arriving just in time for the first performance. The attitude of the production manager can help tremendously in avoiding misunderstandings. From an early date the production manager should work closely with the director and the team to ensure that as few problems as possible will be encountered once the play reaches the stage.

The production manager will probably be looking for an efficient stage management team, each member of which should be committed to working for children, or at least be willing to approach the project with an open mind. The director is advised to insist on having a say in the choice of staff, to meet them and gauge whether their attitude will be positive and helpful, both in the rehearsal room and in the theatre.

If you're a stage manager who likes late nights and hates early mornings, then children's theatre is not for you. When your last show finishes at 4 p.m., you won't find the front of house bars open, and coming into the theatre at 9 a.m. (and sometimes earlier), to put your set up for the fourth time in a week is not particularly enjoyable after eight pints, a vindaloo, and a three-hour discussion on adapting Dostoevsky for the stage.

However, if you love working with sets and props, then you will find that children's theatre is a wonderful place to be. Big, Bright and Colourful – the B.B.C. – are very often the order of the day.

Anybody involved in the technical side of children's theatre needs just a slightly thicker skin, a touch more patience and preferably a slightly bigger sense of humour than your average stage manager.

The 'Ooh' of the audience when the house lights go down, and the various expressions of awe, inquisitiveness and sheer excitement that a child can radiate when coming backstage to see the set and props, is something adult shows will never be able to match. It is something that every stage manager should experience, something nobody should ever devalue, and in my opinion is the essence of theatre itself.

Neil Hillyer, stage manager

Casting

Lindsay Anderson once told me that good casting was 90 per cent of good directing. He often took six months to cast a film.

In professional children's theatre, it is often necessary to spread the casting net wider than agents, and advertise in broadsheets like the *Production and Casting Report*. It is useful to keep a list of good actors that you have seen in other productions. Very often, too, actors hear of a production through the grapevine and write, asking for an audition. Directors of amateur productions may have fewer potential performers to consider but, even so, it is worth looking for certain basic qualities.

Actors in children's theatre need all the basic skills: good acting, good movement and possibly good singing. They need a very high energy level, an outgoing enthusiasm which will enable them to enjoy the challenge of performing to children, and the ability to sense when an audience is in danger of becoming restless or losing interest. Each performance of a show varies. Actors need the ability to change the pace and concentrate in order to deal with unusual audience responses.

I have always looked for what I call 'big and brave' performers. These actors approach character with a broad, clear openness. They are brave enough to experiment and are aware that communication with the audience is all-important.

Actors must be thoroughly committed to the show and realize how important it is to give 100 per cent every performance. First-time theatre-goers make up a proportion of the audience at virtually every performance, and it is the actors' hard work that may well decide whether an individual child will want to come again.

High energy levels are needed, given that the actors often perform twice-daily, in the mornings and afternoons. They need to keep their voices and bodies in trim to be able to cope with the workload. They should enjoy being part of a team. There is seldom room for starry behaviour. And they must at all times remember that they are not in a pantomime, where it is permissible to come off the book and add extra dialogue.

Directors will find that many children's plays need performers of varying sizes. A contrast between small and tall performers is often very helpful, particularly in fantasy-based plays. It is also worth remembering that to a child anyone above the age of eighteen is old. Therefore, if you are casting an elderly character it is not necessary to find an elderly actor for the role. It may well be better to find a younger character performer who has the right energy and enthusiasm.

Most auditions are limited to approximately ten minutes. It might seem impossible to make a reasoned assessment of someone in such a short time, but most directors agree that, whether it be through instinct or an ability to bring out the best in people, they will normally be able to tell whether the actor has possibilities or not.

When I hold auditions, I always have the choreographer and musical supervisor present. Together we put the actors through their paces in an enjoyable way, giving them the chance to show what they can do.

Most actors find auditions an ordeal and enter the room somewhat nervously. I try to put them at their ease by referring briefly to their previous experience and telling them something of the play we are doing. But I am aware of the fact that they may not be listening very carefully, because they are worried about singing their song. So I ask them to sing first, to get that part of the audition out of the way. When they sing, I'm not looking for the most beautiful or even the most tuneful voices. The musical supervisor will monitor their sense of rhythm and whether they can sing in tune. I am more interested in them putting over the song well. Some actors come along with a well-known children's song. This is not always the best choice. Such songs often encourage the actors to be rather twee or indulgent, giving a patronizing air to the performance. This is the last thing I'm looking for.

Next, I often ask the choreographer to try out a few simple steps with the actor. This is mainly to see whether the actor has a basic sense of co-ordination. It is not because we are looking for brilliant dancers. Then we may suggest a mime or movement improvisation. This might involve the actor losing inhibitions and leaping around the room as an over-enthusiastic dog. This is not necessarily intended to show us what a brilliant mime artist the actor is, rather to show us whether he or she will enjoy performing in an exuberant, eccentric manner.

I tend not to ask them to perform set pieces or speeches from other plays, rather to acquaint them with the play we are working on, and ask them to read.

When I read scenes with auditionees, I will often ask them to read the character two or three times in different ways, to display their versatility and to assess whether they yield to direction and can understand the ideas I suggest. Again, I am looking for them to be big and bold, to offer a caricature, just to show how far they can go. It is at this stage that my instinct will often tell me whether the actor has an aptitude for the work, or whether they would really rather be doing an adult play. However exotic or fantasy-based a character I may be asking them to read, I still want them to play it 'for real', somehow to find a basic truth in the lines, rather than speak them tongue-in-cheek. This is actually more difficult than it sounds. Some actors genuinely feel they are demeaning themselves by playing fantasy characters, whereas others relish the idea of playing animals or even inanimate objects.

Finally, I like to have a chat with the actor about some of his or her favourite parts. Such a chat reveals the enthusiasms and the openness of the actor, and I think I can usually tell whether they could become good company members as well as play a part successfully.

During all these stages of the audition, we are getting an idea of the person we are watching, the personality of the performer, whether he or she will enthusiastically share the creation of a play for children.

Director's Homework

I work out, in some detail, the whole concept of the production in advance. It is the director's duty to the actors to be prepared. By the time I reach the rehearsal room I like to have the whole play blocked out in my mind and on paper. Obviously things are learned in rehearsal, and changes are made, but over the years I have found that having a very clear idea of what the final production will look like helps the team push forward in the same direction.

I work with the stage ground-plans, sometimes even using toy figures or coins to represent each character. I work out entrances and exits logically, appropriate certain areas of the stage for certain scenes, and thus visualize the 'geography' of the play. Early in rehearsal I 'block' the scenes with the actors, sometimes making changes along the way but without wasting time on detailed work or characterization, trying to give the actors a general impression of how the production will work. To some this may seem dictatorial but, as an actor myself, I have always resented time-wasting in rehearsal, and if the director has no clear plan, the first week can easily fly by without anything much having been achieved.

I also work out a tight schedule of work. If there are songs in the show, time must be found for singing and choreography rehearsals as well as acting rehearsals. It can be very useful to have the use of two rehearsal rooms, so that while some actors are rehearsing a scene, others can be rehearsing a song. However, I find it very helpful to have the choreographer present for acting rehearsals so that each character's movement will be consistent throughout the play. The timetable will often also include rehearsals of puppetry sequences or special sessions in other skills. It is no good leaving these to the last moment.

The director should schedule regular production meetings at which all departments can swap the latest information and make sure they really get to know the play and its potential problems. Ideally, there should be a very clear understanding of how the production will work before rehearsals start.

Work will have started on the building of the set and the making of the costumes. The choreographer will have worked out some basic movement ideas. The musical supervisor will have devised harmonies and basic ideas for incidental music. The lighting designer will have a good idea of how the show will look. The sound designer will have started assembling the sound effects.

Every department must be totally involved and committed to the project and give enough time and consultation to understand what the director is trying to achieve. As little as possible should be left to chance. When the actors arrive in the rehearsal room, there should be a feeling of confidence that the production team knows what it is doing and the challenge of translating the play from page to stage can commence.

Section 2. Rehearsals

On the first day of rehearsal, when the whole team (actors, stage management and production team) assembles together for the first time, I use my introductory welcoming speech to encourage every-body's commitment to the production. I make it clear that no-one must look upon this production for children as less important than one for adults. If it is not already clear to the participants in the room, I talk about the nature of the audience and tell the actors that this may be one of the toughest jobs they ever undertake. I emphasize that children's theatre is not an easy option, but a specialized branch of theatre and an art form in its own right.

Then, before we have a read-through of the play, I talk for a while about the background to the play and anything I feel might be of interest. For example, when preparing the company for *More Adventures of Noddy*, I felt it was important to talk about Enid Blyton and the world of Noddy she had created. I pointed out that although Noddy is a toy living in a world of toys, he is really a child growing up in a world of adults, who help him learn about life. Children identify with Noddy, who has three of the things they often aspire to – a house, a car and a job. I spoke of Enid Blyton's skill as a writer and her appeal to children in that she uses toys, children and the supernatural – all elements that 'work' well in children's stories.

I pointed out that criticisms of the *Noddy* books for political incorrectness were no longer relevant – the books were amended some years ago. But I admitted that I felt her female characters were not very proactive, and explained that this was why I had strengthened the role of Tessie Bear. I also admitted that I found some of her writing twee, and that with the blessing of her estate I had tried to avoid such sentimentality and coyness. I hoped that an understanding of my attitude to the work would be useful for the entire team in case they were asked by the media to give a comment on the play, as well as persuade them to respect the integrity of the author. I explained how the stories helped reinforce children's recognition of right and wrong, and appealed to their sense of fairness. I told them how Enid Blyton encouraged children to help worthy causes, many of which she set up herself. For this reason, I had chosen charity collecting as a relevant theme in one of the two adventures I had created. I had copies of the books for the company to look at, and also Susie Caulcutt's costume designs and set model for everybody to see.

When rehearsing a musical production it is a good idea for the cast to get the songs under their belts as quickly as possible. The musical director and cast work together a fair amount of time in the first few days. As soon as the songs are learnt, they can be choreographed. The sooner this is achieved the better.

Alongside the music and choreography, I do a basic blocking of the play as quickly as possible.

Blocking and Focus

Take a look at an audience of children watching a play. You will notice that their heads move from side to side as they follow the action. Adults, on the other hand, will usually keep their heads still. The eye-span of a child is narrower than that of an adult, and the child cannot take in the whole stage at one glance. The director must always establish where the focus of the audience should be when plotting the moves.

The focus should never be changed too sharply. For instance, if something important is happening downstage left, be careful not to have a sudden entrance and bit of business upstage right. By the time the children's eyes have swung round, they may have missed something important.

Also, the actors must be aware of where the focus should be. Any extraneous movement away from the point of focus needs to be avoided. Sometimes actors find this strange. Obviously, they should not completely turn off and freeze if they are not within the main focus, but they must control any desire to wander round or move unnecessarily in case they cause a distraction.

Focusing the audience's attention is all part of a production's clarity. Children, more than adults, need to be directed to the things that matter most. I once saw a production of *The Gingerbread Man* in which the song 'Come the Light' (a prayer that everything will turn out right by morning) was sabotaged by a director getting the focus wrong. In my stage directions I suggest that at the end of the song the characters should go to sleep and then, accompanied by tick-tock noises and the gradual arrival of dawn, the hands of the cuckoo clock should turn until they reach 8 o'clock. The director of this production decided that the clock hands should turn slowly during the whole song, so that by the end of the song morning had arrived. What he hadn't foreseen was the fact that the children would become far more interested in the moving hands than in the characters' singing. As a result, the focus was in entirely the wrong place and the emotional spell of the prayer was missed.

It is sometimes fun, when blocking the play, to use the auditorium for certain entrances, exits, chases or hiding places. Children undoubtedly enjoy the close physical presence of the actors. Indeed, some young children, until the moment when an actor comes into the audience, think the whole performance is on film or video. But always make sure that the theatre is suitable for auditorium activity. It is no use having exciting things going on in the stalls if nobody in the circle or upper circle can see it. Disembodied voices and shrieks of audience enjoyment are no consolation to the section of the audience that is missing out.

In the early days of rehearsal, the director should work through the play scene by scene or section by section. With the actors one should consider carefully what each scene is about. What is its place in the story? What are the important plot developments? What will the audience learn from the scene? When the objective is agreed, a shape will emerge and, hopefully, a logical way of playing the scene will be found.

Pace

Looking through the script for *Rupert*, I am shocked at the amount of pace and energy needed. I've got notes on every page! 'Keep the scene up. Keep it moving. Positive. Contained but huge energy. Big. Lots of excitement. Very big and animated. Keep up the pace.' Towards the end, I had written, 'Although the play is winding up, energy needs to stay up.' And, on the very last page, after 'The End', I wrote, 'PHEW!!!'
Rachel Gaffin, Rupert, *Rupert and the Green Dragon*

Pace should not be confused with sheer speed. Simply saying the lines fast is not helpful at all. It will lead to gabbled dialogue and the audience may well not be able to understand it.

Pace has more to do with pursuing a through-line with energy and intensity. It involves picking up cues deftly. In every moment something (music, light, action, speech) is carrying the momentum forward. Keep the action going within the scenes and when moving from one scene to another. Don't give the audience the opportunity to become bored.

There should be no unnecessary pauses or hiatuses. Sometimes the actors will want to allow time for a change of thought or a transition of mood, but they must try not to think of every moment too naturalistically. They must think and react more quickly.

It is like playing a ball game where the participants try to keep the ball in the air and never let it hit the ground. A good pace holds the audience's attention and makes them keen to know what comes next.

Respect for the Play and the Audience

Skilful directors treat children's plays with the same respect as adult plays. They look carefully for the problems characters face, the turning points in the action, the crises and climaxes and what the play is trying to say.

A major problem occurs when the director cannot take the play seriously.

> I was invited to see a foreign production of one of my most successful plays, *The Gingerbread Man*. If someone had given me an injection to put me to sleep, taken me off on an aeroplane and sat me in an auditorium where I woke up watching a play in a foreign language, I would have had no idea that I was watching my own play. The setting was no longer a Welsh dresser but a draining board with a sink and a swinging tap. Sleek the Mouse was played (legitimately) as a cowboy manqué; but it did seem odd when he entered on a real horse.
>
> In another foreign production I saw, of *The Witches*, the director had decided that it would be fun for most of the witches to be played by male actors in drag. This went directly against Roald Dahl's starting point that any woman, even your teacher, might be a witch. These witches were not real women, they were bizarre, camp figures from an adult drag show. Also, the director decided that in fairness some of the male characters in the play should be played by women. He decided that one male character should actually be changed into a female character, then added to the confusion by having the part played by a man.

This betrays a lack of respect for the audience as well as for the playwright's intentions.

Directors shouldn't assume that a children's play is no more than an amusing trifle and should be directed as a breezy romp in an atmosphere of relentless, forced, jollity. They should realize that a children's play, however fantasy-based, is not by definition silly or lightweight. If a director cannot enter the mind of a child through the play, encouraging the actors to play with sincerity, the result will be bland and uninvolving.

Part of the problem lies in the fact that some fantasy ideas have, for an adult, a funny side. Yet children see the serious side. For example, in *Nutcracker Sweet* the nuts are in danger of being engulfed in chocolate by Professor Jelly Bon Bon, the ace confectioner with his giant nutcrackers and terrifying chocolate-squirting machine. The notion is amusing, but not to the nuts who are in danger of dying. The children see the situation from the point of view of the nuts; it is a matter of life and death, a potential tragedy. For a director to deny the importance of this situation by encouraging the actors to play it superficially or jokily is sabotage, a pointless dilution of a highly dramatic, exciting idea which cries out to be played for real.

Furthermore, in the case of Seagull in *The Selfish Shellfish*, it is well known that if a bird tangles with an oil slick, it is sadly doomed. It would be wrong for the director to pretend otherwise by trivializing or glossing over Seagull's death. Tragedy is not out of place in children's theatre.

The Script: Interpretation and Clarity

> I think being a parent helped me to see first-hand the very magic world of story-telling. Children know every detail of a story. When they know a book character, then that is what they want to see on stage. When it comes to acting a well-known character, I felt that it must be like lifting the picture off the page and giving it life.
>
> Leni Harper, Meg in *Meg and Mog Show*

The director's job is constantly to monitor certain basics: pace, audibility, clarity of ideas and speech and sincerity of playing. The challenge is to sustain the audience's interest, ensure comprehension, emotionally involve them, make them laugh, be moved and feel concerned for the action. Part of the director's job is to ensure that the meaning of every line, movement and action is clearly understood by a young audience witnessing the performance for the first and only time. The logical exposition of the story is all-important. If children can't understand what is happening they will soon turn off.

The director must always make sure, from scene to scene, that the actors understand where their characters are in the story, and how they should develop as the plot proceeds. Nothing must detract from the through-line of the story. For example, in the opening scenes of *The BFG*, Sophie and the Big Friendly Giant get to know each other. Sophie, having been snatched away from the orphanage, is clearly in a state of shock. The BFG should be quite frightening and a potential threat at this stage. Will he harm Sophie? Will he eat her? There should be no clues at this stage that the two will form a bond of friendship and co-operation. Yet I once saw a production of the play in which these opening scenes were played in a very friendly, almost joky manner. There was no sense of danger. This meant that the actors had nowhere to go. Friendship had been established too early. The story was not served well and the audience missed a vital part of the developing relationship.

A skilled director uses directness and simplicity. If you are tempted to try being clever or tricksy, be very careful. Don't try to overload a scene with subtexts or hidden meanings. And sometimes in a script there are no layers to pull back. For example, in *The Witches* there is a scene in which Grandmother and Boy are on a boat sailing to England. They are discussing the subject of witches. The scene contains important information which the audience needs in order to appreciate later developments. It should be simply played, with Grandmother and Boy leaning on the ship's rail. In a Dutch production of the play, the director decided to introduce another character into the scene. A woman was leaning over the rail near by. As the scene progressed, she scratched under her wig and began sniffing, to suggest that she could smell a child. These clues led the audience to suppose that she must be a witch. Fair enough, but the whole purpose of the scene was changed. The audience didn't listen attentively to the important dialogue. They naturally concentrated on the witch, wondering what she was going to do. Was she going to try to kidnap Boy? She wasn't, of course, and we never saw her again in the production. This piece of invention was destructive because it took away from the clarity of purpose intended in the scene.

Another aspect of clarity involves sharing the play with the audience. This is a technique for involving the children in the development of the story. This can sometimes be attained by speaking strategic lines 'out front'. The actor should not look directly at the audience, as though expecting them to contribute, rather look out above their heads when considering a situation or coming to a definite decision. Sudden ideas and realizations can be played in this way. It helps break down the barrier between auditorium and stage and means that important statements will be more clearly understood. If you are directing a play where the main character is telling a story, make this main character give the audience a clue when the story is about to go into a different area. Any new information needs to be acted with urgency.

The director will find it worthwhile to underline in the script the first mentions of any characters, locations or important ideas, and to encourage the actors to emphasize them clearly.

Sincerity

In workshops I sometimes use a short scene from *The Gingerbread Man* to illustrate what I mean by sincerity. The Gingerbread Man has been found lying inert on the worktop of the dresser. Salt, Pepper and Cuckoo realize that he will not 'wake up' until he has a face. They search for currants for his nose and eyes and a piece of glacé cherry for his mouth, sit the Gingerbread Man on the rolling pin and 'create' his face. The Gingerbread Man sits with his back to the audience, so that we don't see the face until he comes to life and turns round.

HERR VON CUCKOO: One eye.
SALT: Aye.
HERR VON CUCKOO: Two eyes.
SALT: Aye, aye.
HERR VON CUCKOO: Three eyes.
SALT AND PEPPER: No!
HERR VON CUCKOO: One nose. One mouth.

The scene looks very simple. It's just a case of pressing in the currants and cherry. Most students, when attempting the scene for the first time, will play it in a matter-of-fact or joky way. They'll pick up the pun on the word 'eye', and find funny the idea that Cuckoo rather stupidly nearly gives the Gingerbread Man a third eye rather than a nose.

But on closer examination, there is much more to be found in this scene. The scene is transformed when played with great concentration and intensity. There is nothing matter-of-fact about what they are doing. They have never done it before. The audience are anticipating the coming-to-life of the Gingerbread Man. Will he be nice? Will he be nasty? The characters should also be aware of the potential danger of the situation. Are they creating a monster? They need to approach the task almost artistically, wanting to make sure they position the currants and the cherry correctly. When Cuckoo nearly gives the Gingerbread Man three eyes, the others should rush to correct him with a serious suddenly of concern, rather than laughing at silly old Cuckoo getting it wrong. All three should display a growing admiration for the face as it develops and an excitement and anticipation as it is finished. The more pleasure and pride they get from the task, the more the audience will become involved and eagerly await the moment when they see the face for themselves. The scene is fun, yes, but more fun when played with a serious tension. Music can punctuate the positioning of each eye and build to a climax as the mouth is positioned. The scene may be very short on paper but it is a vital part of the story and the director must give it full emphasis.

This example shows how easy it is to go on first impressions and miss the whole power of the writer's scene. The more fantasy-based the writing, the more 'real' the performances must be. The characterizations may be large and eccentric, but the situations and concerns of the characters must be taken seriously. Every character, whether human, animal or inanimate, will be expressing human emotions, fears and joys. The play will only come alive and involve the audience if the actors are playing it 'for real'. The director must always look for the reality within the fantasy and not be afraid to encourage the actors to find a truthfully sincere level of performance.

I have often seen amateur productions which I consider more effective and faithful to the playwright's intention than professional ones. The sets may be less lavish, the production may be raw and less tight, and the actors' skills in movement, dancing or singing might not be above average, yet the power of the story-telling and the resulting audience appreciation is greater because they play the lines simply and sincerely without sending up the whole thing.

Characterization

For several years my career focused more on professional acting than writing. I performed in many adult plays on stage and on television. I found that very often at the read-through and in the early stages of rehearsal the more experienced actors gave very little indication of the characterizations they would eventually adopt. They spoke their lines without much expression, aiming, as rehearsals progressed, to develop their own ideas and those of the director from a blank canvas. They realized that first impressions of the role were not necessarily helpful. They didn't want to plunge in with a simple caricature, rather grow gradually towards a rounded character.

A children's play demands a somewhat different approach. The director should encourage the actors swiftly to find several basic, obvious aspects of their characters and play them to the hilt, even at an early stage of rehearsal. As we have seen, most children's plays have boldly drawn characters whose basic traits establish themselves early on in the story. This helps the children know immediately what the characters are like, which leads to clarity of understanding and instant involvement in the action. This does not mean that the characters will not develop and maybe change their attitudes by the end of the play, but quickly sets up the basic premise of the story.

For instance, in *The Selfish Shellfish*, the Great Slick is a villainous oil slick. His villainy and oily quality need to be boldly drawn from the start. In *The Plotters of Cabbage Patch Corner*, the Red Admiral is pompously authoritative and posh. Salt in *The Gingerbread Man* is a jolly sailor. Encouraging the actors to find these basic qualities early in rehearsal is essential. The actors may sometimes feel that they are being asked to provide merely caricature performances, but it should be pointed out to them that these basics are merely the essential starting point. In the early stages of rehearsal the director should not be looking for too much subtlety. Villains must be played as villains and the audience needs to understand that they are evil. A cheeky character must be played cheekily. A friendly character must be overtly friendly. This will help the audience know how to react to the characters, picking up their strengths and weaknesses and becoming involved in their actions.

For this reason, the director should avoid using actors who insist on working internally or in too cerebral a manner. They may be unwilling to let go, to act with the big, bold brushstrokes the work needs. They may also find difficulty later in communicating with the audience. Such actors may be worried that this initial approach is too 'obvious'. Just because a character is called 'Mussel', they won't want to play the part too overtly as a muscle-bound strong man. It is true that by the time the production opens, the character will have developed other characteristics and sensitivities, but unless that basic sense of brawn rather than brain is immediately apparent, the rest will not follow naturally. The basics should not be watered down or smoothed over.

The actor must be encouraged to see things from a child's point of view. For example, a child will have a fairly fixed idea of what a witch might look and sound like. Roald Dahl's witches are, of course, exceptions, and therein lies their strength. But most children will perceive a witch as a crone dressed in a black cloak and pointed hat, with a sinister, whiny, snarly voice. An actress playing a witch should use that obvious interpretation as a starting point. Sometimes in auditions I ask an actress to imagine she is playing a witch on the radio rather than in the theatre. I ask her to read in a voice which would leave no child in doubt as to what she was, even without being able to see her. The actress who can deliver such an instant, bold characterization is likely to have both the bravery and the imagination to create the character successfully on stage.

Here is an example of how I would talk to an actor playing Cuckoo in
The Gingerbread Man:

> I encourage you to see the situation in human terms. Therefore, here
> you have Herr von Cuckoo whose job it is to cuckoo the time – he lives
> in a cuckoo clock, he's perfectly happy, he does his duty every day and
> comes out on the hour every hour. Suddenly, his world is blown apart
> when he comes out one morning and starts to cuckoo and finds that his
> throat is very sore. He realizes he may be losing his voice. He may lose
> it altogether which would mean he couldn't do his job properly, and
> that could well lead to the situation where he is thrown in the dustbin
> by the Big Ones, the human beings.
>
> It's happened before if something doesn't work – there was a jelly
> mould on the dresser that was cracked and it got thrown away,
> boom, in the dustbin. Nobody's ever seen it again. He doesn't know
> necessarily what the dustbin is, but it's a threat – he knows that he
> might disappear. Now if you think of that in terms of a human being,
> even you, the actor, playing the part – one day you find that you are
> losing your voice. Maybe it's going to go completely. That is your
> livelihood. That is a tragic occurrence. Unless you, the actor, feel that
> panic and that sense of desperation, and make the audience feel it,
> then the whole mainspring of the plot – which is to find a way of
> getting your voice back – isn't going to work. When we hear you say
> the line 'Ich my voice have lost', that has to be genuine and
> concerned, so that we in the audience are involved. It can't be done in
> a joky or light-hearted way because it denies the importance of the
> moment, the importance of all the things that go on in this fantasy
> world.

Directing Suddenlies

Sudden ideas, revelations, entrances, sounds, movements and changes
of mood keep the audience on their toes, forcing them to attend,
giving them no time to get distracted, making them want to know
what happens next.

Suddenlies may make the audience jump but shouldn't be forced.
They should be legitimate moments of excitement which don't allow
the audience to relax. The director can help the actors emphasize the

suddenlies and explain how important they are in involving the audience.

For example, here is a short scene from *The See-Saw Tree*. The tree folk have evacuated the tree, fearing the Big Ones will soon cut it down. Adjacent trees have already been felled and bonfires have been started. Amid the lingering smoke, the tree folk assemble at the foot of the tree, nervous and afraid, like homeless refugees. Mistlethrush perches on her improvised nest. Dunnock and Cuckoo fuss round her. (The numbers in brackets indicate suddenlies.)

MISTLETHRUSH: I think the eggs are OK. Ta ever so, Dunnock. (*to Cuckoo*) And you, dearie.

CUCKOO: Quiet, Mistlethrush. Try to rest.

MISTLETHRUSH: No, I'm very grateful. And if we come through all this, Cuckoo, feel free to dump your rotten egg on me as usual.

CUCKOO: Thank you.

(1) BAT (*tuned in*): Owl! (*after a pause*) Rabbit.

(2) RABBIT *enters, breathless*
All listen eagerly
OWL: Well?

RABBIT (*not defeated*): The field's a right old mess, Owl. They've filled in the burrow. Killed all my friends and relatives. They're burning the trees. Chaos it is, chaos.

(3) BAT (*tuned in*): Big Ones approaching.
Music

(4) *The rumble of a heavy vehicle approaching*

(5) OWL: We'd better move on.

RABBIT: No. There's nowhere to move on to. And this is the last tree. We can't let it die like the others.

SQUIRREL: Hear, hear!

OWL: But we can't stop the Big Ones.

RABBIT: Maybe not. But we can show a bit of resistance. Stand up for our home.

JAY: Go down fighting, eh?

BAT: Right on!

MISTLETHRUSH: We can't fight them.

DUNNOCK: But we can't desert our home.

RABBIT: Good for you, Dunnock. What do you say, Owl?

(6)   *The heavy vehicle stops. Doors slam. As voices are heard approaching, Owl makes her decision. Standing centre, she stretches out her hands. The others, as if mesmerized, join her. They defiantly, bravely, form a chain in front of the tree*

VOICE 2: Right, boss. Let's get it down. Charlie, how are you doing?

VOICE 3: Nearly ready.

The sound of machinery being unloaded

VOICE 2: Big one, this. What do we do, boss? Start up top?

VOICE 1: I reckon.

VOICE 2: Polish this one off, be home in time for tea, eh?

(7)   *Laughter. Suddenly a yellow cable swings into view*

VOICE 3: Chainsaw ready, boss.

VOICE 1: Electrics ready?

VOICE 2: Ready!

VOICE 1: OK, Charlie. Turn on.

(8)   *The ghastly noise of the chainsaw. Reflections from the savage metal glint on the faces of the tree folk. Suddenly, accompanied, as it were, by the noise of the chainsaw, they sing, loudly and defiantly*

Music

(9)   TREE FOLK (*singing*): Save our tree
                             Don't let it fall
                             Save our tree
                             Save us all.
                             Save its trunk
                             And leafy dome
                             Save our tree
                             Save our home.

Look again at the nine suddenlies in this scene:

(1) Bat interrupts the conversation, having picked up something on his radar. All freeze until he announces who is coming.

(2) Rabbit enters, in a sorry state.

(3) Bat interrupts again. All freeze. This time he picks up the fact that the Big Ones are approaching, which instils fear into the others.

(4) A sound cue suddenly. Frightening rumble noise.

(5) Owl suddenly breaks the tension with her line. The next nine lines are all suddenlies of a kind. The tree folk discuss what to do. New ideas. Sudden uncertainties. Discussion. Sudden rays of hope. Sudden hopelessness. The argument swings back and forth.

(6) More suddenly sound cues. Doors and voices.

(7) A visual suddenly as the cable swings into view. The tree folk react in fright.

(8) Another suddenly sound cue. The ghastly noise of the chainsaw.

(9) The tree folk suddenly galvanize themselves into protest action and song.

If all those suddenlies are played to the full, I defy the audience to get bored or to remain indifferent to the plight of the tree folk. If the scene is played for real, it must grab the children's attention. I have chosen a 'busy' scene on purpose to highlight the suddenlies theory, but directors will find it useful all through the play.

Directing Climaxes

To help keep the momentum of the play going, the director should look for sequences of dialogue or action which build to a climax. The actors should be encouraged to find a rhythm in these builds, precisely catching the meaning and level of each moment.

Some climaxes are obvious. The build-up to the end of Act One of *The BFG* involves the Giants preparing to travel to England to find children to eat. They freeze in stylized fashion while Sophie and the BFG work out a plan whereby the Giants' intentions can be foiled. To keep up the tension and excitement, it is important that the BFG and Sophie play the scene with great urgency and intensity, mixing the special dream they will blow into the Queen's bedroom window, and preparing to leave in pursuit of the Giants. A musical pulse helps keep up the tension. Finally the Giants unfreeze and set off, pursued in silhouette by the BFG and Sophie. A further build occurs as Buckingham Palace appears and the curtain falls.

More subtle climaxes can often be found within scenes. When characters are discussing a situation or a possible course of action, the combination of climaxes and suddenlies breathes life, energy and variation of pace into the scene.

Here is an excerpt from *The Selfish Shellfish*. The Great (oil) Slick is approaching the rock pool. The creatures are in danger. They discuss what to do. I've divided the scene into four sections:

(1) MUSSEL: What are we going to do, H.C.?

H.C. (*crossly*): How should I know?

STARFISH: Please, H.C., you're a thinker, aren't you?

H.C. nods

Then think of a plan. Quick.

H.C. (*standing*): Very well, I'll try. Now . . . he's had no message from Sludge, right?

URCHIN: Right.

H.C.: So he might not come.

STARFISH: Right.

H.C.: On the other hand, he might come *looking* for Sludge.

MUSSEL: Right.

H.C.: And even if he doesn't, he still poses a future threat.

MUSSEL: He could destroy the rock pool.

STARFISH: He could destroy *us*.

(2) H.C.: But aren't we safe up here?

MUSSEL: Hopefully, yes, but with a strong tide anything's possible.

Pause

H.C.: There's only one thing for it.

STARFISH: Yes?

H.C.: We must invite him to come. Send a message on his drum.

URCHIN: I could do that. I heard Sludge do it last night.

H.C.: Excellent.

MUSSEL: But why, H.C.? Why invite him to come?

H.C.: Because we've got to get rid of him once and for ever.
STARFISH: Yes, but how?

(3)   H.C.: You said he came last night.
STARFISH: Yes.
H.C.: What made him leave? Why didn't he destroy the rock pool there and then?
URCHIN: Of course, the storm!
H.C.: The storm. I see.
MUSSEL: The wind made the tide turn. The Great Slick was carried off with it.
H.C. (*having an idea*): There must be another storm. A storm so violent he'll never dare to return.

(4)   STARFISH: But we can't just make a storm happen.
Pause. Urchin suddenly turns to the audience
URCHIN: *We* can't. But *they* could!
H.C.: How?
URCHIN: They could make *noises* like a storm. Big, frightening noises. (*to the audience*) Will you help us again?
AUDIENCE: Yes.
URCHIN: You will?
AUDIENCE: Yes!
URCHIN: Thank you.
H.C.: Excellent. Let's get organized.

The scene already has a built-in tension. The creatures know they have to do something. Otherwise their lives are in danger.

Each section marked provides a separate climax.

In section 1, H.C. sums up the situation. His thoughts build logically and each thought is confirmed by another character. Mussel and Starfish continue the build, ending with the devastating thought, 'He could destroy *us*'.

H.C.'s flow has been interrupted. He brings in a new thought – the fact that they may not be safe where they are. Then there is a suddenly, as H.C. has an idea. He exclaims, 'There's only one thing for it.' Another build towards a climax begins as H.C. sets out his plan. Urchin joins in with enthusiasm – another suddenly – 'I could do that.' The build continues until the climax is reached with Starfish's desperate question, 'Yes, but how?' In effect, she pulls the rug from under H.C. He has thought of a plan, but still has no idea how to get it started.

Thus a third sequence begins. H.C. carefully thinks 'in the moment'. The others make contributions. The climax comes as H.C. triumphantly cries, 'There must be another storm.'

Again, the rug is pulled from under him as Starfish points out that they cannot just make a storm happen.

Then another suddenly starts another build as Urchin introduces the idea that the audience might help. Using the audience, who are asked to shout out their willingness to help, this sequence builds through to H.C.'s climax, 'Excellent. Let's get organized.'

The twists and turns of this scene, the highs and lows, the desperate quest to find a way out of a life-threatening situation – all must be played with truth and energy, clearly setting out the development of the idea. A sense of climax gives variety and texture to what otherwise might be rather a static, wordy scene.

Positive Negative

To keep up the energy levels, the director needs to help the cast play negative statements positively.

Imagine the different ways an actor could interpret the line 'I'm so unhappy, I don't know what to do.' The thought behind the line is clearly negative. The speaker is upset, maybe desperate. It would be possible to play the line tearfully, defeatedly, in a whisper or in a state of hopelessness. Such interpretations might be ideal for an adult play, but in a children's play the actors should be encouraged to play the line – albeit negative – positively. It should be given the same emphasis and energy as a line like 'I'm so happy. I've never been so happy in my life!' By playing a negative line positively, it gives it negative strength rather than negative weakness, and thus keeps the attention of the audience.

Here is a short scene from *The Gingerbread Man*. The cantankerous Old Bag on the top shelf of the dresser has been visited by the Gingerbread Man, who wants some of her honey to cure Cuckoo's sore throat. (The numbers in brackets indicate the positive negatives.)

OLD BAG: I mean you're not getting him any. I'm glad, delighted he's lost his voice. I've always hated that stupid noise every hour of the day and night. 'Cuckoo, Cuckoo, Cuckoo.' Now perhaps I can get a bit of peace and quiet.

GINGERBREAD MAN: But the Big Ones may throw him in the Dustbin.

OLD BAG: Good riddance. And good riddance to you, too. Clear off. (to the audience) And *you* can clear off too. All of you.

GINGERBREAD MAN: What have *they* done?

(1) OLD BAG: They don't like me.

GINGERBREAD MAN: How do you know?

(2) OLD BAG: Nobody likes me. I'm all alone. All the other tea bags in my packet were used up ages ago. The Big Ones missed me and I hid in the teapot. No-one ever visits me.

GINGERBREAD MAN: Well, it's not easy getting here.

(3) OLD BAG: It's not easy *living* here.

GINGERBREAD MAN: Are you lonely?

(4) OLD BAG: I never said that.

GINGERBREAD MAN: I'll be your friend, if you like.

(5) OLD BAG: Huh. Bribery. Get round me. Let's be friends. Then I give you the honey. Whoosh, down. Never see you again.

GINGERBREAD MAN: No! We'll all be your friends. (*encouraging the audience to shout 'Yes'*) Won't we?

OLD BAG: Don't believe it.

GINGERBREAD MAN: Why not?

OLD BAG: People have to like you to be friends with you.

Look again at the five positive negatives. I have seen productions where the actress has overtly played these lines for sympathy, speaking them rather coyly and negatively. It works far better if her complaint of unfair treatment is played with positive petulance and resentment; this is much stronger. It still might gain some sympathy for the Old Bag, but it is not over-sentimental, and will not shift the scene into the area of pantomime, where the audience would be encouraged to say 'Aaaaaaah!'

Humour

Creating laughter in the theatre is always rewarding. As discussed earlier, children do not always laugh at the same things as adults. Children differ from adults in that they enjoy repetition, particularly when the humour is physical. Plus, while much adult humour revolves around language – witty remarks, irony and clever turns of phrase – these are not enough for children. Children enjoy word play such as spoonerisms, nonsense words, puns and jokes, but humour from characterization, movement and recognition is just as important. A skilled director will make sure the production stays within the realm of children's humour.

Roald Dahl recognized that children enjoy anarchic humour. In my production of *The BFG*, the biggest laughs came in the scenes where fun was poked at figures of authority. Children loved it when the pompous heads of the Army and Air Force, summoned by the Queen, laughingly dismissed the notion of giants and then got a huge shock when they turned to see the BFG. They loved it when a child in class was able to 'fluence' a teacher and make her dance in an extrovert manner; it was even funnier when the headteacher arrived, told off the teacher for her disgraceful behaviour in class, but then was 'fluenced' himself. Needless to say, the BFG's whizzpoppers caused much hilarity too. Such scenes need to be directed with gusto and a sense of the ridiculous.

Highlight the humorous ideas based on things that children will recognize, such as arguments between parents and naughty children. The problems of getting dressed were very familiar to the children who laughed at Noddy mistakenly putting both legs in one trouser leg.

Children find the downfall of a villain very funny, but make sure that the actor paves the way for a fall by being excitably triumphant beforehand. The greater his confidence and cockiness, the bigger and funnier his come-uppance. Stylized chases and knockabout falls always work well, as long as they are integrated to the action. I have often found that it is the actor's reaction to the fall that is funnier than the fall itself.

Explore the humour that springs naturally from the situation – unexpected funny happenings, pulling the rug from under a pompous character, the audience knowing in advance that something untoward is about to happen.

Emphasize the humour rising from language – playing with words, rhyming, using nonsense words and spoonerisms.

Create humour through movement, for example, stylized fights or chases can employ clowning techniques. Pure slapstick comedy from the world of the circus can be appropriate.

Avoid putting in so-called theatre in-jokes which the children cannot be expected to understand. I don't mean blue jokes or innuendo, which certainly have no valid place in a children's play. I mean inventive 'gags' such as the one used in a production I once saw of *The Gingerbread Man*. The villainous Sleek the Mouse entered, showing off and asserting his authority. He was lit by a follow-spot. Just as he was making sure the audience knew who was boss, the follow-spot moved, leaving him in the dark. Trying to assert his authority, he called the follow-spot back. It came, but moved again. The gag was repeated several times. In fact it is an old music hall gag which works very well with adults, but the children in the audience were totally confused. They turned round to see the source of the light. Some of them may have wondered if it was meant to be the moon shining down. But every one of them was confused as to why this light was moving, and, when Sleek ordered it back on him, they wondered who he was talking to. The joke was out of context. It was a theatre in-joke. It not only had nothing to do with the story, but it caused a real problem for the actors in that it took them quite some time to retrieve the attention of the audience.

Audience Participation

Some children's theatre practitioners completely avoid the use of audience participation. Perhaps they feel it smacks too much of

pantomime – 'He's behind you!' or 'Oh yes I will, oh no you won't!'
But children do enjoy joining in, and provided participation is used
creatively and not simply to whip up the audience into a frenzied state
of hysteria, it is worth directors considering using it sparingly and
orchestrating it carefully. There are four basic uses for audience
participation.

1. Getting ideas or information

If a character is confronted with something he has never seen before
or doesn't understand, and if that something is recognizable to the
audience, there is every reason for asking the audience what it is. It
gets them involved. They enjoy helping and showing off their
knowledge. For example, in *The Ideal Gnome Expedition*, the
innocent Gnomes rescue a clockwork toy from the dustbin. They
have never seen anything like it. The audience tell them it is a duck.
Similarly, when asked, the audience inform the Gnomes that the
sudden circle of light that hits them is caused by a street lamp, and
that the things that roar dangerously past them when they are trying
to cross a road are cars. The dresser folk in *The Gingerbread Man*
have never seen a gingerbread man before. When they find one, what
could be more natural than to ask the audience what it is. It is
essential that actors stay in character when these requests are made,
rather than appear to step outside the action.

Once the audience have been given to understand that they are
allowed to make a contribution to the play in this way, the danger is
that they will answer any other question that happens to come up in
the dialogue. One way of avoiding this is for the director to give clear
directions to the actors that if they are not actively searching for an
answer, they should keep their eyes averted from the audience when
asking the question.

The first time a character directly asks the audience a question, he
may get rather a muted response. An initial shyness or uncertainty
will make the audience hesitate. It is then advisable for the actor to
repeat the question or, as though unable to understand, to say, 'I beg
your pardon?' This will often make the audience respond with more
enthusiasm. And although audience participation should not become

a test of the actor's ability to get the audience shouting loudly, nevertheless a good solid response is always welcome.

2. Warnings

An audience will always be willing to help the characters by giving warnings of impending danger. If a character is unaware of the approach of a 'baddie', and if the principle of audience participation has already been established, the likelihood is that a warning cry will echo from the auditorium unasked for. This is always a good sign, because it means that the audience have become involved with the action and instinctively want to keep the characters they identify with out of danger.

Directors can help such moments by not rushing them. Make sure that the audience can clearly see the 'baddie' enter, let him signify his intentions of, say, catching the 'goodie', and then, with exaggerated paces, set off with relish. This should achieve the desired response. Such audience participation often depends on a form of dramatic irony, whereby the audience knows something that the characters do not. Such knowledge is enjoyable to the audience, and children will be only too willing to share it.

3. Asking for help

Another form of audience participation is asking for direct help. Here are three examples: In *The Owl and the Pussycat Went to See ...* , Owl, Pussycat, the Quangle Wangle and the Runcible Spoon are on their journey to find a ring and someone to conduct the wedding ceremony. When they get tired, they want to go to sleep. But they are worried that the Plum Pudding Flea, who has expressed his desire to eat Owl and Pussycat, might suddenly arrive. They ask the audience to warn them if he comes. The audience willingly obliges. In *The Ideal Gnome Expedition,* Chips the Cat asks the audience to help him teach the principles of road safety to the Gnomes. This is done by teaching them a song, which they in turn teach the Gnomes. In *Noddy,* when Big Ears' magic spell fails to work, he asks the audience to join in the words. Because of their help, the spell works. This gives the audience a feeling of achievement, and really does make them a part of the action.

4. Set Pieces

Sometimes the help required is more elaborate. It involves rehearsing the audience in a sequence of lines, noises or movements. Such set pieces provide the ultimate sense of involvement for children. I usually use them towards the end of the play, making a satisfying climax.

In *The Selfish Shellfish,* the audience create a storm to fool the Great Slick. In *Meg and Mog Show*, the audience help Meg and the witches by making springtime noises to encourage Meg's garden to grow.

In such sequences, the director must make sure that every step is taught clearly to the audience, and that a certain discipline is maintained. It is much more fun in the long run if the audience 'perform' well and in the right places, and don't anticipate by participating too early. But the actors mustn't turn into bossy schoolteachers. They must stay in character and retain the urgency of the situation which has led them to ask the audience to help. Watch out for actors going on to 'automatic' when setting up the plan and rehearsing it with the audience. The actors must keep it fresh, remembering that this is the first time they have ever had to use the plan.

Ensure that the actors don't confuse the children by asking overcomplicated or convoluted questions. Go for a good, clean reaction. Unless, of course, the whole point is that the audience is meant to divide. In *The Plotters of Cabbage Patch Corner,* some of the audience vote 'Up with the Big Ones!' and some vote 'Down with the Big Ones!' In this instance, the play is structured to take both opinions on board – indeed, the audience are merely reflecting the differing views of the characters.

Once the audience have been invited to join in, they will feel free to participate whenever they wish. It is up to the director to help the actors prevent this. The audience can 'get in' if the slightest of pauses is left between lines or even words. I have seen actors take a quick breath, only to find that the audience are shouting out. Normally their contribution is positive, but sometimes it is unwelcome. Keep up the pace and you should keep unwanted interruptions down to a minimum.

Finally, the actors should always be directed to thank the audience if they have helped. The children's co-operation can usually be guaranteed but should not be taken for granted.

The Technical Rehearsal

Most theatre folk swap nightmarish tales of technical rehearsals they have endured. The euphoria of a couple of successful run-throughs in the rehearsal room often evaporates as soon as the technical rehearsals on stage begin. There always seem to be problems with the set, with props that don't behave as expected, with entrances that seem to be in the wrong place, blocking that has to be changed, costumes that don't fit or scene changes that seem impossible.

I shall never forget, as an actor, sitting in the wings of a freezing-cold Bristol Hippodrome at three o'clock in the morning of the day of opening night. We still hadn't reached the interval and yet another problem had brought the rehearsal to a standstill.

Not surprisingly, my motto as a director is 'I hate surprises'. I spend the pre-production period aiming for the fastest and smoothest of technicals, trying to think ahead and avoid the usual problems. This has been forced upon me because schedules and budgets are tight and there is very little time to waste, particularly in children's theatre. An average schedule might involve getting-in the set and lighting it on the Sunday, spending Monday in technical rehearsals, having a dress rehearsal on the Tuesday morning and opening on the Tuesday afternoon. Taking into account the knowledge that staff overtime means considerable extra production expenditure, it becomes essential to make every effort to stay within schedule.

There will always be problems, of course. That is part of the excitement and fun of working in the theatre. But with careful pre-planning these problems can be kept to the minimum. It is worth setting down the requirements of each department because there is often a lack of liaison and that is when the dreaded 'surprises' begin to surface.

Before anyone sets foot in the theatre, a complete blueprint of the production should have been worked out. The stage management team, in consultation with the director, will know exactly what is required of them. Who will be doing what during the scene changes? Where exactly should every prop be set?

The production manager and the designer will already have communicated the technical requirements to the resident stage crew. Each flying bar will have been numbered, and they will know which flying piece should be attached to which bar, how the set will fit together and where some of it will be stored until it makes its entrance.

The lighting designer will have seen several rehearsals and worked out the lighting rig on paper so that as soon as access to the stage is possible, the electrics crew can rig the lanterns, colour them up and focus them in the right positions. The lighting designer will know the geography of the play as well as the director.

Hopefully, the costumes will have been fitted and completed well before the technical, and the wardrobe person will make sure she knows who wears what, who has to make quick changes and which side of the stage they come off in order to make them. He or she will also have watched rehearsals and know the play well.

The sound engineer, in collaboration with the sound designer, will have been in the rehearsal room too. The sound cues will have been played in rehearsal and volumes established. The sound engineer will have all the cues written down and understand what is required.

Long before the actors arrive, the director, in consultation with the stage manager, should set the positions of the scenery. Trucks and furniture which move on and off during the course of the production should be marked on the stage floor. This will save time during the technical.

Hopefully, the lighting designer will be able to do his basic plotting before the technical starts. With the director he will have worked out what each lighting cue should achieve. The stage manager, who will be cueing the lights, needs to be present at the lighting session and insert every cue into the prompt script.

The music department will make sure that the musical director has a clear view of the stage and that all the music and synthesizer settings are agreed.

The actors should arrive in good time for the technical, so that they can put on their costumes and make-up. Directors of adult plays sometimes don't insist on the actors wearing costume and make-up in the technical, because they simply want to concentrate on technical problems. But in a children's play the costumes will very often be an integral part of the performance, and it is essential that the actors get used to playing in them, and discover whether there are any adjustments or alterations that need making. This is particularly true of padded costumes and headdresses. Make-up, particularly in a fantasy-based play, is an important part of the characterization, and it is important for the director to see it under light as soon as possible, in order to be able to suggest changes.

Before the technical I explain to the actors that although the main purpose of the rehearsal is to make everything technical work smoothly, the rehearsal is for them too. If anything proves problematic or if they have important questions to raise concerning technical things, it is up to them to stop the rehearsal and ask. But they must be sensible about this. If a button comes off or if a microphone is playing up, there is no need to stop the rehearsal. The button can be sewn on later and it is likely that the sound engineer will know about the problem microphone and be trying to sort it out.

The director, too, must use the time wisely. Don't waste time directing the scene or trying to change an actor's inflection. Such things should have been done already, in the rehearsal room. If an entrance needs changing or a scene needs re-blocking because of a sight-line problem, that is a different matter. But the director should always be aware that at this rehearsal it is the technical detail that really matters.

The excitement of the technical is that, for the first time, all the elements of the production come together 'for real'. For the first time we see what it looks and sounds like. The director becomes rather like a musical conductor, co-ordinating each department, carefully putting all the elements together and trying to make them into a unified and satisfying whole.

Some directors like to sit in the auditorium alongside the lighting designer, with the choreographer and the designer close at hand. The sound designer will probably be with the sound engineer. In modern theatres everybody is in communication with each other, and with the stage manager on stage, using headsets. However, I find this rather restricting. I like to be free to move around, checking sight-lines, making sure that the action is clearly visible from all parts of the theatre.

I also like to let people know what is going on. For an actor it is frustrating to be kept waiting without knowing what the problem is. By keeping them in the picture, they become part of the process rather than pieces of scenery. I find it useful to wear round my neck a referee's whistle. A technical involves stopping and starting, and to ensure that everybody in the building knows that it is necessary to stop, I have found that a shrill whistle does the trick. Some people may think it is a sign of a power complex. Maybe it is. However, the only time I have found the whistle caused problems was when Mr Plod had one too, and every time he blew it, the technical stopped unnecessarily.

Much of the technical will be to do with timing. However exact the mark-up on the rehearsal-room floor, entrances will never be exactly the same on the real set. They must be timed carefully. The exact timing of lighting cues and sound cues must be fixed, too. The length of a fade up or down can make all the difference to the mood created. Flying cues and scene changes will need practising several times, to find the most fluent effect.

The director must watch out for any hiatuses. Try to keep it moving. Make everyone understand that the story will only be told properly if the scenes run smoothly from one to another.

After the technical, let the actors have a rest. But gather the production team round to share their impressions and notes. Do any costumes or props need modification? Is the set working smoothly? Are there any lighting cues that need re-thinking? Is there time to put things right before the dress rehearsal?

The Dress Rehearsal

The dress rehearsal of a children's production differs very little from that of an adult production. Everybody, in all departments, concentrates to deliver a performance with no stops, exactly as if an audience was 'out front'. However, if the play contains audience participation, the production team and anyone else sitting watching the proceedings will need, just as in earlier rehearsals, to respond and react in the way they think an audience of real children will join in. However much enthusiasm the adult substitutes may muster, they will never achieve the volatility and gutsiness of the real thing, and until the actual first performance, director and company will never really know exactly how the audience will react. That is all part of the challenge.

Section 3. The Opening Performance and Beyond

The first performance of any play, for adults or children, is an exciting and daunting experience for the whole production team. The actors are nervous. The director and the production team are nervous. The writer, particularly if this is the première performance, is nervous. For the first time their efforts are exposed to outsiders. The fun and adventure of the rehearsal process must be forgotten. This time it is for real. How will the audience react? Will they laugh at things we found funny in rehearsal? Will they become involved in the story? Will they find any sections tedious? Quite simply, will they enjoy it? Add to that the worry that something technical might go wrong, that an actor might not achieve a difficult costume change in time or that the stage management might forget to set that vital prop, and it becomes understandable that the first performance is living dangerously, living on the edge, as we all enter the fray.

For theatre, unlike poetry, novel writing, art or sculpture, is a collaborative medium. Many cogs drive the wheel. Each cog has a vital part to play. Any cog can make a mistake and affect the flow. Thus the challenge becomes greater. At this stage, the director has to let go of his or her baby; now it must enter the world and stand on its own two feet.

The first performance of a children's play can be even more nail-biting than its adult equivalent. The volatility of an audience of children creates even more potential hazards and unknowns. I always think of the audience as another character in the play, the final actor in the jigsaw, the actor who has never attended rehearsals. This actor may not stick to the script, is quite likely to throw in an unexpected comment and may differ considerably from the audience of partisan onlookers we had in the rehearsal room. The director will have hopefully prepared the cast for possible audience reaction. He or she, guided by the writer, will have endeavoured to anticipate audience participation, particularly in a play which needs it to propel the plot. But no director can be absolutely certain of what will happen once the new character actually arrives. And it is the director's duty to watch the first performance – and, indeed, subsequent performances – to see if any changes or improvements can be made as a result of the audience's response.

The director's job is made more complicated by the fact that no two audiences of children will react in exactly the same way. That is part of the challenge. Not only that, there are several different types of audience, all of which will pose different problems.

Let us imagine we are producing *The Gingerbread Man* for a number of performances. Some will be daytime performances, aimed at school parties. Some will be weekend or holiday performances; some of these will be daytime matinées, some will be early evening performances. The ideal age to see *The Gingerbread Man* is probably between and five and nine, although there are many children of three and four who will, without understanding it all, derive much pleasure from it; and children of ten and eleven, although they may sense that the story is a little young for them, should certainly not feel patronized by the play.

If you have been working your way through this book, you might recall my classification of different types of audience in Part 2 (pp. 15–29). As a reminder, here they are again, in more detail.

Different Types of Audience

1. The Weekday Performance for School Parties

This is my favourite. Children of the right age – lots of them. The only adults present are teachers, perhaps one teacher for every ten children. It is a special day, away from the daily routine of school. They have had an exciting trip in a coach. For many of them it is a totally new experience. They will possibly be less inhibited among their friends than they would be with their parents. When responding to the play they feel able to let go, without worrying how their parents are reacting to their reaction. They offer an honest, gut response, which can be incredibly exciting – and sometimes intimidating. I have heard teachers, before curtain up, threatening the children not to misbehave – 'If hear one word...!' I understand the teachers' concern, but believe that they should trust us; now the children are in the theatre it is our responsibility to control them and entertain them. And, in the case of *The Gingerbread Man*, if they literally keep silent, the participation will not work and the play will grind to a halt. Thankfully, if we are getting it right, the teachers have no problem once the play begins. An audience of small individuals leaping up and down, shouting with excitement before the play begins, can quickly be galvanized into an attentive whole. This audience tends to be quick and alert and will really keep the actors on their toes. They will be eager to help or hinder the characters and, entering into the spirit of the play, will often believe that their participation and involvement can affect the development and outcome of the plot. I have noticed that this alertness is sometimes greater at morning performances than afternoon performances, when the children sometimes seem to have a little less energy.

2. The Weekday After-school Performance

This normally takes place at 4.00 or 4.30 p.m. It offers the opportunity to parents to bring children whose schools have decided not to bring a party. This performance is particularly valuable in times when school budgets are tight and in areas where teachers feel unable to ask the parents for extra money for school trips. Again, it is usually one parent who brings the children, many of whom will be the ideal age for the play. However, they may be accompanied by sibling infants and babies, who will not fully comprehend the nature of a theatre visit and can certainly not be expected to sit silently throughout the whole performance. They may indeed find more enjoyment in banging the seats or scampering up and down the aisles. And the babies may well cry.

This audience can be very tough to play. In a family audience you can often hear adult voices explaining things to their children. This can be frustrating because often the explanations are quite unnecessary. 'Oh look, it's getting dark, it must be night-time!' 'Oh, look at Noddy's car. Isn't it lovely!' 'Oh dear, here comes that nasty goblin again.' Such comments are well meant, but do tend to distract other members of the audience and contribute to the surface noise in the theatre.

But this performance can be rewarding in its own right. The response may be more gentle, but the rapport with the children, as individuals rather than *en masse*, can be very endearing. And, if the actors persevere, playing with energy and sincerity, even the very young ones will become intrigued by the pictures they see and the sounds they hear, and settle down to an enjoyable afternoon, even if the complexities of the plot defeat them.

3. The Weekday Daytime Performance

Many theatres will advertise this performance to the public as well as targeting school parties. This means that a weekday daytime performance may well be attended by a number of school parties plus members of the general public. These tend to be parents and pre-school children. Normally only one parent attends, presumably because the other is at work. The pre-school child may well have infant or baby siblings, who cannot be left at home. So they come too. This audience mix can be tricky. Before the performance, the excited babble of noise from the school parties tends to be overpowering, making some of the pre-school children nervous and some of the babies cry. This sometimes continues through the performance, distracting the main bulk of children and affecting their involvement. Furthermore, a mother or father will tend to talk to the small child, either to reassure it or to explain helpfully what is happening in the story. The child will be too young to understand the story fully, but may well be enjoying the colour, the music and the general atmosphere. But running commentaries from parents cause a continual background whisper, which can be distracting to the school-party children. I often wish that school-party performances could be closed to the general public, but commercial pressures usually make this impossible.

4. The Weekend or Holiday Audience

This is my second favourite. A matinée on a Saturday or Sunday, or during school holiday-time. This performance may be attended by parties of children from Sunday schools, brownies, cubs or club outings, but the vast majority of the audience will be made up of families. Children accompanied by mothers, fathers, grandparents and other relatives, maybe a group of friends coming as a birthday treat, children for whom theatre-going has already become a regular experience and first-timers. Because most families don't want to employ a babysitter, there may well be babes in arms and infants, too. There may even be a number of adults attending without children, theatre practitioners with an interest in children's theatre or adults who enjoy witnessing children enjoying themselves. This audience has the widest variety of age. It contains more adults than a schools' performance, and the family group rather than the school party becomes the focus. The play becomes more of a shared experience between the children and parents. Younger children will happily talk to their parents, and vice versa, throughout the entire show, asking questions and sharing the experience, rather like sharing a bedtime story. When younger children get excited, they want to share that excitement with the parent. Older children may be more aloof. They may become a little embarrassed about displaying too much enthusiasm or overt reaction. And infants and babies may be a problem. I remember the opening performance of one production of *Meg and Mog Show*. My elder daughter, aged seven, was already a veteran theatre-goer, but her sister, aged three, had never been before. Within a minute of curtain up, Meg's alarm clock rang. That was enough for Rebecca. 'I don't like it,' she cried, and was immediately taken out by my long-suffering wife. This was the right action, in my view. Why force a child to be frightened? Then again, it may have been easier for us, as a family, to make that decision because we hadn't paid for the tickets. Many parents persevere with their tiny ones, in the hope that they will be won round. Many are, but some will never settle.

This audience usually has a happy buzz and genuine warmth flowing between the stage and the audience. The response may not be as 'clean' and big as from school parties, but the mix of ages and generations somehow makes the performance something special, when everyone joins in the fun and shares the ups and downs of the plot. The director must encourage the actors to sense this atmosphere of celebration; there will undoubtedly be a certain amount of surface chatter as parent and child exchange comments, but the actors must realize that this is all part of the event, and must not be put off by it. This performance, when it really swings, provides a true 'feel-good factor' for both cast and audience.

There is a danger, however, in the presence of so many adults. Sometimes they will find something funny which, to the child, is quite serious. The director must encourage the actors not to start playing to the adults rather than the children. Adding innuendo should be prohibited because the reactions of the adults can be distracting to the children. For instance, when the Gingerbread Man is castigated by the Old Bag, some adults are tempted to give a sympathetic 'Aaaaaaah' in rather a tongue-in-cheek fashion. It is a reaction often played for in pantomimes, for instance when Buttons is spurned by Cinderella. We can't stop adults doing it, and we can't stop the children being rather bemused by it, but we mustn't pander to it. In the long run, the adults will enjoy the performance much more if the children are enjoying it.

These four audiences offer very different reactions to the same play. The director must make sure the actors understand this and are not thrown by it. It can be off-putting, having played to several gutsy school-party houses, reacting vociferously in unison, then to play a family audience whose response is less immediate. The actor must realize that both reactions are valid and that probably the play is working perfectly well for both, although on stage the response will feel quite different.

5. A Note on Babes in Arms

The problem of babies and toddlers spoiling things for their older brothers and sisters has never, in my opinion, been properly addressed. It would help parents if theatres had clear guidelines on the appropriate age group for the play. Maybe there should be an announcement before the performance asking parents of little ones who become disturbed kindly to remove them from the auditorium. One ideal solution can be found in the children's theatre in Minneapolis, Minnesota, where, at the back of the circle, there is a large room, divided from the auditorium by a sound-proof plate-glass 'wall'. Parents are encouraged to take unsettled children there, where they can watch the show and hear it through loudspeakers; meanwhile, the screaming infant is no longer disturbing the rest of the audience. Polka Theatre in Wimbledon has now banned children under three from attending plays in the main auditorium, but Polka is fortunate in having a second auditorium which specializes in plays for very small children. As a practitioner I welcome the move, but recognize the fact that many parents may object until they understand the reasons. Each individual theatre needs to address the problem and find its own workable solution.

After the Opening Performance

The opening performance has been and gone. With a children's play this is likely to have been an opening morning or afternoon rather than an opening night. For the writer, actors and director there will hopefully be a feeling of exhilaration and satisfaction, but there will always be a few things that haven't gone quite as expected. Some problems, like a delayed lighting cue or a fudged scene change, can be sorted out immediately. But the director is advised, assuming the play is running for a good number of performances, to wait before making any significant changes to the production. Let the play settle and the actors find their way before launching into major adjustments.

Very often the reaction of the first audience is not truly representative. This is partly because the actors may be a little nervous, understandably. The audience may react in unexpected places or fail to react to moments that in rehearsal seemed sure-fire. But the first audience may well not be a true sample of audiences to come. The audience may be specially invited, so that it contains an unusual mix of adults and children. There may be critics out front. There may be adults on their own, connected with the production company or friends of the actors. These adults may give a false impression of future reaction, laughing or applauding in the wrong places or not wholeheartedly joining in the audience participation. Sometimes actors' friends, thinking they are being helpful, actually overdo their vocal participation, intimidating the children. The sound of hearty guffaws and adults joining in, helpfully pretending to be children, unsettles them. When the first performance of a children's play takes place in the evening it is because critics often find it difficult to come during the day. This again can mean that there are fewer children present than usual, particularly in term-time when parents do not like their children to have late nights.

The first London performance of *The Plotters of Cabbage Patch Corner* was affected in this way. There were no school parties present, so the reaction and participation was diluted. That Christmas I also had *The Owl and the Pussycat Went to See ...* on in London. It had already opened and the company was invited to the first performance of *Plotters*. They all sat together and, with the best of intentions, demonstrated their enjoyment by overreacting. I'm afraid to say that the rather 'in' laughter and loud response coming from the back of the auditorium caused the rest of the audience to clam up. I hasten to add that the general reaction to the show was not seriously affected and the critics gave us splendid reviews. But I remember wondering whether it had been a good idea to invite the *Owl* company whose good intentions, rooting for the new play, nearly backfired.

Interpreting Audience Reaction

At the end of a performance of an adult production, it may be difficult to gauge quite how much the audience enjoyed it. If it is a comedy, the amount of laughter will be a good guide, but in a straight play the audience will remain passive and quiet whether or not they are responding with pleasure. A children's audience is different. Hopefully they will react with laughter and, sometimes, participation. But if the play or production is not working, they are likely to become restless, to talk and even to want to leave the auditorium to go to the lavatory. Conversely, they may voice such vociferous disapproval towards a villainous character that it becomes difficult to stop them and continue the play.

This volatility is a tremendous help to the director and the actors in ascertaining where the problems lie, where any dead patches may lurk, and where some fine tuning is necessary.

1. Restlessness

If restlessness starts in the middle of a scene, continues for a while, then subsides as a new scene begins or an exciting suddenly grabs the attention of the audience once more, then the following possibilities may help to locate the problem: too wordy – too static – lack of clarity – lack of focus – audibility problems – unhelpful lighting – songs not working – legitimate restlessness.

Too wordy

If the play is generally working well, and the restless patch is an isolated one, it may well be that the scene is too wordy or too static. Because I normally direct my own plays, I'm lucky in that I can adjust the dialogue, making cuts if necessary, without an angry writer complaining that I am ruining his or her work. But most writers do not object to a little judicious cutting, as long as the clarity of the scene is maintained.

Too static

If the scene does seem too static, see if there are any legitimate ways of making it more physical. See if you can find any suddenlies in the dialogue which can be emphasized with movement and 'new idea' exclamations.

Lack of clarity

If the scene carries important plot information, check that it is being played clearly. Are the audience really understanding what is going on? If not, it could well be that the pacing of the scene needs looking at. Maybe important points are not being stressed adequately. Maybe the actors, trying hard to prevent the audience becoming restless or interrupting, have forced the pace too much. Maybe they need to slow down their delivery. This does not mean they should allow unnecessary pauses between the lines, but they should be encouraged to present the developing story-line clearly and deliberately.

Lack of focus

Check whether, in the blocking, the focus of the scene has been properly established. Are the actors in good positions? Are they too far upstage? Is there anything else going on at the same time as the dialogue which is distracting the audience?

Audibility problems

A more basic question is, can the audience hear the scene properly? Is there a problem with the sound? Are all the microphones and speakers working? Is the balance correct between the spoken word and the musical underscoring or is the music drowning the voices? Has there recently been a very loud sound effect or a vociferous piece of audience participation which has made the dialogue sound too soft? Can the actors project more? Certainly, if the audience can't hear properly, they can't be expected to follow the scene. Actors normally have no problem with voice projection, but in a children's production they need to use it well.

Unhelpful lighting

The lighting designer may need to pin-point more precisely the area of the stage where the scene is taking place. To light such a scene in general coverage lighting, particularly when there are areas of the stage or characters that do not need to be lit, makes it difficult for the audience to focus attention in the right place. Make it easy for the audience. Make them look where you want them to look.

Another problem might be the lighting levels. In some of my productions, in order to achieve an exciting atmosphere, I will ask the lighting designer to keep the lights fairly low. This can sometimes be counter-productive. If the actors' faces cannot be seen, it is more difficult to follow their speech. Somehow children – and adults, I suspect – need to see mouths moving to register immediately what is being said. So maybe you need to increase the level of the lighting by a few points. This may sacrifice some of the atmosphere, but far better to do that than lose the dialogue and thus lose the audience.

Sometimes children will react to lighting very differently from adults. It may be tempting to have a complicated lighting plot simply for the sake of it, but the lighting should always enhance the narrative rather than obscure it. In *The Selfish Shellfish*, we had a lighthouse on the horizon behind the rock pool, looking as though it was miles out to sea. In one scene, the lighting faded very slowly, over a period of several minutes, to suggest the onset of darkness. The lighting designer thought, to his credit, how effective it would be if a small speck of light were to shine from the lighthouse, becoming more noticeable as the main lighting decreased. It worked beautifully. In the dress rehearsal we were most impressed. But in performance this one tiny pin-prick of light became so interesting to the children that they commented on it and discussed it all through the important dialogue running through the scene. In the end we had to change the timing of the cue so that the lighthouse lit up at a moment when nothing else was happening.

Songs not working

Sometimes children become restless during songs, particularly if the songs are not driving the story forward. This does not necessarily mean that the song is bad or that the performances are not good enough. It could well mean that the song is too long and would benefit from having a verse and chorus cut. Or it could mean that the song is in the wrong place in terms of the developing audience involvement.

For example, in *The Gingerbread Man* there is a song called 'The Dresser Hop'. It is quite early in the play and establishes the fact that every night the dresser folk meet up on the worktop for some fun and a dance. In truth, the information contained in the song is not vital to an understanding of the plot. Over a period of fifteen years I directed the play many times, always feeling in my heart that the audience was not really very interested in the song. The Gingerbread Man, the character the children have come to see, has not yet appeared on stage. The song holds up his arrival. As a result the audience was turning off slightly. But I liked the song. I still do. So I resolutely refused to make a radical change. Eventually, I decided to take the plunge and cut the song altogether. This necessitated changing only one line of dialogue. The effect was almost magical. The story-line was sustained so much better. The audience stayed with it. There was no restlessness. It may have taken fifteen years, and I personally regret the loss of the song, but I know it was the right decision.

Legitimate restlessness

It is worth keeping in mind that in some instances, the children's restlessness will be perfectly legitimate. In fact it is not restlessness at all, rather an enthusiastic rustle of approval. In such situations the director need not change anything. But it may be an idea to explain what has happened to the actors, so that they can ride over the moment confidently, knowing that all is well. For instance, after a particularly exciting piece of action or a theatrically visual surprise, the children will enthusiastically comment upon it to each other. This reaction is certainly not boredom, rather the reverse. In *The BFG*, when the glowing dream jars are first revealed, their magical visual quality usually inspires a gasp, followed by excited whispers. Such a moment is gold dust and should not be trampled on; it must be allowed to breathe.

In *Rupert and the Green Dragon*, the appearance of the Baby Squirrels was always greeted with delighted squeals and laughter. During the first few performances, I was pleased by the reaction, but concerned that the subsequent dialogue, even though it wasn't important plot-wise, was getting lost. The solution proved simple. In the script I had written the following:

SQUIRREL: It's warm enough for my babies to leave the nest. (*calling*) Come along, babies.
The Baby Squirrels, squeaking noisily, appear on the branch
They loved your peanut butter sandwich, Rupert. Thank you.

The second half of the speech was getting lost. All we had to do was to delay the entry of the Baby Squirrels, so that, in the published version of the play, I changed the text as follows:

SQUIRREL: It's warm enough for my babies to leave the nest. (*calling*) Come along, babies. They loved your peanut butter sandwich, Rupert. Thank you.
The Baby Squirrels, squeaking noisily, appear on the branch

In this way, the audience reaction to the Baby Squirrels came as Rupert said goodbye to Squirrel and set off for home. The audience reaction continued nicely until Rupert arrived in the next scene.

2. Comments Made by the Children

The director can also learn a lot from the comments made by the children in the interval and after the show. I often hover in the auditorium or the foyer listening to comments. Children tend to be positive rather than critical. They talk about the things they liked. For instance, the way Bat was hanging upside down on the tree in *The See-Saw Tree*, or the way the frobscottle bottle in *The BFG* had bubbles which went down instead of up, or the way a silken cloth was used to represent the tide coming in and going out in *The Selfish Shellfish*.

Sometimes children eagerly discuss the problems raised in the play or speculate on what will happen in the second half. I remember a performance of *The Plotters of Cabbage Patch Corner*, in which the audience are encouraged to make up their minds whether they think the behaviour of the Big Ones is acceptable. In the interval I went to the gents', and found three boys cornering a fourth rather threateningly, eagerly asking him, 'Are you Up with the Big Ones, or Down with the Big Ones?' I waited to see that the poor child wasn't bullied for his beliefs, then came out rather pleased that the play was causing such debate.

It is not often that the children will actually criticize something they didn't like. I often wish they would. Perhaps it is their lack of critical faculty that makes them react positively rather than negatively when it comes to a discussion. But I have sometimes overheard questions indicating that they haven't quite understood something. 'Why did Blotch have that blue mark on his shirt?' asked a child after a performance of *The Papertown Paperchase*. He hadn't realized that Blotch was made of blotting paper, and had been 'wounded' by a splash of ink from the Ink Well in Papertown Square. Perhaps the child had never come across blotting paper, although when the play was written it was still in daily use. As a result of his comment, I slightly changed a couple of lines introducing the character, attempting to make it clearer.

Sometimes a child will pick up on a logical flaw, which none of us has spotted in rehearsal. For example, in *The Gingerbread Man*, there is an elaborate set piece in which the Gingerbread Man is hoisted with a rope up to the top shelf. He had been unable simply to jump up and climb on. But in the interval I heard a child saying that surely he could have stood on the rolling pin and reached the shelf with ease. I realized that at this point in the play the rolling pin was very close to the shelf. I didn't want to lose the sequence with the rope, so simply found a way in which the rolling pin was positioned much further downstage. This meant that it was henceforth unlikely that anyone would connect the rolling pin to the shelf, and the rope solution was now both logical and acceptable.

3. Audience Participation
The whole area of audience participation needs monitoring carefully. The director must check that it is working successfully, and if not, ascertain why not.

Audience participation should never become rabble-rousing, and the director should always nip such excesses in the bud. The director needs to ask: are the actors communicating it clearly enough? If not, they should be asked to be firmer with the audience, really spelling out the intention. This must not involve coming out of character, but demands a brave, determined approach. Or perhaps the participation is getting out of hand because the audience are becoming over-excited. If so, perhaps the whole sequence needs toning down somewhat. Perhaps the actors are pushing too hard and giving the audience the impression that they want them to go over the top. Toning down can quite easily be achieved simply by moderating the tone of voice or the intensity of feeling.

For instance, in *The Gingerbread Man* there is a sequence where the Old Bag threatens the audience. This is always a dangerous thing to do. In the scene, she tries to prove that the audience don't like her. She does this by asking how many children like to drink tea, rather than a fizzy drink. The idea is that because on the whole children don't like tea, they don't like her. Over the years I have had to moderate the scene, partly because today's children react with less inhibition than when the play was written and they tend to respond with reasonable vehemence. The fun of audience participation is lost when the antagonism becomes too real. Another reason for modifying this scene was that, as the years have gone by, it has become noticeable that more and more children actually profess to like drinking tea. Whether this is a form of bravado on their part, or a genuine change in children's taste buds, is immaterial. The fact is, when the scene didn't work, it was necessary to change it.

Occasionally an audience-participation sequence will not work unless certain obvious pointers have been carefully put in place. One device I have used several times involves a character being asked to guard something in case a 'baddie' approaches. The character then proceeds to fall asleep. The audience will usually shout out to wake up the character. The business is usually repeated two or three times, before the character finally goes to sleep and the 'baddie' appears. This leads to pandemonium and excitement in the audience, until the character wakes up and some sort of chase or action sequence begins.

As the writer and director, I try not to be too blatant or obvious when making the request to the audience to keep watch. In *The Owl and the Pussycat Went to See ...*, the Quangle Wangle says he will stay awake to guard the others. The Runcible Spoon suspects that he, too, will go to sleep. The audience pick up from her the likelihood of a problem and, without much encouragement, shout out the moment the Quangle Wangle yawns. In *The Ideal Gnome Expedition*, one of the Gnomes goes to sleep while looking after the Clockwork Duck. The audience are not asked to help, but automatically start shouting when Chips the Cat appears and threatens the Duck.

But when I used the same device in *More Adventures of Noddy*, leaving Bumpy Dog to guard Noddy's house in case Sly the Goblin comes, I had bargained for a slightly older audience. Very young children did not automatically shout to Bumpy Dog to 'Wake up'. This necessitated adding a line for Tessie Bear, as she and Noddy set off in the car. She said, 'And don't go to sleep!' I didn't really want to put this line in, because I felt it was signalling the audience too much. But, for that younger age group, it proved essential.

Directors should note than pre-school children need a more gentle introduction into audience participation than older children. The actors should be directed to take their time to gain the audience's confidence, if necessary repeating a question to encourage a more positive response. But coming out of character and using a patronizing approach should obviously be avoided.

It is only after seeing the play with an audience that you realize, as the director, some of the things you hadn't thought of. Silly things such as asking the audience to do something, but not letting them know when to stop doing it. This is normally self-evident, but not always. In *Save the Human*, the audience of school parties were invited to bring to the theatre an animal mask that they had made at school. During the performance, in the Conference of Animals scene, the audience were invited to put on their masks to become animals at the Conference. In rehearsal, I had forgotten to put in a line asking them to take off the masks. This resulted in many children keeping them on during the next scene and even the scene after that, to their own discomfort.

After several performances of *The See-Saw Tree* I noticed that children's hands remained raised long after the vote to save or cut down the tree had been taken. So I asked the actress playing Miss Wise to watch out for this and, when necessary, insert a line telling them they could put their hands down now.

In *The Ideal Gnome Expedition,* the audience is invited to help teach the Gnomes road safety. This involves learning a song, complete with actions. The audience is asked to stand up at the beginning of the sequence. But, writing the play and in rehearsal I foolishly omitted to insert a line asking them to sit down again at the end of the sequence. For several performances this resulted in half the audience remaining on their feet. Needless to say a new line was put in and the problem never occurred again.

4. Not Enough Reaction
After the first few performances, the director may well find that a certain moment in the play that was expected to be particularly exciting is 'going for nothing'. This will not necessarily be the case. As we have seen, children will not necessarily clap when they think something is effective. But it is worth investigating whether the moment in question is being given its full weight. For example, in *The BFG* we had a wonderful Giant, 14 feet tall, sitting (like the illustration in the book) on a grand piano, with a table supported by four grandfather clocks. The Giant itself was manipulated by the actor inside. It was incredibly impressive. At the technical rehearsal, everybody, cast and crew, enthused about it. We couldn't wait for the reaction of the children when they saw it. Of course there was a good reaction. A certain amount of gasping. Occasionally even applause. But as the weeks of the tour went by, I was aware of the fact that the reaction was not as great as I had hoped for. Why was this?

To begin with, the BFG was trundled in on his own truck by two or three of the cast, playing maids in the Palace. As they became more and more proficient in manipulating the truck and finding its position, the entrance was getting faster and faster. The actors were treating it matter-of-factly, as though they brought this Giant into the Ballroom every day of their lives. The truth was, they *did* bring it in every day – as actresses. I explained to them that at every performance it must look as though they are doing it for the first time. They must be slightly wary and not make it look too easy. This immediately slowed the entrance, making it more effective.

I also suggested to the lighting designer that before the entrance the side of the stage where the Giant came from should be darker, and that the lights should increase slowly as he entered. I also asked for the musical fanfare accompanying his entrance to be slower. All this gave the moment room to breathe and allowed the audience time to take in the ingenuity and enormity of the Giant. The result was a much bigger reaction, which pleased us, and the audience.·

We found a similar problem in *The Witches*, but managed partially to solve it in rehearsal. Towards the end of the play there is a major climax in which the witches turn into mice. We knew that this would involve exciting music, eerie lighting effects and strange, discordant sound effects. Our illusionist adviser had come up with a splendid way of making the Grand High Witch turn into a mouse. Realizing that her plans had been foiled, she removed her glamorous face mask, revealing her true ugly face beneath, then challengingly approached the other characters in the hotel restaurant, trying to escape. Forced on to a serving trolley, she inadvertently stepped into the soup tureen (from which the soup containing the magic mouse potion had been served to the witches) and sank into it, eventually disappearing completely. Then a bedraggled mouse appeared from the tureen. Meanwhile, the other witches had disappeared and suddenly mice were seen to climb on to the table and also run along the tops of the ornate walls.

We rehearsed the sequence many times in an exciting, realistic style. But there was something lacking. It all happened too quickly. It didn't have the nightmarish quality I had envisaged. The solution we found was to do the whole thing in slow motion. The sequence now took four or five times as long, and every moment was focused and controlled, because the movements were slow and stylized. Exaggerated arm and leg movements, reactions of horror and terror, everything became heightened, weird and nightmarish.

In the theatre, with the lighting and sound contributing to the effect, I was very pleased with the result. But the first few performances still didn't have as much effect on the audience as I had hoped. Although the illusions worked and I don't believe the audience understood how all the witches had disappeared, somehow the audience wasn't going through the cathartic experience we were trying to give them. The solution was twofold. First, I slowed down the sequence further, which made it even more bizarre. Second, I asked the lighting designer to focus more specifically on each relevant area of the stage as the sequence developed. Thus the audience were looking in the right place at the right time. The disappearance of the Grand High Witch became more central for its duration, and then the appearance of the mice was made far more obvious and effective. The result was often a stunned silence followed by enthusiastic applause and cheering, particularly from the children, as the lights very slowly faded on the anarchic scene.

In *Meg and Mog Show* there is a sequence where Meg, Mog and Owl use Meg's cauldron as a spaceship. It takes off into the sky and, accompanied by a pre-recorded song, Meg, Mog and Owl see various stars, planets and spaceships flying past.

The Arts Theatre, London, where I directed the play five times, does not have the facilities actually to fly the cauldron. So we used a smoke machine to give the impression of lift-off and the actors mimed appropriately. Black tabs flew in behind and then cut-outs painted to pick up ultra-violet lighting were carried across the stage on rods by actors dressed completely in black. The effect was quite magical, but in the first performances I was disappointed with the audience reaction. They enjoyed the cut-out spaceship and planets, but the whole sequence felt grounded and unmagical. In retrospect the solution was quite simple. We used a mirror ball. This is a large revolving ball, suspended above the stage, covered, mosaic-like, with small pieces of mirror. When lights are directed upon it, it throws out moving specks of light which not only fill the stage area but circle round the auditorium. The whole effect is rather like a magical night-time snowstorm. The effect on the children was immediate. This was real magic. The whole sequence worked for the first time.

Part 6 Acting in Children's Theatre

Twice as Difficult, Twice as Rewarding

> Anyone who imagines that acting in children's theatre is a soft option hasn't done it.
>
> Susannah Bray, The Old Bag in *The Gingerbread Man*;
> Owl in *The See-Saw Tree*

An eminent theatre professional once came to Sadler's Wells to see one of my productions for the first time. Afterwards he thanked me for an enjoyable afternoon, saying how much he had enjoyed the play. Then he added, with evident surprise, 'And weren't the actors good!'

The general perception of children's theatre relegates it to the second division. More specifically it is often assumed that the people who work in it do not need to be as 'good' as their counterparts in adult theatre. This is patently ridiculous, yet actors who perform for children are often thought to be there because they couldn't get a better job, that is to say, a job in adult theatre. They have, as it were, taken refuge from the real world by doing something less prestigious and therefore less demanding.

The truth is that acting for children is far more difficult than acting for adults. I always tell my actors, on the first day of rehearsal, that this will probably be the most difficult job they will ever do, including Shakespeare. The dedication and energy they will be expected to give will be enormous. The volatility of the audience, as described earlier, makes every performance a challenge.

Many actors who are wonderful in adult theatre would run a mile from the challenge of working for children. They simply wouldn't have the necessary qualities to sustain them through the experience, and many would be terrified by the thought of appearing in front of hundreds of primary-school children. Yet for those who have the necessary qualities, it can yield genuine rewards.

Skills

So what does an actor need to succeed in children's theatre?

A good basic acting ability is obviously essential; clarity of voice, good vocal projection and a good ear for accents will be helpful.

An interest in and a willingness to learn special skills such as puppetry, conjuring and acrobatics, plus circus skills such as juggling and stilt walking, will be advantageous.

Versatility is a great help. The actor needs to enjoy playing a wide variety of characters.

A relish for playing larger than life characters is essential. Can you act in a big, broad style when required? Can you be uninhibited? Do you enjoy communicating with an audience? Do you enjoy working straight out front as in a music hall or cabaret performance? Does the idea of 'working' an audience appeal to you? Children's theatre is not as broad and free as pantomime, but requires much of the same expansiveness and recognition of the live audience as an integral part of the performance.

Underlying all the basic skills, the actor must be willing to work hard to meet the challenge of grabbing and sustaining the audience's interest. This will necessitate having the right attitude towards the work.

Attitude

> One of the basic rules for any performer, in my opinion, is that you must always try 100 per cent, whether it is for adults or children. It really doesn't matter if it's 16 million watching on TV, or four tourists and a whippet in a pub theatre, there is no point in doing it any other way.
>
> Clive Mantle, Securidog and Wacker in
> *The Ideal Gnome Expedition*

Children's actors should have an openness and generosity of character which will give them the flexibility and commitment to work as part of a team. In a children's production there is no room for stars or for selfish performers who concentrate on the creation of their own character to the exclusion of everybody else's. Such actors create their own little world within the play and rarely work with other people; they merely work alongside them. The following anecdote comes from my own experience.

> I was once in an adult play in which the leading female role was played by an American actress trained in the 'Method' school. She was a very talented actress, but her only interest in the other characters was how they affected her. It was impossible to experiment openly within the scenes, because she was only willing to experiment with her own thought processes and reactions. The director found it difficult to relate to her. If something didn't feel right, she simply wouldn't do it. Things came to a head in the dress rehearsal when the leading actor entered the room to play a scene with her, but couldn't find her. She was hiding behind the door. A children's production cannot accommodate this kind of blinkered self-indulgence.

Liking children is not, in my view, a prerequisite for entertaining them. But certainly the actor must respect children and actively want to please them, inspire them and give them an exciting theatrical experience. I found that not all actors see their performance working in this way.

> Some years ago, I was auditioning an actor for the role of Turkey in *The Owl and the Pussycat Went to See....* I explained to him that the character kept getting his words muddled up when performing Owl and Pussycat's wedding ceremony, and that the children would much enjoy shouting out to correct him. The actor's eyes widened. 'If the little buggers shout at me,' he said indignantly, 'I'll shout right back at them!' Needless to say, he didn't get the part.

In an adult play, the emphasis is often on the spoken word, dialogue, conversation. In a children's play, the physical acting out of situations will usually be as important.

> The energy required is the same as you must use in a full-scale musical, and then some.
>
> Maureen Lipman, Meg in *Meg and Mog Show*

> I remember when I was first employed by David to play this part. I was terribly nervous. I was young and fairly new to the game and would be

joining a cast of very experienced professionals. I was in prime fitness, having just finished musical theatre training at drama school. I didn't know at the time of auditioning that the demands of the show would act as a total assault on the mind and physical senses. After the first performance, I thought I had done it all: played it for real, stayed on my toes, kept up pace and focus. Unfortunately, it was not enough. A note passed back to a very exhausted me said, 'We need more energy.' 'More!' I thought to myself, 'I'm half dead already.'

Shelaagh Ferrell, Pepper in *The Gingerbread Man*

Many first-time children's actors are genuinely surprised at how much effort they have to put into rehearsals and performances. And it never gets any easier. Every performance requires the same amount of energy; it is impossible to cheat or play at half-steam. Children's actors need to be physically fit or they will soon collapse from exhaustion. I find the audition usually weeds out unsuitable actors.

Once, when I was casting a production, an agent rang me and told me that there was an actress I really had to see. She would be perfect for the play. Unfortunately, she was working in Plymouth, but the show had already opened, so she could come up for a morning audition. On the only possible day, she also had a 2 p.m. matinée. So it was arranged that she would get a very early train, come to audition at 9.30 a.m., and return straight to Plymouth. My choreographer, musical supervisor and I met up at the rehearsal room, and the actress duly arrived. She looked pretty rough, complaining that she had hardly slept the night before, worried that she was going to oversleep and miss the train. The train journey had been traumatic, and she was feeling like death. When asked to sing and dance, she complained that it was far too early in the morning to expect her to be able to show off her skills, and proceeded to do her stuff grudgingly. When I asked her to read, it was quite obvious that she was a clever actress, but the reading lacked any sparkle or enthusiasm. When I tried to chat to her, it was obvious that she was worried about staying too long in case she missed her train. She wasn't offered the job. She was very talented, but maybe she wasn't a 'morning' person.

Even healthy young actors cannot combine a madly social night-life with early morning shows. No-one can work to children on automatic pilot. It demands considerable concentration to deliver the necessary precision when 'living in the moment', carefully positioning one's suddenlies and allowing for adjustments to one's performance necessitated by the volatility of the audience. Actors contemplating working for children should seriously consider whether they are able to operate on all cylinders during morning performances. Self-discipline is required.

The most difficult issue for any actor to come to terms with in children's theatre is the seriousness of the story. In my experience, it is always the darker side of a story that grabs the children's attention. Yet very few actors and directors take the content seriously. As a result, the biggest impediment to the success of children's theatre is a misguided assumption that a children's play must be played with a superficial jollity or gaiety and any serious issues must be played tongue-in-cheek. This is despite the fact that the plays have been carefully constructed with crucial emotional issues for children. Time and time again, the heart of the play is destroyed by this blindness. Actors and directors slam the door shut on any idea of genuine threat or danger. There is little comprehension of the importance of letting children's emotions respond to something quite raw. Actors often believe that fantasy roles have to be played in a jokey, silly way. When you have characters who are bumblebees, or slugs, the temptation is to think, 'Oh isn't it fun.' It is not necessarily fun. It certainly isn't fun if you are a walnut, about to be covered with chocolate.

It may well be an advantage for actors to have retained a certain childlike sense of wonder. By this I don't mean that they should be psychologically stunted or that they have never grown up. What I mean is that actors should be able to share with the audience a genuine delight in the story being presented and find a real pleasure in the fantasy and the magic. It helps if actors can suspend disbelief and enter into the spirit of the play like a child. Such actors will almost automatically play 'for real', with no cynicism, finding a truthful and honest performance.

Cynicism

Cynicism is something one must always avoid. It manifests itself in different ways.

- An actor may simply feel embarrassed playing an animal or a twittering Jumbly or a villainous, bouncing Plum Pudding Flea. As a result, the actor may play the part without real conviction, as though winking to the adults in the audience, 'I know this is daft, and I'd much rather be doing a bit of Shaw or starring in a musical, but this is the best I could get...' Children won't be fooled. They won't reward such a performer with their full attention.
- An actor may play a role over the heads of the children in the audience towards the adults, as if to say, 'Look how clever I am at entertaining the children!' This leads to a kind of complicity with the grown-up section of the audience, almost ignoring the children, except when getting them to shout out, and avoiding any notion of taking the character seriously. This is most obviously seen in pantomimes, where there seems to be a rule which says that at no point should there ever be a sense of real danger; even in adversity, the characters should act with a detached jollity, refusing to take the plot seriously, for fear of being caught doing 'proper' acting.
- An actor may be unable to 'let go' because he or she finds it difficult to enter the imagination of the play. If, in *The See-Saw Tree*, one of the creatures living on the tree cannot really believe that the tree is in danger or that he may soon be homeless; if he cannot translate the fears of the tree folk into human terms; if he cannot play 'for real' the potentially tragic situation – then the audience will never become truly emotionally involved in his performance. It stands to reason that if the actor doesn't believe it, the audience won't. Just as the audience is expected to enter into the spirit of the play, so must the actor.

Actors' Pitfalls

Acting for children requires you to consider not just what you are doing, but what the audience is doing. I have played The Old Bag on several occasions and can picture myself waiting in my teapot for my first entrance, carefully listening to the audience reaction to the opening scenes, trying to gauge the appropriate level for this particular audience. While I'm mentioning sitting in teapots, I would like to add that although working for David Wood is satisfying it is usually also dangerous. I am resigned now to a first day of rehearsals where I will be leaping off a shelf six feet high, climbing trees and generally taking my life into my hands.

Susannah Bray

When I perform for children I always imagine a piece of elastic stretched between me and the audience. It needs to be kept taut if I am to retain their attention and keep hold of them. Because of the volatility and instant response of a children's audience, it is not difficult to sense when their interest is beginning to wander; the onset of restlessness is quite palpable. The elastic starts to slacken; this could lead to a loss of control. Now is the time to use one of the techniques to bring them back and tighten up the elastic again. A change of pace, a sudden burst of movement or an increase in vocal volume; a deliberate challenge to the children to make them concentrate again, to regain their attention. Of course, when you are acting with others, you cannot suddenly do your own thing with no regard for anyone else; but with experience, the whole cast can simultaneously gauge the tension of the elastic dropping and use a spurt of energy to stop the attention drifting any further. It must become instinctive. Monitoring the audience is far more important in a children's play than in an adult play. And every audience will bring different challenges.

Before the first performance of a children's play I try to warn the actors of certain dangers they may not have encountered if they have never played to children before. These thoughts are not meant to intimidate the actors, rather to make sure they are prepared for any eventuality.

- Never be patronizing. Never talk down to the audience in a singsong voice. Don't think of them as infants. Remember that they will probably be more alert than an adult audience and will instinctively sense if they are being talked down to.
- Don't fall back into a silly, childish style of acting. Respect the audience and they will respect you.
- Don't underestimate their ability to absorb information, as long as it is clearly presented. Children's immediate memory is often far better than adults'. The manager of the theatre where I first directed *Flibberty and the Penguin* expressed his amazement over one particular incident. Near the beginning of the play, the Penguin opens his suitcase, revealing three items (a photo of his mother and father, a bar of soap and a toothbrush). As the play progresses, each item is used for a specific purpose. What was surprising to the manager was that near the end of the play, ninety minutes or so after the items had been shown, the audience was asked to remember the third item. No problem at all. Every child remembered.
- Although it is vital that the audience can hear all the dialogue in order to understand the story, this must not be taken as a reason for shouting or unnecessarily exaggerating every word. Stage whispers can be remarkably effective. If the children are interested enough to hear what is being said, they will listen carefully. It is up to the actor to gauge how much he or she can control the audience by carefully modulating his or her voice. In these days of sophisticated sound and radio mikes, it is particularly important to recognize that high volume does not equal clarity.
- Actors should never forget to share the story with the children's audience. Communication is vitally important. Even in a play where there is no direct audience participation, the audience must feel part the whole experience. Too much conversation spoken with heads side-on or looking upstage is likely to alienate the audience. This is why actors should find ways of playing key lines out front, not talking *to* the audience but rather sharing information *with* them.

You must learn to engage the children's contributions when you want them and how to silence them completely when it's important that they listen. And you can't do it by bullying and hectoring or pleading, but only by engaging their imagination. It's like the best teaching, in that sense, unpatronizing but solidly focused on the 'now'. 'Only this very minute', as Joyce Grenfell said, 'and I'm in it.'

Maureen Lipman

Always remember that, although you know what is coming next, the audience doesn't. Never anticipate reactions or fudge moments of surprise or changes in the plot. Always give them their full value. Try to retain this freshness through every performance.

- Be aware that there may well be unexpected interruptions or comments from the audience. Some of them will be funny. Sometimes a child may make a genuinely witty comment. Sometimes a child may get the wrong end of the stick and say something which is not helpful.
- Be on your toes. Be very careful how you react to such interruptions. Never acknowledge a witticism or try to ad-lib a counter-remark. This will immediately change the tone of the scene and invite a free-for-all. If the comment is correct or helpful, and if there is a danger of the child repeating it, or of other children picking it up and echoing it, acknowledge it quickly, showing that you have understood and that the child has indeed said something valuable. But don't come out of character and laugh. Keep going.
- If you have inadvertently paused and allowed the audience in, try to keep going until a suddenly diverts the audience, or acknowledge them quickly and carry on. Don't get into a debate.
- There may be a situation in which a response is invited, but an isolated voice in the audience gives an inappropriate response. For instance, in Vicky Ireland's play, *How Does Your Garden Grow?*, the friendly gardener asks for a few examples of what vegetables people grow in gardens. At the performance I saw, one child said with absolute gravity, 'jelly'. The temptation here is to find the response funny. This will sometimes be difficult to resist because the adults in the audience will probably laugh. But it is essential, as

happened in the Polka production, that the child's response should be taken on board, considered, and then kindly and politely rejected.

- A problem that sometimes arises is that the audience will shout out something which the actor cannot understand. In this case, the solution is to ignore it. By the time you have tried to find out what is being said, anarchy might have set in. On the first performance of my production of *The Ideal Gnome Expedition,* the Gnomes rescued the Clockwork Duck from the dustbin and, as per the script, asked the audience what it was. The response sounded somewhat different from what we expected. Instead of the word 'duck', the audience seemed to be shouting 'book'. I could see that the Gnomes were thrown by this. They asked the question again. Again the reply, 'book'. Thankfully, the actors realized, round about the same time as I did, what had happened. We were playing in a theatre in the Midlands, where the local accent pronounces 'duck' as 'dook'. The answer was correct, but simply sounded different from the pronunciation we were used to.

In *The Witches* it was very difficult at times to control one's own laughter in 'stage silences' while 'magic' was happening and visual effects, because you'd hear a tiny voice yell, 'Don't do it!' or, 'Bruno be careful', or once a small boy saying, 'Ha. Ha. She's poisoned.'

Janet Whiteside, Grandmother in *The Witches*

The actor's natural temptation might be to 'corpse' when an unexpected comment comes from the auditorium. But control is essential. I'll never forget a performance of *The Selfish Shellfish* when Seagull was in his final death throes, having been coated with oil by the Great Slick. This was a very moving moment, as the other characters surrounded him in reverent concern. The audience fell absolutely silent, sharing in the moment. I was delighted. Suddenly a loud voice from the front of the stalls, where a party of brownies was sitting, echoed through the auditorium. 'Stupid little bird.' Thankfully, the actors kept their cool and continued concentrating. There were a few titters from the audience, but to my relief, another sound took over: the sound of the other children shushing the culprit in no uncertain terms. The interruption could have proved disastrous, completely breaking up the atmosphere. Instead, it galvanized the audience into a determination to experience the cathartic climax of the play. The vast majority of the audience had become totally involved and was determined not to let one child spoil things.

● One of the most common concerns expressed by actors after the first performance of a play is actually a huge compliment. This occurs when the actors expect more laughter and general verbal reaction than they receive. They come off stage complaining that the audience can't have enjoyed it much, because they were so quiet. But the fact is that if children are quiet, it means they are listening, and if they are listening, they are always enjoying the play. If they are not enjoying it, they would be talking and rustling. Actors must never feel they are 'getting it wrong' if the audience is quiet. The reverse is true. Children don't always find funny the things that made us laugh in the rehearsal room.

Characterization

It is a temptation for an actor to believe that a character in a children's play will usually be one-dimensional, a caricature, and that this somehow makes it easier and less challenging to work on than a character in an adult play. This is dangerous. It is true that many characters will have one specific quality or frailty which provides the basic tool for characterization. The Cowardly Lion in *The Wizard of Oz* is indeed cowardly. Captain Hook in *Peter Pan* is a heartless villain. Such obvious pointers are not only useful to the actor, they are essential in clearly establishing the character with the audience. Indeed, it is often useful for the actor to start with the very basic, fundamental aspects of the character.

But most characters in children's plays will have much more to offer, and, as in an adult play, actors must explore their roles and find nuances and subtleties, and chart carefully how the character develops or changes. Treat the material seriously and the results will be rewarding. The Old Bag in *The Gingerbread Man* is a crabby recluse. But that is only scraping the surface. She turns out to be lonely and vulnerable. She has magical healing powers, thanks to her herbs. By making friends with the Gingerbread Man, her life is transformed. And she becomes something of a heroine when she cures Cuckoo's sore throat. The actress playing the role has a very challenging task. She has to invoke the audience's loathing early on, display her vulnerability enough to secure a little sympathy, and then convince them of her good intentions. In the simplest terms, the actress has to turn the audience round. Part of her job is to make the audience understand that first impressions can change. This is harder than it sounds, because a child's instinctive reaction is to see life in terms of black and white. To portray convincingly the various shades in between, which represent the complexity of most human characters, is no mean achievement.

Audience Participation

Actors encountering audience participation for the first time should try hard to approach it with relish rather than dread. Assuming it is integral to the play and not simply an excuse for rabble-rousing, it is a perfectly legitimate device to further the involvement of the children in the story. Therefore, it is important that the participation is indeed part of that story, rather than a section grafted on for the sake of it.

When inviting participation, never come out of character. It is not you talking to the audience, it is the character. There should always be a valid reason. As we have seen, children will readily help by giving information or advice, and will certainly be happy to help the goodie or hinder the baddie, should the opportunity arise. The more seriously and genuinely the character addresses them, the more eager and vociferous will be the response. If you want advice urgently, ask for it urgently, keeping up the momentum and letting the audience see how vital their contribution is.

Make sure that you address the audience clearly, repeating questions if necessary. The earlier in the play the participation comes, the more important it is to make the audience understand that you really do want them to participate. If the first response seems a bit thin and tentative, ask the question again with added intensity, encouraging a bigger universal response.

Never anticipate a reply. Encourage it, but never make it seem that you knew the answer in the first place. Receive their reply and let your face light up with understanding. And always say thank you. This is not simply a question of politeness, it gives the children pleasure to feel that they have been of use, and helps to make them feel they are an important element of the play.

If you are inviting the audience to take part in a set piece, for instance, making the garden grow in *Meg and Mog Show* or catching the ugly insects in *The Plotters of Cabbage Patch Corner*, don't undervalue the importance of carefully rehearsing the audience. It is more fun for them to 'get it right'. Therefore, don't be afraid to repeat a section, or 'have another rehearsal'. As long as they see that you mean business, and how important it is to you (your character) that they do it well, they will respond with care and enthusiasm. If you make it seem that it doesn't really matter anyway or pretend not to notice when they start saying a line early, the whole thing will lack discipline, the audience will be less inclined to do it 'properly', and a very muddy sequence will follow. In *The Gingerbread Man,* when Salt and Pepper, helped by the audience, catch Sleek the Mouse under the mug, the excitement and sense of anticipation can be truly electric. But sometimes the desire to give Sleek his just deserts proves so irresistible that the audience jumps its cue instead of waiting for Salt to blow his nautical whistle. It takes tremendous strength of will as a performer to assert one's authority and make sure the sequence doesn't get out of control. But it really does pay dividends to be firm. And, if you stay in character, the children will accept your pedantic insistence on getting it right as a way of making sure the plan is successful.

When the audience help Meg and the other witches to make the garden grow, it can be wonderfully exciting and moving. If Meg and the witches play absolutely for real, making the audience understand that the noises of springtime they make might really fool the garden into thinking it is springtime, the children will try really hard to make the magic happen. The effect is further enhanced if Meg and the witches remain unsure of a happy result. They must keep up the tension and the feeling of hope. They must not approach it as a matter-of-fact sequence. It is desperately important. The huge cheer that will greet the eventual transformation will prove the point and be a heart-warming reward.

In *The See-Saw Tree*, which is for a slightly older age group than *Meg and Mog Show*, the whole audience is invited to make a decision as to whether the building of a new playground on a piece of wasteland is a good idea. The twist, of course, is that on this piece of wasteland is a very old oak tree, which will have to be felled to make way for the supermarket. It is essential that the public meeting be conducted by the actors with utter seriousness and that every decision the audience is asked to take is put in a very clear and balanced way.

By treating the children, if you like, as adults; by asking them to vote; by inviting them to hear different arguments and make up their own minds; by convincing them that their views matter and that whatever they decide will win the day – all this gives the play a sense not only of theatre but of an important event. Such audience participation owes an enormous amount to the type of audience involvement used in Theatre in Education. It is my view that *The See-Saw Tree*, more than any of my other plays, fuses the basic concepts of children's theatre and Theatre In Education and hopefully achieves the best of both disciplines.

Someone once asked me, 'How do you ad-lib?' My response was, 'I really don't think you should ad-lib.' The play should be structured in such a way that apart from the reinforcement of an instruction, ad-libbing should be unnecessary.

In front of a small audience, there is a danger of the performance dropping because the actors are getting less audience reaction than usual. But they should avoid raising their eyebrows and somehow insinuating that the members of the audience that *are* there are to blame for the poor attendance. They should take it *more* seriously. In fact, they should give even more than they would to a normal-size audience.

I remember being offered my first job working for David Wood on *Flibberty and the Penguin*. When I told my friends of my good fortune

they began to regale me with all the old horror stories of working with
an audience of children and the hell one would go through. If you ran
through the audience, they would spit at you or try to trip you up as
you ran past.

Stephen Reynolds, Policeman in *Flibberty and the Penguin*;
Dong with a Luminous Nose in *The Owl and the Pussycat*
Went to See...

A student once asked me what to do if you get attacked when going
through the audience towards the stage. The simple answer is not to
go through the auditorium. By the sound of it, this student had been
in a play where characters had gone through the audience as baddies
intimidating the children or baiting them to get a reaction.

I have seen two productions of *The BFG* in which the Giants
entered through the audience and did just this. My own feeling was
that the children were absolutely justified in attacking these
characters who were invading their space and relying on their good
nature. The fact is the Giants are meant to be frightening. They are
far more frightening to an audience if they are acted straight on the
stage and not prancing around provocatively in the audience.

A chase is one area where having the cast going through the
auditorium is sometimes fun. A director may use the chase because
there is a difficult scene change to accomplish and obviously it diverts
the attention away from the stage. That can work because the
intention of the actors in this situation is not to interfere or interact
with the audience. The moment you set up an interactive situation,
you dilute the impact of the characters considerably and you risk
frightening some smaller children in the wrong way. It becomes a
direct threat rather than a staged threat. It's like a villain coming out
of the TV screen and touching you.

I remember doing a play in the round and one of our cast was spat
at. She just had to carry on, and hope the rest of the audience would
respond positively. Another time, I was playing an old man, and one
child was deliberately nudging another to take his attention away
from the play. I kept in character, looked them straight in the eye and
moved closer to them. I forced them to look at me, but in a way so
that no-one else knew what was happening. They ended up blushing,

but they stopped fooling around and were attentive for the rest of the show.

In the rehearsal room, whenever there is any type of audience participation, anyone who is not performing a character at that moment should become the audience, so that actors can anticipate responses. This gives the actors practice in clearly communicating with an audience.

The First Performance

Don't expect an audience of children to clap in the places where adults might be expected to; for instance, at the end of songs. In an adult production, if a song finishes with a final climax and flourish the audience usually accepts it as a cue to clap. Children will not automatically recognize such a cue because the notion of clapping hands together to show appreciation is not yet part of their social language. If the performance is a family one, at which many parents are present, it is likely that the adults will indeed clap, and that some of the children will join in. If it is a school performance, the actors should never expect applause and should certainly not show disappointment when it doesn't come. Finish the song clearly and neatly, then go straight into the next line of dialogue.

You may also notice the lack of volume in the clapping at the curtain call. Often this is amply compensated for by cheering which seems to be to children a more instinctive way of showing appreciation. As a director, I try not to keep the curtain calls going too long for this very reason. It's fine if there is some action to music going on, or a reprise of a song, but it is probably best not to have too many bows. If there is little or no enthusiastic clapping, the actors will naturally complain that it felt 'eggy'.

Part 7 The Business Side

The Market

Children's theatre, like adult theatre, is highly competitive and there are limited outlets for professional productions. It is important to remember that children's theatre is a branch of showbusiness, and 'business' is the operative word.

Just as in any other business, it is important to get to know and understand the market. For a first-time children's playwright it is probably best to find out what kind of plays are being performed and the companies that perform them. It is worth going to see productions, reading published children's plays, and looking in the trade newspapers and magazines for information and guidance.

When approaching a theatre company or producer, it is possible to send the completed play for consideration but it is not essential. In the first instance, a synopsis should suffice. It may even be an idea to write for advice first. What sort of plays are they looking for? Could you go and talk to somebody about possible ideas? Making personal contact can be a real advantage.

Some writers worry that their ideas may be lifted by unscrupulous producers. It is certainly true that it is impossible to copyright an idea. Some writers, however, deposit a dated copy of their synopsis or play with a solicitor, in order to register their work in case of plagiarism. However, cases of stolen ideas are rare in the theatre, which still, thankfully, tends to be a fairly 'gentlemanly' profession.

Many playwrights use literary agents to help place their work. However, there are very few literary agents who specialize in children's theatre or have comprehensive knowledge of the field.

The best advice, to begin with anyway, is 'do it yourself'. Several of my plays for children had already been produced before I managed to secure the services of the legendary play agent Margaret Ramsay. Even so, when she took me on her books, she pointed out that the agency had little expertise in my chosen area, and I was advised to continue making personal approaches to theatre companies, sending them regular mailings, and trying to establish a working relationship with them. Having said that, an agent is often the best person to look after the business side. They know the ins and outs of contractual arrangements and can often secure a better deal than the writer.

When applying to theatre companies, it is counter-productive to offer them a play which clearly does not fit into their recognized pattern of work. A small-scale theatre company touring schools and arts centres will never be able to perform a play written for a large cast, requiring complicated settings. This is why it is so important to study the market. It avoids time-wasting and disappointment.

On the strength of a good idea or synopsis, some theatre companies will commission the play from the playwright. A commissioning fee will be offered. The size of the fee will obviously depend upon the experience of the writer and the resources of the company. Often the fee will be against royalties. In other words, when the play is performed the production company will deduct the commissioning fee from the performance royalties. This may seem unreasonable, but it safeguards the playwright: should the play not be performed for any reason, the commissioning fee will stay with the playwright and at least pay something towards the time and effort it took writing the play. The commissioning fee will often be paid in three instalments. The first will be on the signing of the contract, the second on delivery and acceptance of the manuscript and the third on the date of the first rehearsal or first performance. Copyright in the play remains with the playwright, but the producing management will sometimes receive exploitation payments should the play be performed subsequently by other companies. There is normally a time limit imposed on such an arrangement. Similarly, if the commissioning producer fails to produce the play within a certain time, all rights revert back to the playwright, who can then try to place the play elsewhere.

Every deal is different, and an agent is really the best person to do the negotiating.

Sources of Information

In Great Britain, *The Stage* is a weekly newspaper that covers mostly professional work. *Amateur Stage* is a monthly magazine. *Plays and Players* may be less helpful concerning children's theatre. The magazine of the National Operatic and Dramatic Association gives details of mainly musical productions. The catalogues of Samuel French Limited list many children's plays, and the Samuel French Theatre Bookshop stocks plays not only on their own lists but from other publishing houses. The Association for Professional Theatre for Children and Young People is a useful source of information about plays, theatre companies and directors. Children's theatre companies and Theatre in Education companies are listed in various Theatre Directories, often found in libraries. There is also a section in *Contacts,* a trade book which is updated regularly.

The *Writers' & Artists' Yearbook* (published annually by A & C Black) lists agents and the major professional children's theatre companies.

Professional Children's Theatre Companies

In Great Britain theatre companies which occasionally produce plays for children can be roughly divided into three groups: small, medium and large.

Small

The smaller companies tend to work in schools, arts centres and in the open air. Their productions are usually easily transportable because they very often play only one performance at each venue. They will often have a cast of no more than four, all of whom will also act as stage management and one of whom will drive the company van. Their productions will usually be highly inventive, using the minimum of props and scenery. Sometimes they will devise and write their own material. Sometimes the director will also be a writer. The plays they produce may be educational, reflecting aspects of the National Curriculum, or they may be adaptations of fairy-tales or children's stories. Even if not overtly educational, the plays will offer teachers and parents opportunities for follow-up work and discussion.

Medium

In the medium range, there are several theatre companies which visit mainly theatres, playing full weeks or split weeks. Their productions will tend to be more fully staged and lit, although their cast numbers will rarely exceed half a dozen. These touring companies produce both original plays and adaptations. Like most children's theatre companies their funding is limited and a commercial title is often an advantage.

In the same range are the specialist children's theatre companies in their own theatre. There are very few of them. The best known are Polka Theatre in Wimbledon and Unicorn Theatre in London's West End. Contact Theatre in Manchester also puts on plays for children, although very often their productions are for young people over twelve. These companies usually perform seasons of around six weeks per play, and appeal both to school parties and family audiences. They produce original plays and adaptations. Sometimes the plays are 'in house', written by the director of the company, but they are always willing to read and consider new plays by known or unknown writers. Their plays are produced with skill and care and they have tremendous specialist knowledge of their audience.

Medium-scale regional and repertory theatres, seating 500 or so seats, occasionally produce children's plays as part of their work, but most do not have a clear and regular policy towards children's theatre. Financial constraints make it impossible for them regularly to programme a production for children, except at Christmas time, when they know that it is commercially a good idea to put on a show for all the family. However, most of them choose to do a pantomime title, to ensure box-office success. And even though some of my own plays, like *The Gingerbread Man* and *The Owl and the Pussycat Went to See...* have often been performed in regional theatres at

Christmas time, in recent years the number of productions has dwindled in favour of traditional pantomime titles. Some of the regional and repertory theatres have a Theatre in Education team but many have been forced to cease operations in recent years.

Large

Most of the large theatres in Great Britain are devoted to touring. Therefore, it is not worth writing to them suggesting that they put on your play. They are receiving theatres, not producing theatres. The theatre managers who send out tours are listed in the reference books. When visiting a production in one of these theatres or reading about it, it is always worth noting who the producers are. The producers of children's plays for these larger venues tend to be few and far between. This is simply because a children's production is usually less viable financially than a production for adults. The seat price has to be much lower, thus making it very difficult to make a profit. Naturally there are exceptions. My own production of *The BFG*, presented by Clarion Productions, toured with tremendous success in 1990/91. Although I believe the production was artistically very strong, I have no illusions about the fact that the success of the tour lay in the popularity of Roald Dahl's book. Many schools and families wanted to see it. The title was the selling point. So, when approaching commercial touring managements, it is probably advisable to consider whether the play will have a mass appeal.

Even the plays that tour the larger theatres need to be fairly modest in production terms. *The BFG* had a cast of ten. The settings were imaginative and expensive, but the overall running costs of the production were not excessive. They were comparable to the costs of a medium-size adult play or small musical.

Amateur Theatre Companies

If a professional production proves elusive, an approach to an amateur society is a very positive idea. It must be said, however, that many amateur societies do not regularly perform plays for children.

Perhaps the idea intimidates them. Maybe they have simply never considered doing a children's play.

The state of amateur theatre in Great Britain is very healthy. There are thousands of amateur dramatic societies. Their standards may be variable but their enthusiasm and dedication is unquestionable. Most theatre professionals started as amateurs.

In the first instance it may be advisable to suggest a play-reading. This might encourage an amateur society then to produce the play. It may be worth offering them the incentive of a percentage from your future earnings from the play for a period of two or five years. And it is also worth pointing out to the amateur society how the presentation of a children's play could help foster new and future audiences for their productions.

I have seen many amateur productions of my plays, many of which have delighted me more than professional productions. Although the quality of the sets, costumes and the performances may be occasionally lacking in expertise, the sincerity with which the play is presented is often ample compensation. Professionals will sometimes use their technical skills to 'send up' a children's play. Their tongues will be firmly in their cheeks and they will play over the heads of the children towards the adults. Amateurs rarely do this. They play the story for real, and can thus more successfully emotionally involve the children.

Theatre performances *by* children or young people as opposed to *for* them are really beyond the scope of this book. However, if your play has a large cast or is particularly appropriate for performance by children, it is well worth finding a local school which might be prepared to present the play. Drama in schools has improved beyond all measure in recent years. When I was at school there was an annual school play, nothing more. And those of us who acted in the play were regarded as rather 'cissy'. Now drama lessons, and even drama exams, are quite normal, and school productions are often specially written and developed by pupils and teachers. Similarly, colleges of further education might be worth approaching.

Acquiring the Rights to Adapt a Book in Copyright

Never embark upon an adaptation until you have checked the copyright situation.

Most fairy-tales, myths and legends are clearly in the public domain, and anybody can use them as a basis for a play.

A book written by an author whose death was less than seventy years ago is still in copyright. The author or his or her estate still controls the property, and permission must be sought for stage rights. If an unauthorized adaptation is produced, and if the copyright holders find out, considerable embarrassment and disappointment will follow. An injunction on the production could well be sought, and months of work and planning come to nothing.

Application for Stage Rights

If you have an agent, you can leave it to him or her. If not, the first step is to apply to the publishers of the book. They will tell you who owns the rights. These may be administered by a literary agency on behalf of the author or by the author's estate.

Application can then be made to the right person. The reply may well be that the rights are not available, either because the copyright holder does not want a stage adaptation or because the rights are held by somebody else. If this is the case it is always worth finding out when the option on the rights expires and when you might be able to apply again. Sometimes the copyright holder will have given non-exclusive rights for a stage adaptation, which means that it is possible for another one, again on a non-exclusive basis. This sometimes leads to confusion, with several adaptations in existence simultaneously. But if a production is mounted, the copyright holders are invited to come and see it and if they like what they see, it may well be possible to extend the option for further performances, and even achieve publication of the play. Sometimes, however, a successful adaptation will become exclusive; no other adaptations will be considered.

There is often a difference between British and foreign stage rights. It may sometimes be possible to secure the exclusive stage rights in

Great Britain, but not in other countries. Always check on this when applying for stage rights.

Synopsis

It is likely that the copyright holder will need to see a synopsis of the proposed play before finally agreeing to give an option on the stage rights. Such an option must normally be paid for. The price for a two-year option is not normally exorbitant, and it is often renewable after its expiry, providing the copyright holder has not had another offer which seems more attractive.

Once you have established that the rights are technically available, it is probably necessary to do some speculative work, preparing your synopsis for consideration. At this stage it could also be worth trying to interest a theatre company in a première production. You must always point out to the theatre company that you have not yet secured the rights, but that you know they are available and that you have been given the opportunity to put forward a proposal. Such a proposal will be enhanced considerably if there is a definite offer of a production.

Script Approval

Some copyright holders, particularly those controlling very successful and popular properties, may insist on script approval. This means that even more speculative work is necessary. It may mean that you write the play only to have it rejected. You have to decide whether the investment of your time is worth it.

Royalties

You should also enquire at this early stage what sort of royalties the copyright holder might expect from professional productions of the play. The copyright holders of major properties may well be looking for a very high royalty. Add to this your own hoped-for royalty, plus any other royalties that might have to be paid – to the music composer or to the designer, for instance – and you may find that the whole proposition is totally impractical. No theatre producer would be able to afford to pay such royalties. A compromise can usually be found, but the royalty problem can be a minefield, and if possible it is certainly worth sorting out in advance.

The maximum total royalties should probably not exceed 10 per cent of the gross box office. The average royalties might be no more than 6 per cent. The division of royalties for adaptations varies considerably, depending upon the status of the adaptor and the popularity of the book.

When Clarion Productions asked me to adapt Roald Dahl's *The BFG*, they had already secured an option on the stage rights. I prepared a synopsis, which was accepted by Roald Dahl's agent. Sadly, Roald Dahl died during the time I was writing the play, but my adaptation was accepted by his agent and his estate, and the play toured successfully. The estate subsequently decided that my adaptation should be exclusive and that no other adaptations should be allowed. The play is now the joint copyright of the Dahl Estate and myself. Clarion Productions, in return for mounting the first production, receive a royalty from all productions for a number of years. If they present the play again, their royalty extends longer. Because of the success of *The BFG*, I was invited to adapt *The Witches*. A similar exclusive arrangement has now been agreed for this play.

For obvious reasons, my adaptation of *The Old Man of Lochnagar*, the book by HRH The Prince of Wales, took quite a long time to reach the stage. I approached the publisher of the book, who put me in touch with the Prince of Wales's lawyers, who put me in touch with the literary agent who looked after the book. They asked for a synopsis, which took many months to be considered and eventually approved. Buckingham Palace insisted, reasonably, on script approval, so I wrote the play and sent it in. After many months the play was accepted. I directed the play for my own company, Whirligig Theatre, and it toured successfully before coming into the West End for a Christmas season.

Getting the Play Published

You are more likely to get your play published if there is a production available for the publisher to come and see. It is true that some plays are sent in on spec and bought for publication, because the publisher believes they will be attractive to amateur societies, but such plays would normally be written by experienced writers.

Try to visit French's Theatre Bookshop in London, or send for their catalogues, particularly the ones that list other publisher's plays. Make a list of the publishers you feel might be most suitable for your work and write to them. Perhaps enclose a copy of the play, but more importantly, invite them to a performance.

These days it is always a good idea to make a video of the production. Certain copyright restrictions exist, but, assuming you have the permission of the actors and assure everybody that the video is not for professional showing, there should be no problem. A video may not be able to convey the atmosphere of the performance as it happened live, but it is a very good way of keeping a record of the production. If a publisher is unable to visit a performance, sending a video is the next best thing.

Afterword

When I started out in children's theatre, it appeared to me that most people – theatre folk and the general public – assumed that anyone who worked in children's theatre was one of three things: a beginner, a failure or a crank. In thirty years we have moved on. The talent is there, the commitment is there, but we still have to bang our own drum.

Hopefully, this book will encourage more practitioners to sample the satisfaction and sense of achievement children's theatre can offer. May our endeavours lead to the importance of the work being truly recognized at last. May the annual drama awards include it as a respected category. May we live to see a National Children's Theatre.

David Wood was born in Surrey, England, and studied at Worcester College, Oxford. Since 1967 he has written more than forty plays for children which are performed throughout the world. Many of them he has directed for his own touring company, Whirligig Theatre, the premier children's theatre company in the United Kingdom. The London *Times* has called Mr. Wood "the national children's dramatist." He also writes children's books and is a professional children's magician. He lives in London.

0660